This book is dedicated to the memory of

Jacob Kladder,
The ultimate do-it-yourselfer
and

Marjorie Kladder
A most determined and intentional woman
and

R. William Field
A remarkable researcher, gifted teacher, and a compassionate human being

© 2023 Center for Environmental Research and Technology, Inc.

Protecting Your Home from Radon

Disclaimer

The Center for Environmental Research and Technology, Inc. strives to provide accurate, complete, and useful information. However, neither Center for Environmental Research and Technology, Inc., nor any person contributing to the preparation of this document makes any warranty, expressed or implied, with respect to the usefulness or effectiveness of any information, method, or process disclosed in this manual. Each person who uses the information or methods disclosed in this manual is thereby assuming any and all risks associated therewith and shall have no claim against the Center for Environmental Research and Technology, Inc., any author, or contributors to this manual for damages or expenses related thereto.

Mention of firms, trade names, or commercial products in this document do not constitute endorsement or recommendation for use.

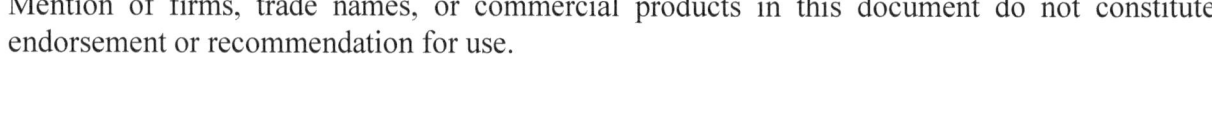

WARNING: If you only read isolated parts of this book, you will not have sufficient details to complete a radon mitigation system. This could result in poor radon reductions and serious injury.

© Copyright 2023 • Center for Environmental Research and Technology, Inc.

Introduction

The first edition of this manual was created by Colorado Vintage Companies Inc. in 1993, at the urging of Ms. Jan Hough, Coordinator of the Radon Project for the State of Wyoming. Since that initial printing, this book has been used by thousands of homeowners as well as contractors to better understand the mechanics of radon reduction such that they can either properly do it themselves or hire a radon contractor with the confidence of an informed consumer.

Through subsequent updates of the original book, *Protecting Your Home from Radon©* has continued to reflect those same practices used by radon mitigation contractors in the United States that allowed the author to say with confidence that "All homes can be reduced to less than the US Radon Guidance Level." Certainly, some projects are tougher than others and can require skills outside of the handy homeowner's capability, but it is all doable with the techniques described in this book.

We are equally pleased that a version of this book has been adapted for use in Canada and it has met with the same level of success and applicability. Although things are done a little differently in Canada due to its more arduous climate, the fundamental approaches still apply and work well.

Since the publication of the first edition in 1993 and second edition in 1995, the radon industry has become more standardized. New standards have been developed for addressing radon in existing and new homes as well as larger buildings such as schools and multi-family structures. The purpose of this third edition is to incorporate aspects of the newer standards to ensure the handy homeowner's work complies with recognized standards and to assist the not-so-handy homeowner to assess proposals they may receive from radon contractors.

Previous versions of this book have also been used to train employees of radon mitigation firms and provide required continuing education for certified radon professionals. We are pleased the Center for Environmental Research and Technology, Inc. has taken up the mantle of continuing to provide this resource for both consumers and radon professionals alike.

Acknowledgements:

We acknowledge the contributions made by several members of the radon industry and in particular:

Denise Brown, Colorado Vintage Companies, Inc., for her years in the radon field and organizational skills

Colin Dumais, Canadian National Radon Training Centre, for his contributions as a true Building Scientist

Jan Fisher, Center for Environmental Research and Technology Inc., for her commitment and attention to detail

Sincerely:
Douglas L. Kladder,
Author
President, Colorado Vintage Companies, Inc.,

PREFACE

Is this book for me, and do I really want to do this myself?

This manual is designed to provide sufficient information to a homeowner to make many of the basic repairs that can significantly reduce radon levels in their home. The techniques described in this manual are not experimental. They work, if done properly. The same methods that are detailed in this manual are identical to those which are used by professional radon mitigators. The only difference between the use of methods described in this book by the professional, as opposed to the amateur, is the time and tools available to do it.

There are, however, certain types of mitigation systems that have been deliberately left out of this manual. These are approaches that involve a higher skill level than those that may be generally held by the typical weekend do-it-yourselfer. There are also some systems that have greater dangers associated with improper installation. The authors recommend that in these specific cases, you seek the advice of a contractor who is a nationally certified radon mitigator or is certified in radon mitigation within your state. A list of web addresses for state radon programs and national certifying bodies has been provided in the Appendix of this book, however it may be easier to simply do a web search entering: "*state radon program* and *Your State*. You should also be able to access specific radon standards recognized by your state from those same state operated websites. Many can also be found at https://standards.aarst.org/

If you really want to dig into radon techniques covering large buildings such as schools and apartments or new construction approaches, the industrious reader may want to review *Measuring and Mitigating Radon in Colorado* downloadable at: https://cdphe.colorado.gov/radon-and-real-estate

The techniques in this book describe methods for reducing radon entry from the soil beneath the home. This applies to the vast majority of problem homes in the world. This book will not assist the homeowner who wishes to reduce radon that may enter the home either from a water source, or if radon emanates from the home's building materials.

Professional help is strongly recommended for the following situations:

1. *If the house is constructed partially or completely over a crawl space that is inaccessible.* To use this manual and perform repairs on houses of this type, you will need to be able to crawl and have good access to the walls of the crawl space.

2. *If the house is constructed partially or completely over a crawl space that has asbestos covered piping or ductwork, or if there is evidence of rodents that may be carriers of Hantavirus.* To perform the repairs described in this book, personal access into the crawl space is required. Working in these areas without suitable respiratory protection is dangerous and should not be undertaken by a person who is not trained and licensed to remove or work in asbestos or high mold containing environments or to deal with decontamination of Hantavirus associated with the urine or feces droppings from infected rodents.

3. *If you desire to reduce your radon levels by increasing the ventilation in the home.* Increased ventilation is one of the least effective radon reduction techniques and the most expensive to install and operate. For this reason, it is not commonly employed unless other indoor air quality problems exist in the home that can only be corrected by increased ventilation. Ventilation systems that minimize the operating costs and the loss of comfort are complex. It would be appropriate to consult with a professional if your intention is to employ ventilation as a radon reduction technique.

4. *If your home has basement walls made out of masonry block and whose internal cores have not been filled with concrete during its construction.* This book will still have significant value. However, if the hollow block walls still allow significant radon entry into the home after the methods described within the book have been followed, a professional will likely be needed to finish off the installation. Systems that deal with removing air from within hollow block walls have a high potential of causing dangerous backdrafting of combustion appliances and should only

be installed by a professional. Generally, the methods described in this book adequately reduce radon levels in the home without having to address hollow block walls, and if not, the same methods described in this book would still be needed with slight modification. Therefore, it is still prudent to use this book, but be aware that these methods may not be sufficient by themselves to totally accomplish the desired radon reduction.

5. *If the house is built over an old landfill or a low-grade coal deposit, or any other formation that may be generating methane gas or have volatile Organic Compounds (VOCs) in the ground or water table.* The systems detailed in this manual collect radon gas and concentrate it for exhaustion above the home. These systems will also collect other soil gases such as methane or VOCs. If these are a problem in your area, consult a professional to ensure that flammable levels of methane are not created or improper discharge of VOCs do not occur.

6. *If your forced air heating or air conditioning system have ductwork located beneath the slab*, the active soil depressurization systems described in this manual may not be as effective as desired. Consult a professional.

The repairs described in this manual apply to more than 90% of the homes in the United States that have elevated radon concentrations. So, unless the above exceptions apply to you, this manual is appropriate for use, provided you have some basic remodeling skills. Tenacity and the willingness to get good and dirty are the other qualifications that you will need to embark upon this project. To do the work in the manual you may find yourself:

> ***Slithering through dark crawl spaces,***
>
> ***Cutting holes through concrete floors,***
>
> ***Cutting holes through the sides of your home or its roof,***
>
> ***Cutting holes through your ceiling,***
>
> ***Applying several tubes of solvent-based caulking,***
>
> ***Digging deep holes alongside your house,***
>
> ***Cutting, gluing, and fitting plastic pipe together.***

The methods described within this book are not that difficult. We have shared every detail from our experience to make the installation go as easily as possible. Each mitigation approach included in this book is broken into three segments:

1. How it works
2. How to plan the installation
3. How to install the system

There are chapters in the manual that support the system installations such as general safety precautions, how to install piping systems, and how to interpret your radon measurements both before and after the installation.

So, if you take your time reading about and planning for the system, you should have little difficulty in installing these systems. If you can do all this, you stand to save a fair amount of money while improving the safety of your home.

Have Fun - Be Safe!

© Copyright 2023 • Center for Environmental Research and Technology, Inc.

Table of Contents

Chapter 1 – An Overview of the Health Effects of Radon 2
    What is radon? 2
    How do radon decay products cause lung cancer? 3
    Why should you reduce the radon in your home? 3
    How much research has been done on radon health effects? 4
    Who says radon is a health hazard? 5
    Is radon everywhere? 7

Chapter 2 - Confirming You Have Tested For Radon Properly 9
    Short-Term vs. Long-Term Testing 9
    How do I identify an acceptable measurement device? 10
    What are some of the most common testing devices? 10
    Confirming the short-term test result by re-testing your home 15
    How do you interpret the measurement results to determine if you should mitigate (fix) your home? 16
    Did my mitigation system reduce my radon levels? 18
    Caution and Advice 18
    Resources for Radon Testing 18

Chapter 3: Radon Entry and Reduction Overview 18
    How does radon enter a home? 18
    Are there other ways radon can enter your home? 19
    How are homes mitigated or fixed for radon? 20
    Why can't I just seal all the entry points into my home? 21
    How do I use this book? 22
    Dimensional Units 22

Chapter 4 - How to Reduce Radon in Homes Built Over Crawl Spaces 26
    How to Achieve the Best Reduction for a Home Built Over a Crawl Space 26
    Planning the Sub-Mcmbrane System 28
    Installing the Sub-Membrane System 35

Chapter 5 - How to Make Use of Existing Water Drainage Systems to Reduce Radon 50
    How to Make Use of a Sump System 50
    Planning the Drainage Depressurization System 52
    Installing the Sump Depressurization Systems 62
    Planning the Exterior Drain Depressurization System 66
    Installing the Exterior Drain Depressurization System 75

© Copyright 2023 • Center for Environmental Research and Technology, Inc.

Chapter 6 - Sub-Slab Depressurization Systems (SSD) 81
When do I need to use sub-slab depressurization? 81
Planning the Sub-Slab Depressurization System 82
Installing the Sub-Slab Depressurization System 99

Chapter 7 – Depressurization System – Fan and Piping 107
Deciding How Much You Can or Want to Do 107
Differences Between Canadian and U.S. Approaches to System Routing 108
Planning the Piping and Fan 110
Installation 131

Chapter 8 – Sealing to Improve System Performance 138
What is the value of caulking and sealing? 138
Planning 139
Caulking and Sealing 149

Chapter 9 – Combining Radon Mitigation Systems Together and Alternate Mitigation Techniques 152
Phasing Installations 152
Tying Multiple Systems Together: 153
Other Mitigation Techniques 157

Chapter 10 – General Safety Precautions & Backdrafting Concerns 160
Basic Personal Protective Gear 161
Ventilate the Work Area to Reduce the Buildup of Chemical Vapors 165
Other Hazards 166
Backdrafting: Possible Effect on Ability of Combustion Flues to Operate Properly. 168

Chapter 11 – New Home Systems 171
Basic Approaches to Installing Radon Control Systems During New Home Construction ... 173
Planning the Sub-Slab Soil Gas Collection System 176
Sub-Slab Design - Using Gravel Beneath the Slab 177
Combining Multi-Level Slabs or Slabs with Crawl Spaces 187
Homes with Crawl Spaces 188
Piping Systems for New Home Systems 189
Working with your Contractor in Planning the Radon System 190

Chapter 12 – Getting Help from Contractors 194
Do I need the help of a contractor? 194
Things to Consider when Selecting a Radon Contractor 195

Resources 203

© Copyright 2023 • Center for Environmental Research and Technology, Inc.

Protecting Your Home from Radon

Radon Reduction Flow Chart

Flow Chart - Page 1
Protecting Your Home From Radon
© Copyright 2022 • CERTI

Warning:

If you only read isolated parts of this book, you will not have sufficient details to complete a radon mitigation system.

This could result in poor radon reductions and serious injury.

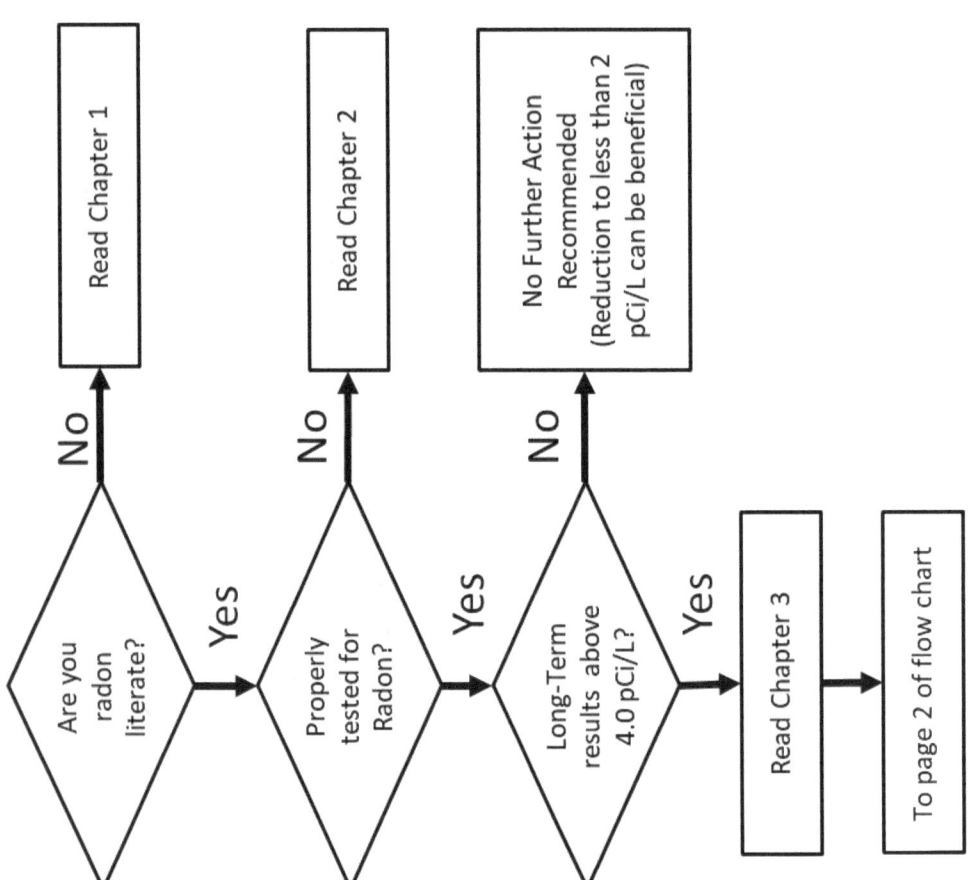

© Copyright 2023 • Center for Environmental Research and Technology, Inc.

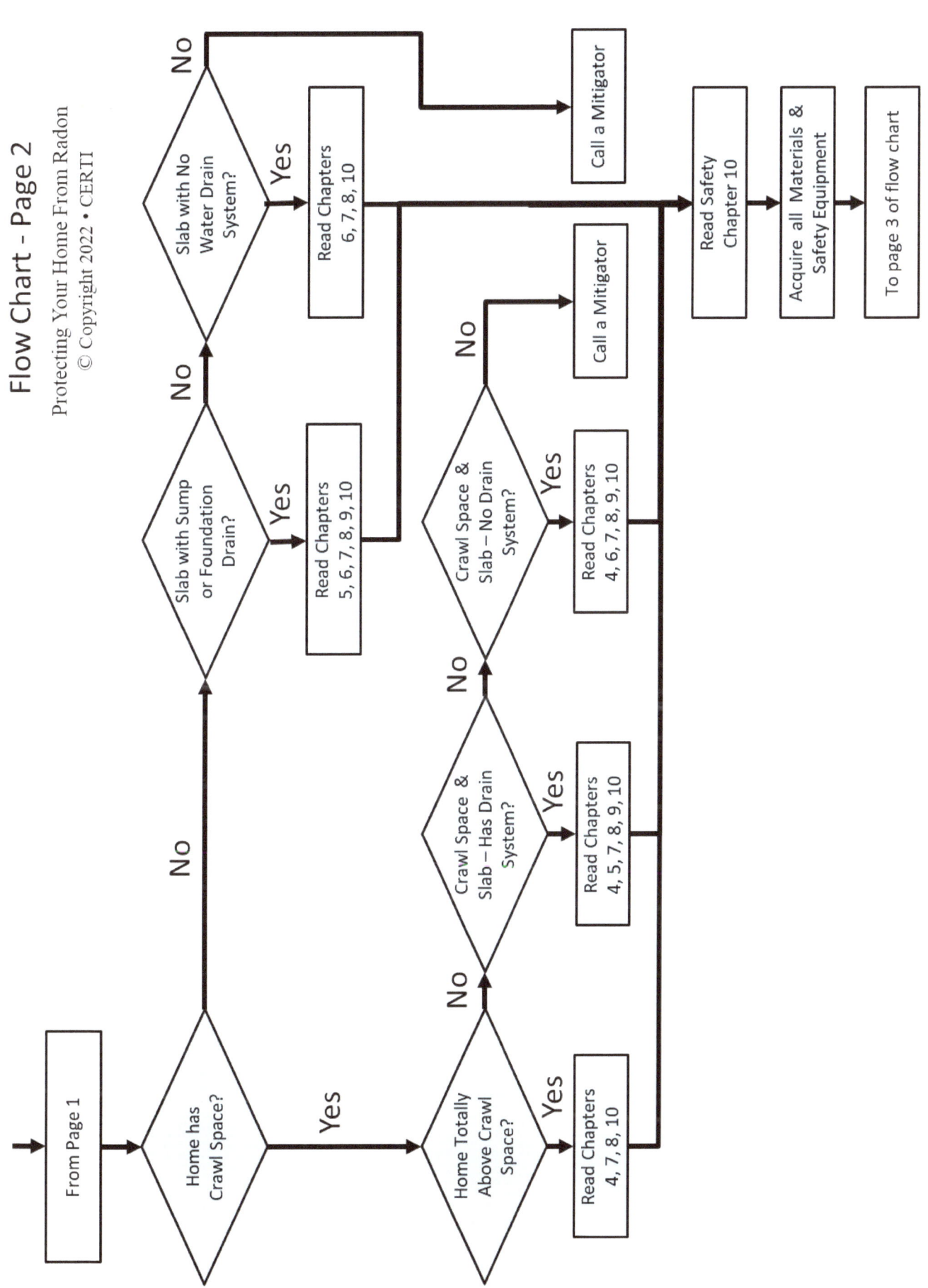

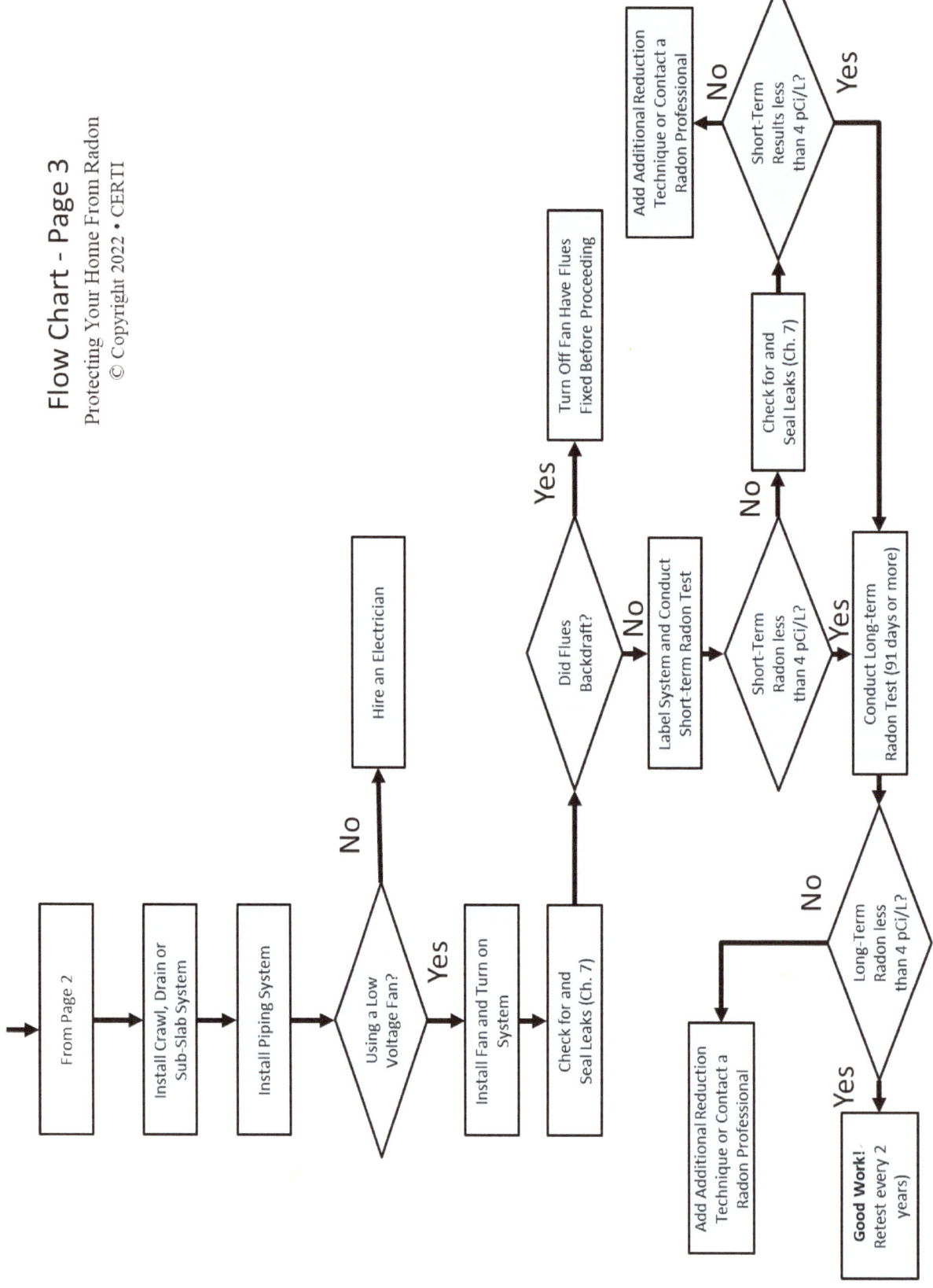

Chapter 1

An Overview of the Health Effects of Radon

What is radon?

How do radon decay products cause lung cancer?

Why should you reduce the radon in your home?

Who says radon is a health hazard?

How much research has been done on radon health effects?

Is radon everywhere?

CHAPTER 1 – AN OVERVIEW OF THE HEALTH EFFECTS OF RADON

Since you are reading this manual, you are probably interested in fixing your home to reduce the radon in it. That's great! But before you invest your hard-earned money (and time) into this project, you may want to have a few questions answered first. In this section, you will learn the answers to the following questions:

1. What is radon?
2. Why should you reduce radon in your home?

So, please set aside your hammer, drill, and caulking gun for a few minutes and read this section. Let's make sure you really are ready to begin the mitigation process.

What is radon?

For billions of years, a very common type of uranium has been gradually changing into radon gas. The uranium, which is found in small amounts everywhere in the soil beneath our houses, does not move out of the soil (see picture below). However, the uranium changes into radon gas, which is free to move up out of the soil and into the air.

When the radon gas makes its way into the outdoor air, it mixes with the vast amount of fresh air in the atmosphere and is usually diluted to relatively low levels. However, when radon enters your home through the basement floor, crawl space, or slab flooring, it can build up inside your house to levels far in excess of that found outdoors.

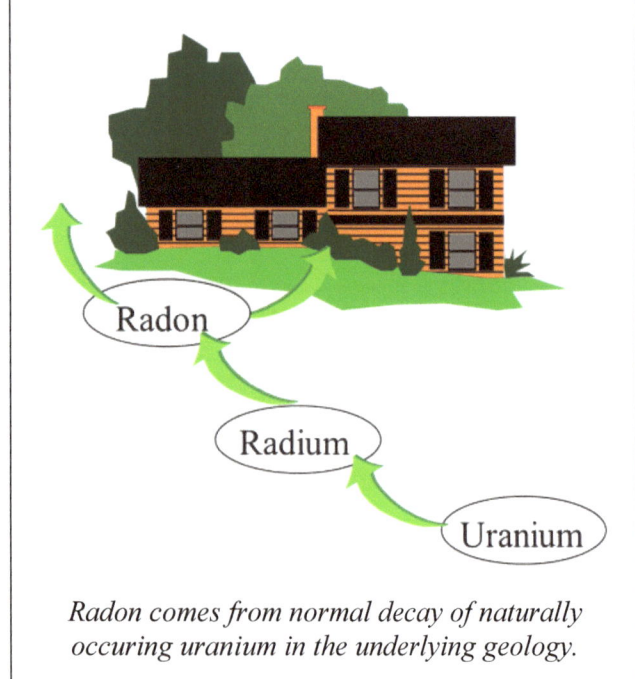

Radon comes from normal decay of naturally occuring uranium in the underlying geology.

As a gas, radon can move through soil and enter the atmosphere where it can be diluted, or it can enter a home where it can present a health risk.

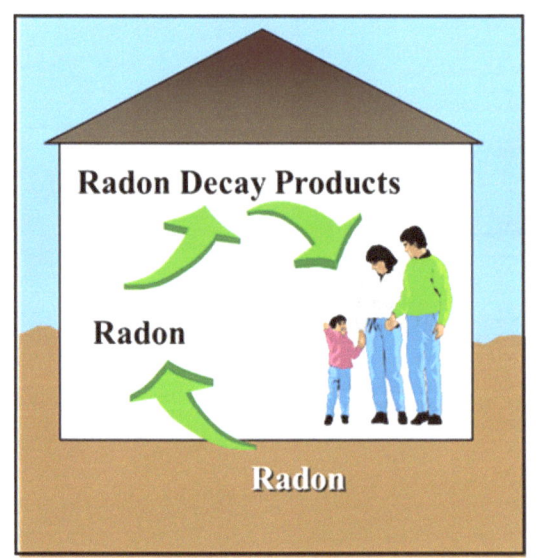

Radon is unstable and further breaks down into decay products which are radioactive solids that can be breathed in.

Over a period of time inhaling radon decay products can increase the potential for lung cancer

Believe it or not, breathing radon is not the main concern. The real culprits of the "Radon Story" are the small particles created by radon as it continues to radioactively decay. These radon decay products are continuously produced by the radon in the air inside the home. It is these radon decay products that cause the damaging health effects when inhaled.

Chapter 1: An Overview of the Health Effects of Radon

How do radon decay products cause lung cancer?

The radon decay products are very small particles. Since they are made within the air inside the home, they tend to float in the air where they can be inhaled. Many of the radon decay products then stick on the walls of the air passages leading to the lungs and on the lung tissue itself.

Two of these radon decay products are especially troublesome: polonium 218 and polonium 214. It happens that these two particles release a high energy particle called an alpha particle. When this alpha particle, which is like a small atomic "bullet," strikes lung cells, the cells can be damaged. The damaged cells, in turn, may become changed in a way that can eventually turn them into cancerous cells.

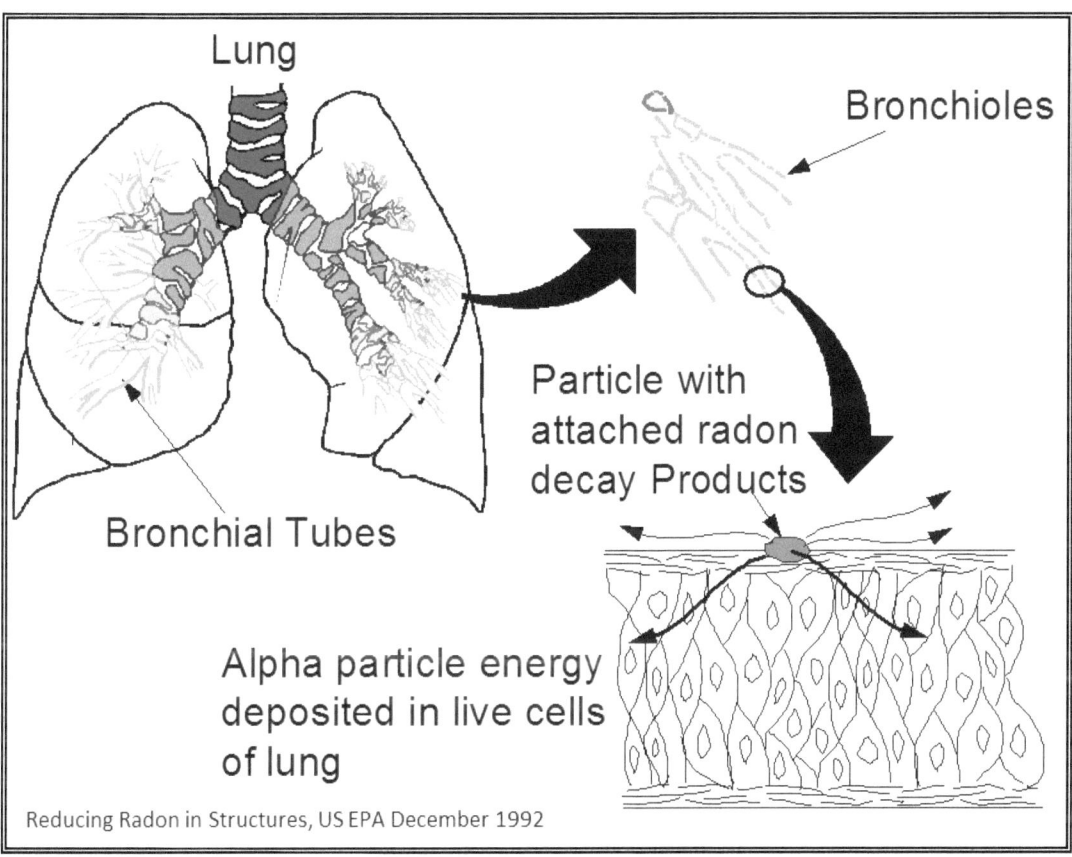

At present, the only recognized hazard from breathing radon (or actually, the decay products of radon) is an increased potential of developing lung cancer. No other health effect has been directly traced to radon, although lung cancer is bad enough. There is no current evidence that breathing radon causes asthma, allergies, colds, flu, or other respiratory illnesses.

Why should you reduce the radon in your home?

There are two main reasons hundreds of thousands of people throughout North America and Europe have already and continue to address radon issues in their homes.

Reason #1: Health Risk

Radon is ranked as a "Group A" carcinogen by the United States Environmental Protection Agency (U.S. EPA). This means it is known to cause cancer in humans. At the present time, the only known health hazard coming from breathing radon decay products is lung cancer. As you would suspect, the higher the concentration of radon (and radon decay products) in your home, the greater your risk of developing lung cancer by breathing the air inside your home.

Fortunately, the effects from radon exposure take place over a length of time allowing one to measure radon over a few months to determine what their exposure actually is under normal lived-in conditions and take considered action to reduce their exposure. In other words, short-term exposure does not mean you will get lung cancer. However, the higher your radon levels are, the sooner you should act.

Reason #2: Future Value and Salability of Home

Increasingly, people and financial institutions are reluctant to take possession or lend on a property that has a defect such as a gas that can cause cancer in its occupants. Taking action to reduce radon levels may also improve the salability of your home compared to another home in your area where such preventative actions have not been taken.

Any level of radon presents some risk and reducing relatively low levels of radon will provide a benefit. By performing the repairs described in this book, it is possible to lower radon levels to below 2 pCi/L. This would significantly reduce radon as a concern in your home. Another way of thinking is to ask yourself the question: How much radiation would I or my family like to be exposed to? If your answer is **none,** then you understand the benefit of reducing the radon level in your home as low as is reasonably achievable.

How much research has been done on radon health effects?

Actually, there has been a lot of research on the effects of radon for quite a long time. Unfortunately, most of the early work was done on occupational exposures in underground miners that led to exposure standards for these kinds of work environments. In other words, it was not felt that homes sitting on radon-producing geologies could be anywhere near the exposures that miners had to be protected against. But because one cannot see or smell radon, that was a very bad assumption.

When elevated residential indoor radon levels were discovered in the mid-1980s many epidemiological studies were initiated that confirmed that exposures in homes were not only common but also presented a significant health risk.

As one can see from the abbreviated chronology shown below, the health effects of radon have been well known for a long time. Guidance continues to be set around the world and is moving to lower and lower exposure recommendations as the technology to reduce indoor radon improves.

1556	Agricola – Identifies Lung Ailment in Miners
1879	Harting and Hess – Lung Cancer in Miners
1945	First study linking radon to lung cancer (miners)
1984	Residential Exposure Headlines (Pennsylvania)
1986	U.S. Environmental Protection Agency Issues 4 pCi/L recommendation
1990's	Relocation Firms begin requiring homes < 4.0 pCi/L (148 Bq/m^3)
1999	National Academy of Sciences confirms risk (BEIR VI)
2003	U.S. Science Advisory Board Reassessment confirms risk
2005	U.S. Surgeon General Advisory on Radon Exposure
2005	North American Pooled Residential Studies Confirm Risk in Homes
2006	American Standard (ASTM) developed for Radon Control in New Homes
2007	Canada drops radon guidance to 200 Bq/m^3 (5.4 pCi/L)
2009	World Health Organization finalizes 3 yr. study - guidance: 100 Bq/m^3 (2.7 pCi/L)

Compliments of R. William Field

Chapter 1: An Overview of the Health Effects of Radon

Who says radon is a health hazard?

The United States Environmental Protection Agency states in *"A Citizens Guide to Radon"* (May 2012) you should fix your home if your radon level is 4 pico Curies per liter or higher.

The United States Surgeon General Health Advisory states: "Indoor radon gas is a national health problem. Radon causes thousands of deaths each year. Millions of homes have elevated radon levels. Homes should be tested for radon. When elevated levels are confirmed, the problem should be corrected."

From *"A Physician's Guide to Radon,"* the American Medical Association writes regarding the evidence of radon health risks ... "Epidemiological studies of thousands of uranium and other underground miners have been carried out over more than 50 years in five nations, including the U.S. and Canada. These studies provide convincing evidence that exposures to radon and its decay products are associated with an increase in lung cancer mortality. The risk of lung cancer is directly proportional to the level and duration of exposure. For example, in one study, miners with cumulative exposures of 30 WLM (one WLM is equivalent to an average exposure of 200 pCi/L for 170 hours) had an increased mortality from lung cancer. Similar exposures might result from people living in homes with average radon levels of 4 pCi/L for about 40 years, assuming 75% occupancy. In addition to the miner data, radon, and its decay products in experimental animals cause lung cancer."

The conclusion that radon is a serious risk is supported by several other respected organizations such as the American Lung Association, the National Academy of Sciences, the World Health Organization, the National Council on Radiation Protection, and the National Environmental Health Association, to name just a few of the growing numbers of organizations.

The table on the following page illustrates some examples of radon risk assessments, modified for people who live in homes (not in mines). This chart has been taken from the U.S. EPA's 2012 publication "*A Citizen's Guide to Radon*" (EPA 402K-12/002).

RADON RISK IF YOU SMOKE

Radon Level	If 1,000 people who smoked were exposed to this level over a lifetime...	The risk of radon exposure compares to...	WHAT TO DO: Stop smoking and...
20 pCi/L	About 260 people could get lung cancer	250 times the risk of drowning	Fix your home
10 pCi/L	About 150 people could get lung cancer	200 times the risk of dying in a home fire	Fix your home
8 pCi/L	About 120 people could get lung cancer	30 times the risk of dying in a fall	Fix your home
4 pCi/L	About 62 people could get lung cancer	5 times the risk of dying in a car crash	Fix your home
2 pCi/L	About 32 people could get lung cancer	6 times the risk of dying from poison	Consider fixing your home between 2 and 4 pCi/L
1.3 pCi/L	About 20 people could get lung cancer	(Average indoor radon level)	(Reducing radon levels below 2 pCi/L is difficult)
0.4 pCi/L		(Average outdoor radon level)	(Reducing radon levels below 2 pCi/L is difficult)

RADON RISK IF YOU NEVER SMOKED

Radon Level	If 1,000 people who never smoked were exposed to this level over a lifetime...	The risk of radon exposure compares to...	WHAT TO DO:
20 pCi/L	About 36 people could get lung cancer	35 times the risk of drowning	Fix your home
10 pCi/L	About 18 people could get lung cancer	20 times the risk of dying in a home fire	Fix your home
8 pCi/L	About 15 people could get lung cancer	4 times the risk of dying in a fall	Fix your home
4 pCi/L	About 7 people could get lung cancer	The risk of dying in a car crash	Fix your home
2 pCi/L	About 4 people could get lung cancer	The risk of dying from poison	Consider fixing your home between 2 and 4 pCi/L
1.3 pCi/L	About 2 people could get lung cancer	(Average indoor radon level)	(Reducing radon levels below 2 pCi/L is difficult)
0.4 pCi/L		(Average outdoor radon level)	(Reducing radon levels below 2 pCi/L is difficult)

Chapter 1: An Overview of the Health Effects of Radon

Is radon everywhere?

The United States, as well as the rest of the world, has a wide variety of geological formations. Some with more radon producing minerals than others. Also, these geological deposits can travel as water and wind erode it and deposit it elsewhere.

Climate and building construction also play a factor in causing more or less radon-laden soil gas to enter a building or concentrate depending upon the amount of ventilation provided. In other words, it can be quite variable and the only way to know how much radon is in your home is to conduct a proper radon test.

However, since the primary source of radon comes from the underlying geology there are some generalized maps available on many state or U.S. EPA radon websites. The map shown below comes from work conducted by the U.S. EPA and the U.S. Geology Survey showing three different radon potential zones in the US.

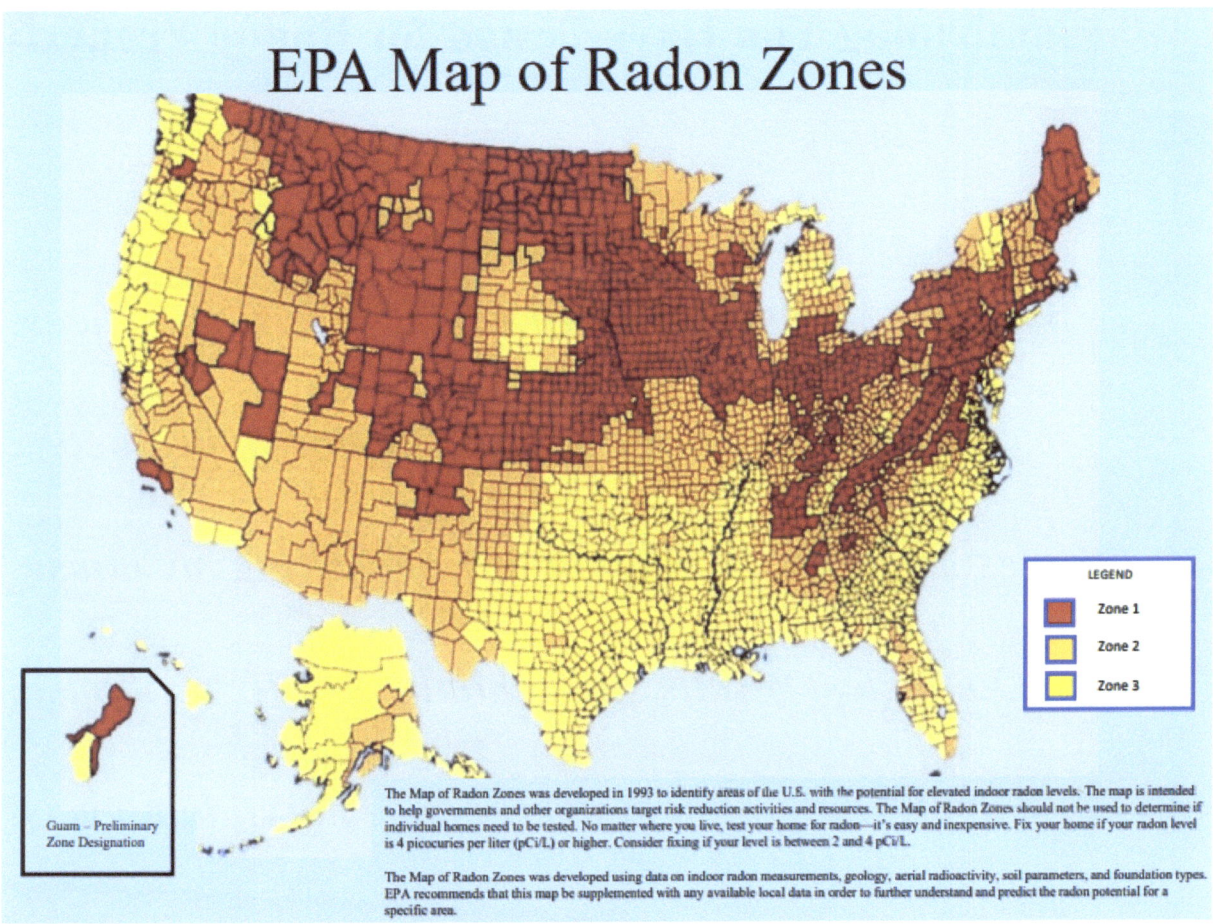

From the map one can see a higher frequency of elevated indoor radon in the higher latitudes where the heating season is longer. But don't be fooled. There have been elevated levels found in homes located in many of the designated "lower zones." This map was not developed to determine where one should test their homes. In fact, the U.S. EPA recommends that all homes be tested, and this philosophy has been embraced by many lenders and buyers at the time of sale.

Chapter 2

Confirming You Have Tested for Radon Properly

What are some of the most common testing devices?

Was my house tested according to protocols?

Are the test procedures different if I am selling my house?

Do the test results say I should now fix my house?

Did my mitigation system reduce my radon levels?

CHAPTER 2 - CONFIRMING YOU HAVE TESTED FOR RADON PROPERLY

Since you may have already tested your house, the questions we will answer in this chapter are:

- What are the common testing devices and techniques? That is, did I do the test right?
- How do I interpret the measurement results to determine if I should fix my home?
- Are the test procedures different if I am selling my house?

When you have finished reading this chapter you should be able to make an intelligent decision on whether or not to mitigate your home and how well you did.

Short-Term vs. Long-Term Testing

Radon levels in homes can vary significantly from hour to hour, month to month as well as season to season. Because the health effects of radon are a result of prolonged exposure rather than instantaneous exposure, a measurement that averages over a longer period, such as a year, is a better indication of the health risk than one that averages radon levels over a few days and certainly over just a few hours.

However, consumers are often unwilling to wait a full year to determine the need to mitigate their home, or if the mitigation system they installed is working properly. Consequently, two different time-based approaches have been developed and are summarized below.

Test Type	Test Duration	House Condition During Test	Purpose
Short-Term	Minimum two days. (Typically, 2-7 days but can be up to 90 days)	All exterior doors and windows closed other than normal entry and exit	Quickly determine radon potential of home
Long-Term	Minimum 91 days up to a year	Operate home as normal	Determine actual exposure in home as you live in it

The graph below illustrates the variations one can have with successive short-term, two-day measurements in the same house and in the same location. As illustrated in this example, the result of a single two-day test could be either well below or well above the actual 90-day average. There can be even greater differences between short-term measurements conducted in summer versus winter seasons.

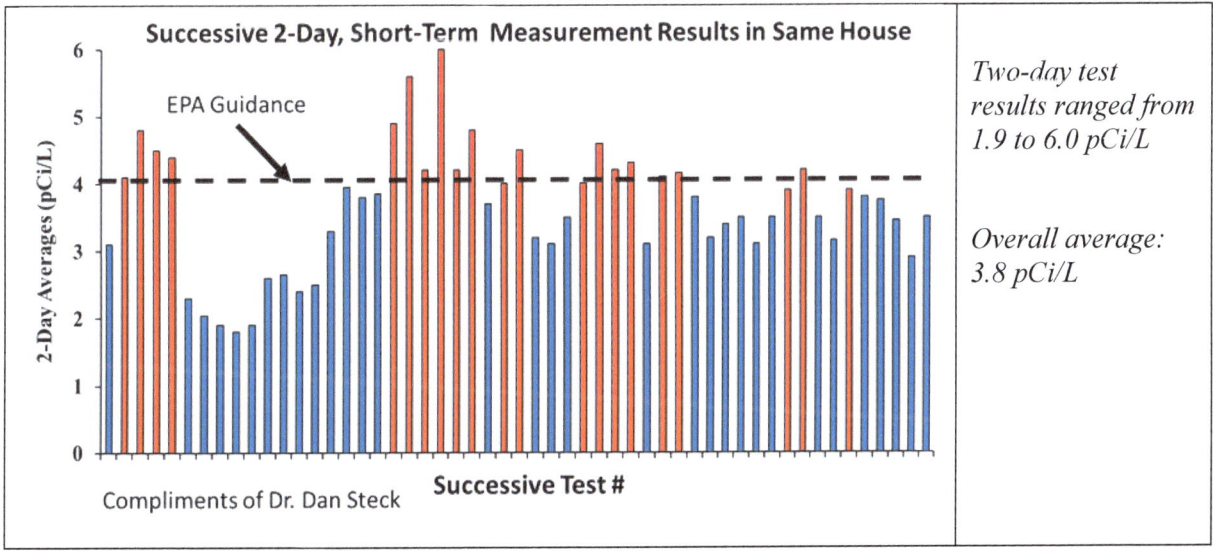

Two-day test results ranged from 1.9 to 6.0 pCi/L

Overall average: 3.8 pCi/L

Because radon entry - and hence indoor levels - can vary hourly and daily, the longer the duration of a test the better the result represents the overall exposure. That is why one has more confidence in a long-term result. On the other hand, one may need to have a quick result for the purpose of determining the home's radon potential such as at the time of purchase in which a shorter duration of 2 days may be appropriate (testing at the time of sale is discussed later in this chapter). Note that any test duration less than 2 days contains insufficient data to decide the need for mitigation.

How do I identify an acceptable measurement device?

Since the year 2000, there has been a significant growth in the radon measurement industry providing more choices for radon professionals and consumers alike. In essence, they fall into two classes: "approved" devices and "unapproved" devices.

An **approved** device is one that has gone through a detailed process of verifying the device or laboratory can accurately measure radon and strict quality control measures are taken in both manufacturing and analysis. An approved device or lab has also received an approved rating by one of two national certification organizations who maintain a list of approved devices and laboratories on their websites:

- The National Radon Proficiency Program (NRPP) (administered by the American Association of Radon Scientists and Technologists) www.nrpp.info
- The National Radon Safety Board (NRSB) www.nrsb.org

Note the US EPA privatized its program in 1998 and defers to these organizations for oversight and radon professional credentialing.

An **unapproved** device has not undergone such an approval process. That does not mean they are not capable of providing good measurements. In fact, these devices can provide a less expensive means for consumers to monitor their radon levels. However, before a final decision to mitigate a home is made or to verify the success of a mitigation, a measurement with an approved device is recommended and prudent.

What are some of the most common testing devices?

Radon Measurement Devices are separated into two categories based upon if they are best used for long-term or short-term measurements. Common examples used by radon professionals and available to consumers are shown below. *Note: Devices need to be posted back to the same laboratory from which you obtained them and don't forget to follow the directions. Some must be returned within a specific time period. Be sure you can meet that requirement before obtaining the device.*

Common Short-Term Devices – Minimum 2-Day Deployment

Activated Charcoal Devices
Several Shown

Short-Term E-Perm

Chapter 2: Confirming that You Have Tested for Radon Properly

Common Long-Term Measurement Devices - 91 Days to 1 Year

Long-Term E-Perm
(With On/Off Mechanism)

Alpha Track Detector
Hanging from ceiling

There are also more sophisticated devices that can measure radon or radon decay products on an hourly basis. They can also detect environmental factors as well as tampering. However, these types of devices are typically used by radon professionals when additional information or results are needed more quickly.

There are also continuous monitors geared for the consumer that can provide hourly data as well as averages. Although they would not be utilized for final determination, they can be helpful as indicators of how well a radon reduction system is performing after installation.

Example Continuous Monitors – 2 days to 1 year Provide Average and Hourly Variations

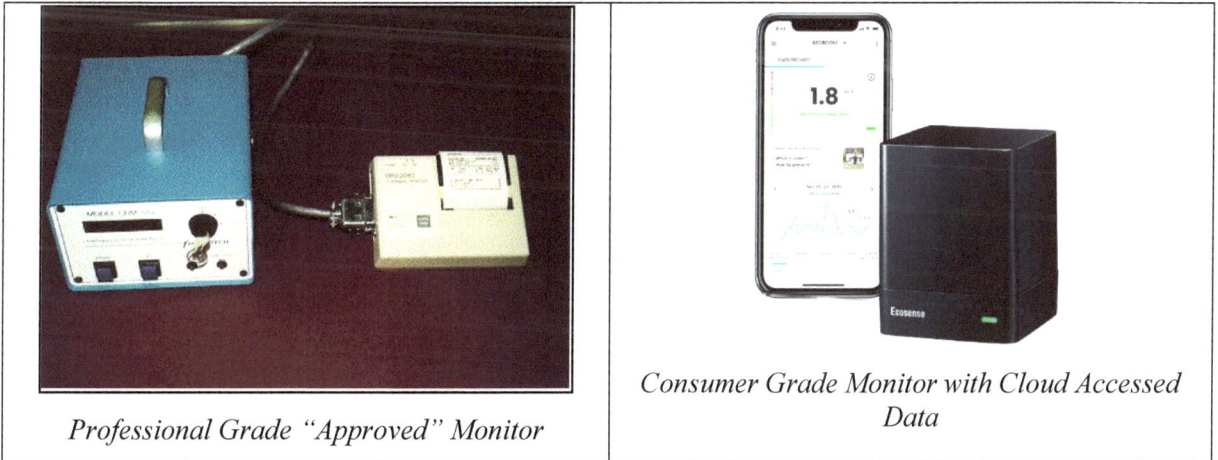

Professional Grade "Approved" Monitor

Consumer Grade Monitor with Cloud Accessed Data

What is a good location for a radon test?

Radon levels tend to be higher in lower portions of the home. That is because radon typically comes in through the foundation in contact with the soil within which radon is being produced. It then moves up through the house, being diluted to lower concentrations than what one would have in the lower level. Consequently, if one has a reading less than 4 pCi/L in the basement you can say with good confidence that radon levels on upper floors are also less than 4 pCi/L. The exception to this assumption would be if there is an unusual source of radon, such as radon in your water or from building materials - either of which is rare.

© Copyright 2023 • Center for Environmental Research and Technology, Inc.

Measurement standards recommend a single test location be selected on the lowest occupied level of the home where you would spend time. Within that lowest lived-in level, you would select a single room where you typically spend time. You could certainly test a basement bedroom or even a basement family room. If you do not have a basement that you use, or if you have no basement at all, you would test on the first floor. It is also recommended that if you also have multiple foundation types such as a basement and a crawlspace, that you test the lived-in area above the crawlspace as well as the basement.

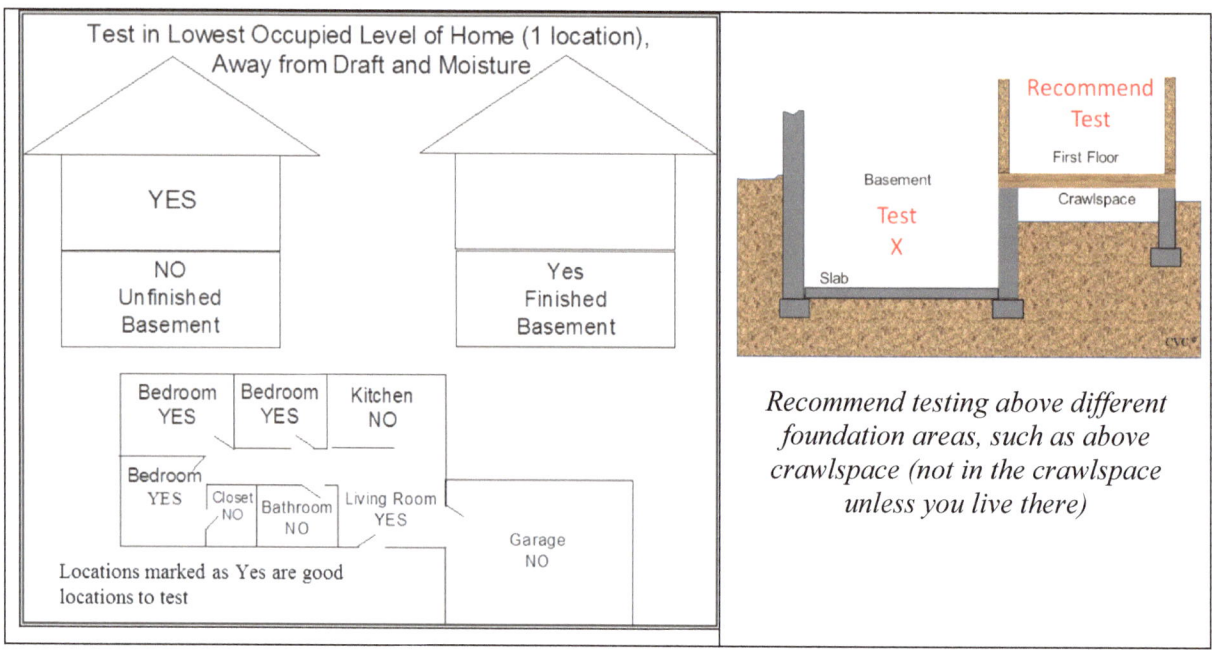

Recommend testing above different foundation areas, such as above crawlspace (not in the crawlspace unless you live there)

One does not routinely test garages as they are outside of the living envelope. We also avoid placing the device in an infrequently occupied room like a closet, a cupboard, or a crawlspace as the air in these locations would not be representative of the air you breathe in the home.

Some devices are affected by high humidity, so, as a rule, we avoid placing devices in kitchens or bathrooms.

The locations marked as a YES on the illustration above indicate good selections for your single test. You don't need to test everywhere on a given level.

Deploying the Device

The test device that you obtain should have specific instructions on how they are to be started, stopped, and sent back to the lab. Additionally, they should provide guidance on where to place them within a selected room. It is always a good idea to follow the instructions provided with the device. The following diagram illustrates proper locations to place a device, maintaining minimum distances from walls, windows and ceilings.

Chapter 2: Confirming that You Have Tested for Radon Properly

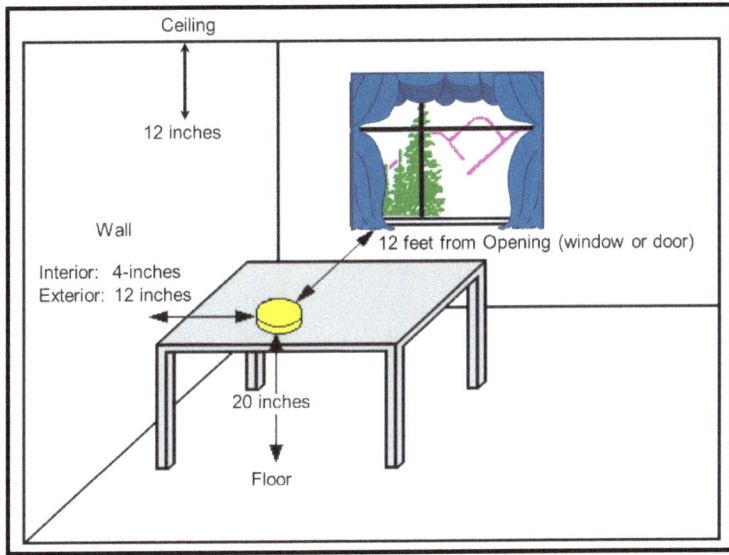

To avoid some pitfalls, here are some rules that apply to all devices:

Object or Feature	Minimum* Distance to Object
Floor	20 inches
Ceiling	12 inches
Interior Wall	4 inches
Exterior Wall	12 inches
Other Objects**	4 inches

…* You can be further from an object as specified - just no closer than is listed

** Objects that might interfere with normal air movement to device like behind a bookcase

Avoid	Examples
High humidity areas	Kitchen, laundry room, bathrooms
Non occupied areas	Closets cupboards, sumps, crawlspaces, foundation nooks
Air currents and heat	• Path of forced air from HVAC system • Over radiators • Near fireplaces • In direct sunlight

After selecting a good location make sure it will not be disturbed or moved during the test period.

Conduct the test per the instructions, and package it up and send it back as soon as the test is completed. Be sure to include start and stop dates and times on the paperwork that will accompany the test device and keep a copy of the information along with the unique ID number of the device before sending it all off to the laboratory.

Protecting Your Home from Radon

House Conditions for Short-Term Tests

Short-term tests are sometimes performed when you want a quick estimate as to how much radon potential a house might have. This could be done as part of a real estate inspection or after a radon mitigation system is installed to verify its performance before conducting a confirmatory long-term test. Remember, short-term tests are indicators and only long-term tests can determine your actual exposure.

Short-term tests are usually 2 to 7 days long in duration and conducted under "closed-house" conditions. Closed house conditions mean the house was closed up for at least 12 hours before the test and for the duration of the test. Exterior windows and doors are kept shut except for normal walking in and out of the doors (don't leave doors open). Also, fans and blowers, which move air from the outside of the house to the inside or exhaust inside air to the outside are turned off. Whole house fans should be off and air conditioners should be put on "recycle" or "max-cool," but not on the "fresh air" setting.

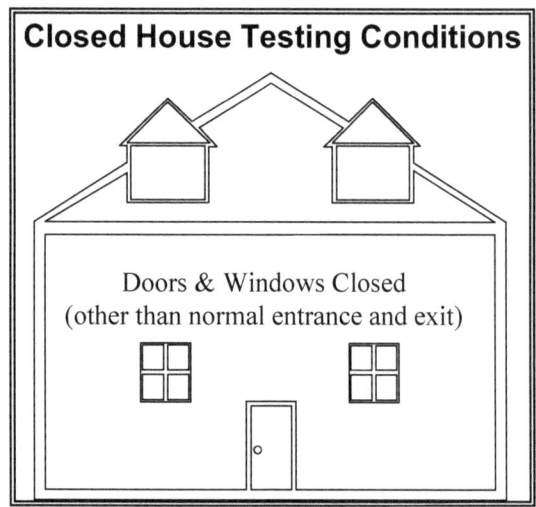

Of course, you *can* live in the house during the testing. Since it is sometimes difficult to keep all the windows closed during warm weather, try to schedule the testing period when it will not be inconvenient or uncomfortable to keep the house closed up. If you must test during warm weather, keep the air-conditioning on, but simply put it on total recycle rather than the "fresh air setting." On the other hand, "swamp coolers" or evaporative coolers that blow air into the home should be turned off during the test.

Note: **Closing up the room in which the test device is placed and opening doors and windows in the rest of the house is not following proper test procedures and can give erroneous readings. This can falsely report the radon as too high, or even worse, too low.**

Chapter 2: Confirming that You Have Tested for Radon Properly

Confirming the short-term test result by re-testing your home

You have now completed the first step of the two-step testing process. To proceed, you should have done a short-term initial radon test under closed-house conditions and obtained a result of 4 pCi/L or greater. If the result of the first short-term test was less than 4 pCi/L, and the test was done correctly, the U.S. EPA would not recommend that further action be taken.

If the initial test was higher than 4 pCi/L, the next step is to confirm the initial reading so that you do not unnecessarily fix your home. At this point, you have an option of either doing another short-term test as the confirmatory measurement **or** doing a long-term test. Ideally, the confirmatory test would be a long-term test (91 days or longer) because this would give you the best data about long-term radon exposures to you and your family. However, if the initial test was in excess of 8 pCi/L, it is recommended the confirmatory test be a second short-term test. In any case, the confirmatory test should be placed in the *same location as the first* short-term test.

If the second test is a short-term test, then closed-house conditions need to be met. All of the testing procedures outlined on the previous pages must again be followed. If the second test is a long-term test (from 91 days to a year) all of the placement procedures outlined on the previous pages should be followed with the exception that it is not necessary to close up the house prior to or during the test. Merely place the test device in the same location as the first test and occupy your house as you normally would. An alpha track detector would be an appropriate test device for this measurement.

Use the checklist below to decide if you should now fix your house.

CONFIRMATORY TEST CHECK LIST		
QUESTIONS	YES	NO
Have you done a confirmatory test?		
If it was long-term - was the result at or greater than 4 pCi/L?		
If you did the test yourself - did you follow the directions?		
Was the test device placed in the lowest lived-in area of the house?		
If the test was done by someone else - are they listed with your state radon program or a national certification program?		
If the second test was a short-term test - was the house closed for 12 hours before the test began (not necessary if the test itself was longer than 3 days)?		
If the second test was short-term – was the home under closed-house conditions?		
Was the test device placed at least 20 inches above the floor?		
Was the test device kept out of drafts and temperature extremes?		
Was the test device promptly read by the laboratory (within a few days of the end of the test)?		
If it was a short-term test - is the average of the first short-term test and the confirmatory short-term test at or greater than 4 pCi/L?		

If you can check yes to all the relevant questions, then you can have confidence in your measurements and can make a good decision regarding the need to mitigate your home. A flowchart summarizing this procedure is located below.

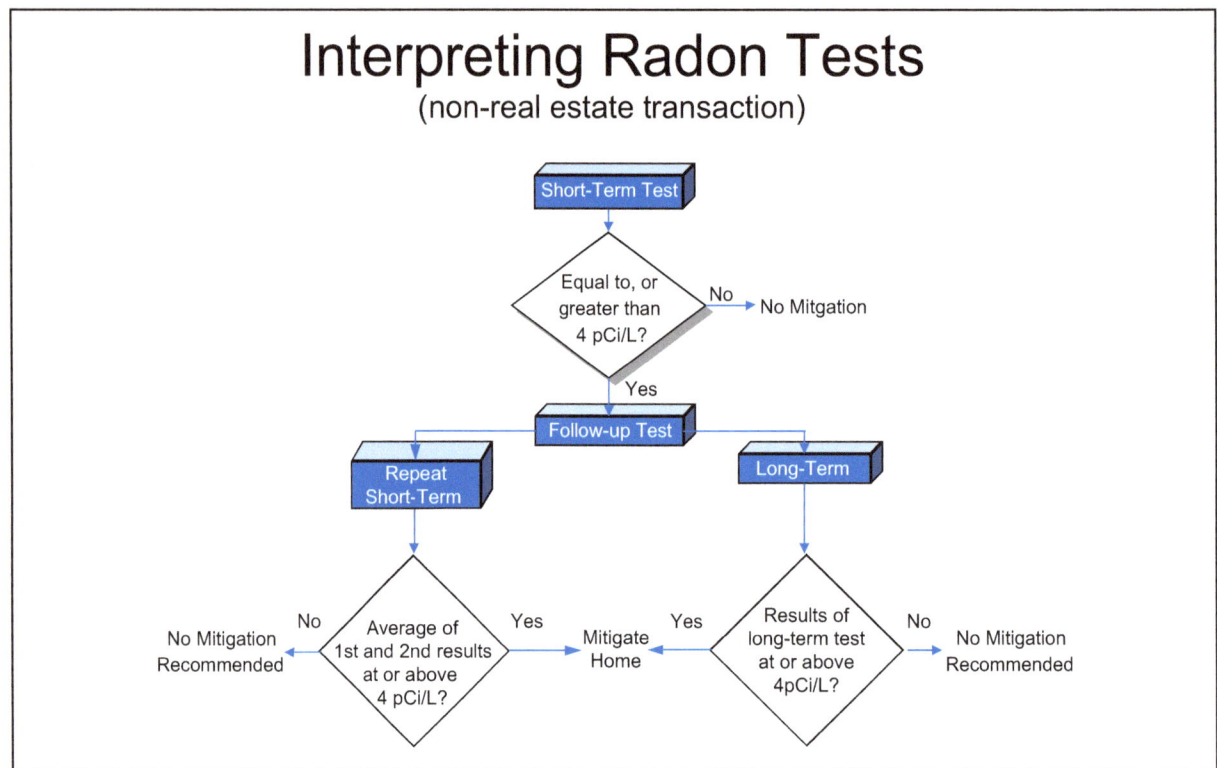

How do you interpret the measurement results to determine if you should mitigate (fix) your home?

Protocols are very clear on this point: If your confirmatory test used a short-term test device, you should average the initial short-term test and the confirmatory short-term test. If the average is at or above 4 pCi/L, then you should mitigate your home. To reduce your exposure, you may choose to mitigate your home even if the results are below 4.0 pCi/L.

If, on the other hand, your confirmatory test was long-term, you should fix your home if the long-term test is at, or above, 4 pCi/L. **Do not** average this result with any other measurement.

The urgency of getting your home fixed is related to the amount of radon in your home. Homes with radon around 4 pCi/L do not present as serious of a situation as homes around 20 pCi/L or greater (there are many homes above 20 pCi/L). Common sense tells you the higher the radon in your house, the sooner you should start repairs.

Chapter 2: Confirming that You Have Tested for Radon Properly

Are the test procedures different if I am selling my house?

It is commonplace for houses at or above 4 pCi/L to be mitigated before they are sold. The money used to fix the home can be part of the negotiations at the time the contract is being written on the house.

If you are putting your house on the market, whether it has been fixed for radon or not, you should not be surprised if the potential buyer insists that a radon test be done.

When the radon test is done in conjunction with a real estate transaction, the testing procedures are slightly different from what was presented earlier in this chapter. You should expect the following changes:

- The testing will probably be done by an independent, certified, testing company. Neither the buyer nor the seller will be placing the test kits in the home. The independent nature of the testing company helps relieve liability from the real estate agent as well as the buyer and the seller.

- The test will be done in the lowest **occupiable** part of the house, whether it is actually lived in or not. (Recall that when you test your home yourself, independent of a real estate transaction, you were to place the device in the lowest **occupied** part of the house.) The reason for the difference of locations is simply because the new owners may use the house differently than you and testing the lowest potentially occupiable space will uncover a radon problem (if it exists) independent of how someone uses the house.

    For example, you may live in a home with an unfinished basement. Although you would not normally test this basement under non-real estate procedures, it **will** be tested under real estate procedures.

- The initial test will be done with either two test devices placed side-by-side, or with a single device called a continuous monitor. The greater confidence implied with duplicate tests (or a continuous monitor) allows the decision to mitigate or not, to be based upon this initial test. Therefore, it is not necessary to have a second, confirmatory test in order to decide if mitigation is necessary. Of course, doing away with the follow-up test saves time, and time is usually important during a real estate transaction.

- Finally, the decision to mitigate is made in this way:

    ♦ If the initial test was performed with two, side-by-side, test devices, with the house under closed house conditions, mitigation is recommended if the average of the two results is equal to, or exceeds, 4 pCi/L.

    ♦ If the initial test was performed with a single continuous monitor placed in a home for a minimum of two days, with the house under closed house conditions, mitigation is recommended if the continuous monitor provided an average radon measurement equal to, or exceeding, 4 pCi/L.

Two side-by-side Passive Radon Detectors

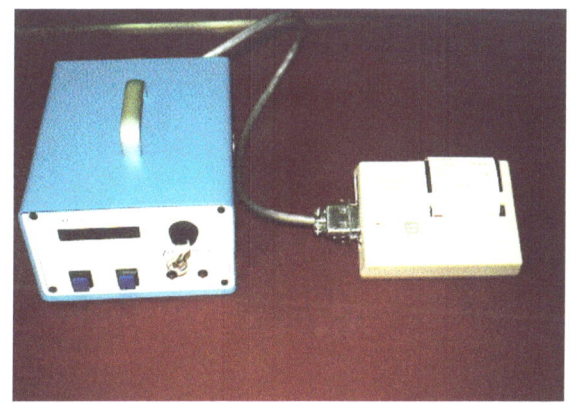

Continuous Monitor that Records Hourly Radon Levels as well as Test Average

Did my mitigation system reduce my radon levels?

A follow up short-term test should be done after you have completed the installation of your mitigation system. This should be done within 30 days of the systems installation, but no sooner than 24 hours after the system is operational. The test should also be done under "closed house conditions."

If the post mitigation test is at or above 4 pCi/L, review the installation of the system for leaks then evaluate the need for further mitigation work. If the post mitigation test is under 4 pCi/L, a long-term test for one year should be done to confirm the short-term results. A test should be performed at least once every two years thereafter to confirm that the radon level is staying low and the system is still performing well. Also, if you remodel your home, retest in the lowest lived-in area to make sure the construction did not reduce the effectiveness of the system.

The simplest procedure for testing your home after mitigation is to always place the testing device in the same location as the very first short-term test. By using the same location, you will have confidence that the post-mitigation readings can be compared to the earlier measurements. You want to ensure the differences in readings were actually due to your mitigation efforts and not from variations seen between different test locations.

Caution and Advice

Test devices used for identifying radon entry points are different than those devices described above. These are referred to as grab sampling devices. Although they can be quite accurate, they only sample the air for a few minutes. Radon levels vary from hour to hour. This is why the minimum sampling time established by the EPA, to provide a reasonable measurement, is 48 hours. **Do not use grab sampling types of devices for short or long-term testing or, in other words, as a basis for determining the need for mitigation.**

Resources for Radon Testing

- US EPA Citizens Guide https://www.epa.gov/radon/radon-resources-individuals-and-families
- US EPA Home Buyer and Sellers Guide to Radon https://www.epa.gov/radon/radon-resources-home-buyers-and-sellers
- ANSI/AARST Standards https://standards.aarst.org

Chapter 3

Radon Entry and
Overview of Radon Reduction Techniques

How does radon enter a home?

How are homes mitigated or fixed for radon?

Why can't I just seal all the entry points into my home?

How do I use this book?

CHAPTER 3: RADON ENTRY AND REDUCTION OVERVIEW

How does radon enter a home?

To understand how radon reduction techniques are able to reduce radon, we should start by understanding how radon enters a home in the first place. There are three factors that affect the amount of radon that enters a home.

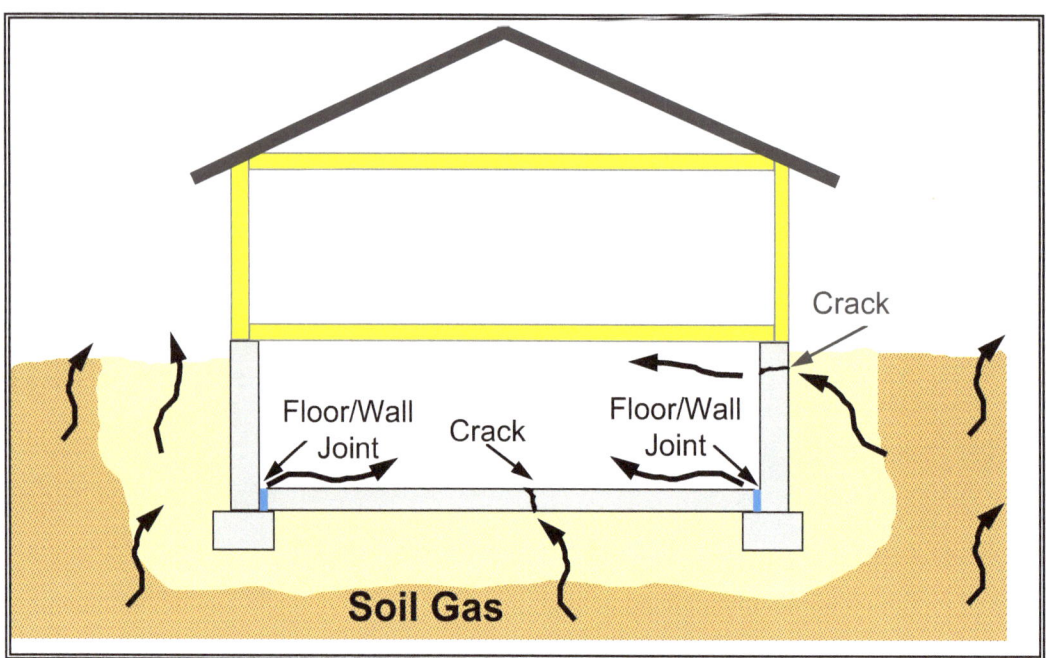

1. **Source.** Radon is a gas that is constantly being created from the decay of naturally occurring uranium and radium in the soil. Radon that is created in the soil can find its way to the surface and either enter the atmosphere or enter your home.

2. **Pathways.** As a gas, radon acts just as air does. It moves freely through the open spaces in the soil. These open spaces can be as small as the space between individual particles of dirt in the soil. The larger the particle size of the soil, the larger the open spaces will be (e.g., gravel versus sand) and therefore the easier radon can move up through the soil. These open spaces provide the pathway for radon to move from its source in the ground (the natural deposits of radium) into your home. Pathways for radon migration into your home may be through the soil below or through cracks and crevices in the soil. Piping trenches and drainage systems that were installed during your home's construction can also be entry pathways, including up around or even through floor drains.

3. **Pressure Difference.** The air inside of your home is often at a different pressure than the air in the soil beneath it. If the pressure inside your home is lower than the air pressure in the soil (or under a vacuum) then air from the soil is sucked into the home potentially carries radon along with it. Vacuums within the house can be caused by exhaust fans as well as the thermal stack effect when it is cold outside and warm inside.

The soil can also be under positive pressure where radon-laden soil gas is pushed into your home. Soil pressure can be caused when wind strikes the side of a hill upon which a home is built.

Either way, air in the soil can be pulled or pushed into your home. If radon is being produced beneath the home, it will be carried along with the air, through pathways and through openings into your home.

The question is not IF your home has openings in the foundation, as all homes have sufficient openings for radon to enter the home.

The rate at which radon is produced beneath your home is a constant, just as the openings in your foundation, for all intents and purposes do not change. However, the pressure difference that causes the soil gases into a home do change as a function of the changes in weather, windows being opened or closed, and intermittent operation of exhaust fans and other appliances.

The figure below is an over dramatization of the vacuums inside of your home drawing radon in. The graph to the right illustrates how radon within the home can increase or decrease as a vacuum within the home increases and decreases causing more or less radon to be drawn in through extremely small openings in the foundation. Vacuums in homes can change as ventilation fans are turned on and off as well as changing weather conditions and outdoor temperatures causing a thermal stack effect. Wind against a hillside can also pressurize the soil pushing radon in. The point is that radon entry is variable unless a mitigation system is installed to control it.

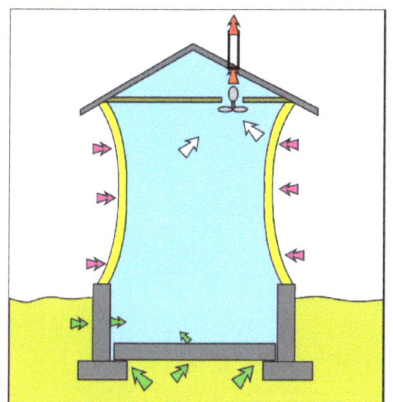
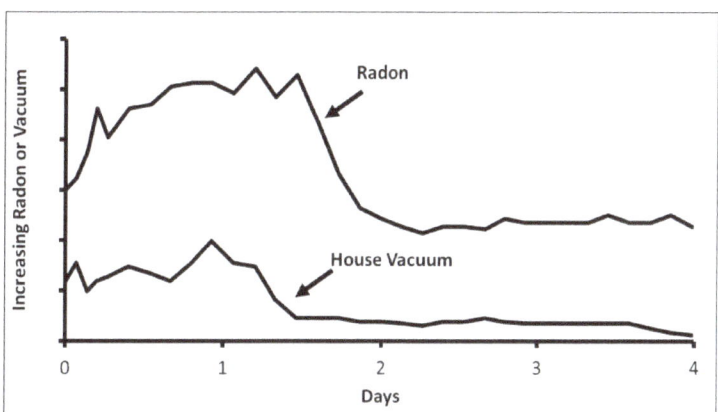

Are there other ways radon can enter your home?

The vast amount of radon that enters homes is via the entry of radon-laden soil gas. However, there are two other ways that radon can enter your home. Fortunately, these typically do not present a major source of radon since their remediation can be more complex and require skills outside the realm of the Do-It-Yourselfer.

Water-Borne Radon

When water is in the ground, it can come in contact with rock or geologies that produce radon. As a gas, radon can dissolve into the ground water and when the water is directly brought into a house, the radon gas will disengage from the water and enter the breathing space, especially under conditions when the water is heated and agitated (like a nice warm shower). This water-borne radon adds an additional amount of radon into the breathing space above that which comes from the soil and represents an additional breathing risk. It is not a significant concern for drinking the water, but rather breathing the radon released from the water.

Once the radon leaves the water it disperses into the volume of the home thereby being diluted. Because of this fact, it takes a significant amount of radon in the water to add a measurable amount of radon in the air. A rule of thumb is that in the typical home using a normal amount of water for showers, laundry etc., the water supply would have to have 40,000 picoCuries per liter of water to cause the indoor air to be at the US EPA guidance of 4.0 pCi/L in the indoor air. And that is a lot!

If your water supply is from a reservoir or a public water supply where it is stored at atmospheric pressure, there is little to worry about. If, on the other hand, your water supply is well water that comes directly into your home without being stored in a cistern AND it comes from a radon producing geology like granite, then it possibly could be a source.

It is always best to test the air first and reduce radon from the underlying soil before taking action to treat well water. And such remediation efforts should be left to professionals who are familiar with treating radon and maintaining water quality.

Radon from Building Materials

Radon can also be emitted from building materials containing trace amounts of radium. Examples have been some granite countertops, some drywalls, and where uranium processing mill tailings have been used as aggregate for concrete or backfill.

If a building material emits radon from the portion of its surface exposed to the inside of the home, it can also add to the amount of radon entering from the soil beneath it. However, the rate at which radon is "emitted" is very slow and typical ventilation rates of a home are more than adequate to dilute this contribution. There have been isolated cases in North America where the combination of a very high source content of the building material AND a very low ventilation rate have been the cause of elevated indoor radon levels. If encountered, mitigation approaches typically increase the exchange of indoor to outdoor air with devices such as Heat Recovery Ventilators which are best installed by qualified heating contractors.

How are homes mitigated or fixed for radon?

Radon mitigation strategies do not attempt to remove the source of radon under a home as that would require a massive excavation process. Nor does radon mitigation attempt to seal out radon by caulking and sealing foundation openings since it only takes a small crack or future crack to allow radon in. What is done is to counter the pressure differentials that cause radon to come in through the foundation through a process called Active Soil Depressurization (ASD).

Active Soil Depressurization is a system that can easily be installed in your home that serves to create a vacuum under your foundation that is greater in strength than the vacuum exerted on the soil by your home, thereby capturing the radon-laden soil gases before they can enter the small openings in your foundation. The system constantly captures these soil gases and exhausts them outdoors before they can accumulate in your home. How ASD is employed is a function of your foundation rather than the indoor radon levels. In other words, the same approach is applied regardless of how much the radon needs to be reduced.

The figure below illustrates how ASD works. In this case, a hole has been cored through the slab foundation and a plastic pipe, typically 4 inches (100 mm) in diameter, is connected to a pit dug out beneath the core. Attached to the pipe is a fan that operates continuously drawing radon-laden soil gas from beneath the slab and exhausting it to a safe location outdoors. By creating a vacuum under the slab, those small openings in the slab where soil air used to come through, interior air now goes down. In other words, an ASD reverses the flow from soil air up to indoor air down.

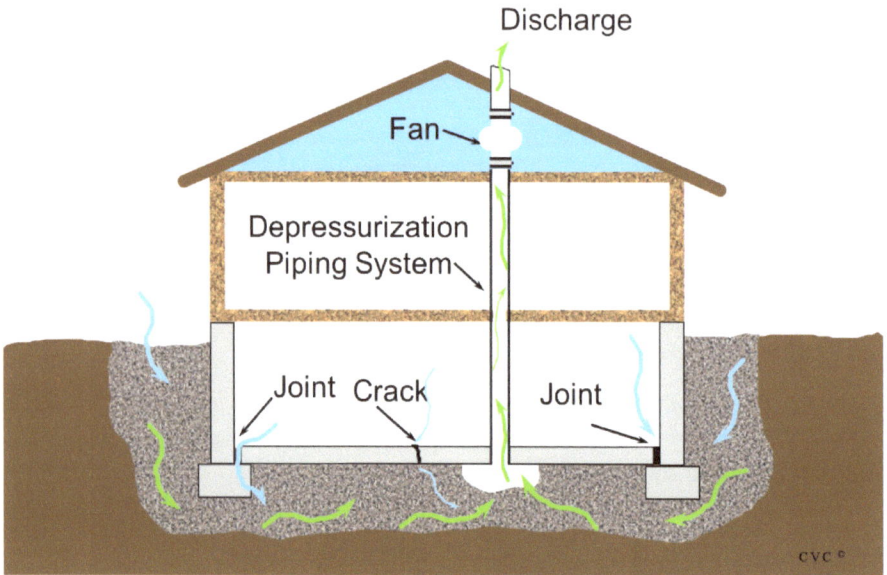

Why can't I just seal all the entry points into my home?

Without counteracting the suction exerted on the soil by the house, radon can continue to enter through extremely small and difficult to seal leak points.

Sealing is not a reliable radon reduction method on its own, however it can improve the effectiveness of an active soil depressurization system and have other benefits for energy conservation in your home.

There are many points in a home through which radon can pass. Most people consider cracks in the concrete floor as the major concern. In reality, they are very small compared to other openings such as:

Concrete Joints. Expansion joints or cold joints are located where the concrete floor meets the foundation wall. These joints can be large radon entry points. Since interior finished walls are often constructed over the tops of the joints, they are generally inaccessible for good sealing even if you wanted to try to use sealing as a stand-alone technique.

Utility Service Lines. There are openings around floor drains, plumbing and electrical conduits where radon can enter the home from beneath slabs or through walls. These openings are also very difficult to access. Often toilets, showers, and bathroom cabinets are constructed over the top of them, which makes getting to these openings for proper sealing very difficult.

Drainage Systems. Drainage systems built into a home that are designed to collect water can provide an easy pathway for radon entry. An example of this would be a sump pit located in the basement that allows ground water to seep in so it can be pumped away. If ground water can get into the sump, so can radon from the underlying soil.

Crawl Spaces and Exposed Earthen Areas. A very large soil opening is presented if your house is constructed over an earthen crawl space. Even if you have crawl space vents or your builder laid down a loose sheet of plastic as a vapor barrier, the radon can still come into the home from the crawl space area. This is because of the house vacuum described earlier. This vacuum draws air from the crawl space into the living space above. There are too many openings in the flooring above the crawl space to stop the radon from entering. The crawl space vents may decrease the suction pressure, but not counteract it completely. Also, the benefit that vents can provide is lost when they are closed in the winter months. Radon entry is often the highest during the winter season, in colder climates.

Is there value in sealing foundation openings? Absolutely. Sealing of accessible cracks will decrease the loss of interior air which has to be replaced with outdoor air and increase heating or cooling cost for the home. It will also increase the strength of the vacuum beneath your slab, thereby improving its radon reduction efficiency. Sealing against inside air loss will also greatly reduce the potential for backdrafting of combustion appliances.

So, yes, sealing is done - not as the only technique but rather to make active soil depressurization systems work more effectively. This is a good thing because it means we don't have to rip out finished walls to caulk floor-to-wall joints. Rather you will be sealing those that are reasonably accessible.

This book will show how an active depressurization system can be applied to:

- **Homes built over crawl spaces**
- **Homes that have water drainage systems**
- **Homes built over basements or are slab-on-grade**

These three applications are those most commonly used by professional mitigators. Although there are other approaches, they are normally used as a supplement to the techniques listed above. By using these techniques, you will most likely accomplish a reduction to below the US EPA guidance level of 4.0 pCi/L. If not, then call a radon mitigation specialist to determine what additional measures may be needed. You will not be wasting your time and effort by installing a system. In fact, you should be able to save hundreds of dollars even if you need additional professional help after installation.

To determine which, or how many, of the techniques will be needed for your home; you will need to spend time inspecting the foundation of your home. You will need to ask questions like: *Do I have a crawl space? Do I have a basement? Do I have both crawl space and basement? Do I have a drainage system that I can use to my advantage?* A "flow chart" style of the decision process is outlined (preceding Chapter 1) to assist the homeowner in deciding which, or how many, radon reduction techniques should be used.

How do I use this book?

There are three basic types of active depressurization systems detailed in this manual, which can either be used by themselves or combined with each other, depending upon your house construction:

- Sub-membrane depressurization for crawl spaces - **Chapter 4**
- Depressurization systems which utilize water drainage systems - **Chapter 5**
- Sub-slab depressurization systems for basements and slab-on-grade homes that do not have drainage systems - **Chapter 6**

A depressurization system is the common element for these approaches. This system consists of the piping and the fan necessary to produce the vacuum for collecting the radon for each of these approaches. Some of the following chapters are applicable to all systems, and some are applicable in certain situations as follows:

- **Chapter 7** describes the depressurization system and applies to all of the detailed mitigation systems described in Chapters 4, 5, 6, 9 and 11.
- **Chapter 8** includes another common element - sealing entry points, which will enhance all of the applied techniques.
- **Chapter 9** describes how systems treating multiple foundations like a basement and a crawlspace can be combined economically using a common depressurization system.
- **Chapter 10** covers general safety practices and is a very important chapter for all systems.
- **Chapter 11** is applicable if you are building a new home.
- **Chapter 12** is applicable if you would rather hire a professional than do it yourself.

Warning: If you only read isolated parts of this book, you will not have sufficient information to complete a radon mitigation system. This could result in poor radon reductions and injury.

Dimensional Units

Many of the dimensional measurements within this book are provided in imperial units with metric units provided on key items. The most commonly used dimension is the nominal pipe size used for the radon vent pipe which is most commonly 100 mm or 4-inch pipe. There may be occasions where smaller pipe such as 75 mm or 3 inch can be used.

Instance	Imperial	Metric
Pipe size	4-inch	100 mm
Pipe size	3-inch	75 mm

Elsewhere where inches and feet are used
1 inch = 2.54 cm
1 foot = 30.5 cm or 0.305 meter
1 meter = 3.28 feet

Chapter 3: Radon Entry and Reduction Overview

To successfully perform the repairs described in this manual without harm to you, follow the process steps outlined below. Pay special attention to the following:

> ## Radon Reduction Process
> 1. Read book (especially safety chapter)
> 2. Identify construction features of home
> 3. Plan system
> 4. Acquire materials
> 5. Reread applicable chapters
> 6. Reread safety section
> 7. Install system and seal leak points
> 8. Have a backdraft test performed
> 9. Install carbon monoxide monitor
> 10. Retest radon levels in home

Step 6 is one of the most important. Be aware that the repairs in this manual will expose you to certain hazards. Some are exposure to solvent-based caulking and glue, while others are physical hazards presented with any type of remodeling work. The caulks recommended in this manual are standard materials that can be found at many building supply stores. However, some people are sensitive to their use. If you are sensitive to organic vapors, you may not want to continue but rather hire a certified professional contractor. If you are not excessively sensitive to chemicals, and *you take the proper precautions outlined in the safety section, and follow the manufacturers' instructions,* everything should work out well.

Steps 8 and 9 are equally critical. At the conclusion of the installation, you will turn on the system. Look for leaks that can be sealed to improve the efficiency of the system. If you have large leaks that extract large volumes of indoor air, you could cause your combustion appliances to backdraft. This could also happen if the system is later broken. This condition is rare, but the effects could be life threatening.

If your hot water heater or furnace backdraft, poisonous carbon monoxide gas can accumulate in the home. *Hire a professional furnace or home inspector who has the proper equipment to evaluate your combustion appliances when you have completed the system.* Proper methods for testing for carbon monoxide are too varied and involved for the untrained individual to accomplish.

Radon reduction systems alone are not responsible for causing carbon monoxide poisoning. However, an incorrectly installed system by a well-meaning do-it-yourselfer or a system that is later broken can cause a serious safety problem. Don't take a chance with the health and safety of your family. Have a backdraft test done. Whether you install a radon system or not, it is recommended to have a backdraft test performed anyway AND to have a continuously operating carbon monoxide monitor(s) installed.

Chapter 4

How to Reduce Radon in Homes Completely or Partially Built Over Crawl Spaces

How to Achieve the Best Reduction for a Home Built Over a Crawl Space

Planning the Sub-Membrane System

Installing the Sub-Membrane System

CHAPTER 4 - HOW TO REDUCE RADON IN HOMES BUILT OVER CRAWL SPACES

How to Achieve the Best Reduction for a Home Built Over a Crawl Space

This chapter specifically deals with how to fix radon entry from crawl spaces. If your house has a basement or a slab-on-grade portion in addition to a crawl space, you need to refer to the chapters in the book which describe those systems (see Radon Reduction Flow Chart preceding Chapter 1).

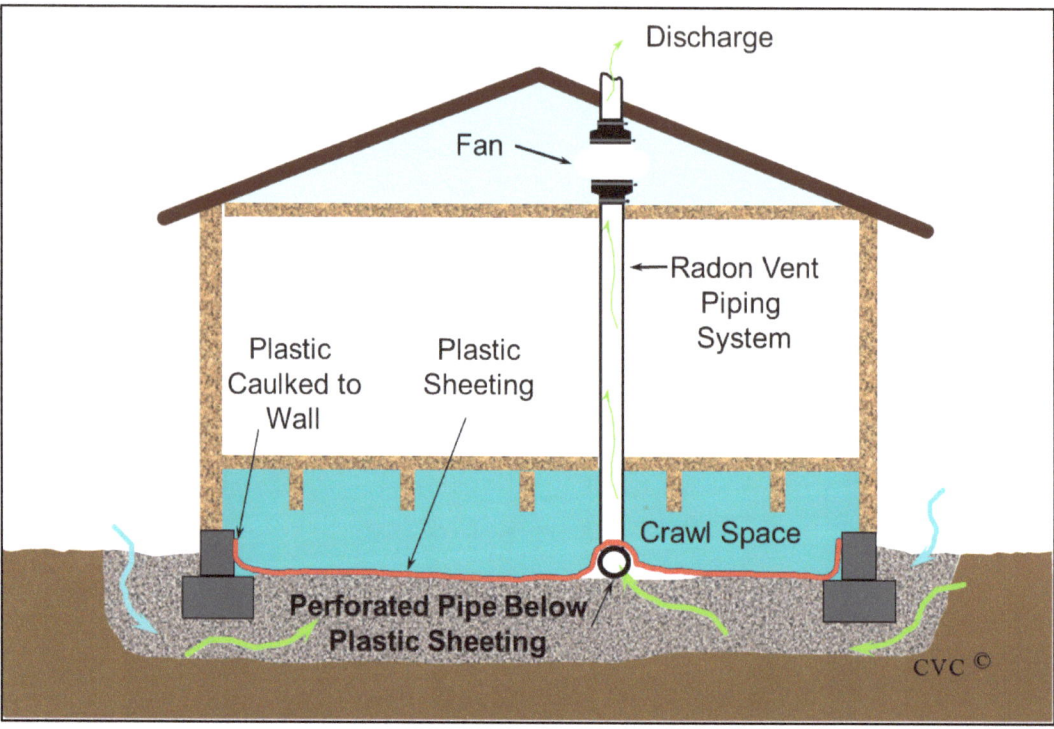

Homes are often built over crawl spaces where the living area is suspended over bare earth. Crawl spaces allow for a large entry of radon into the home even if vents to the outside were installed on the sides of the crawl space. The suction that is naturally created by the house over these crawl spaces can draw the radon, along with other soil gases, into the home. This chapter applies to homes that are constructed:

1. Completely above an earthen crawl space
2. Partially over an earthen crawl space
3. With large exposed earthen areas inside of them

Note if your crawlspace has a thin concrete floor to facilitate storage, treat it as you would a basement slab as described in Chapter 6.

Ventilating the crawl space by blowing outdoor air through it would reduce radon but can have serious side effects. Although this can reduce radon levels, it can cause freezing problems for pipes in the crawl space of homes in cold climates or moisture problems in humid climates, especially if air conditioning ductwork is in the crawlspace. The preferred method for reducing radon entry that does not present this concern; is called a **Sub-Membrane Depressurization (SMD) system.** Refer to figure above.

To construct a sub-membrane depressurization system, a perforated pipe is laid on the ground in the crawl space. A durable plastic sheet is then laid on the ground in the crawl space over the top of the perforated pipe. Next, the edges of the sheet are sealed to the walls of the crawl space and the seams are sealed. A fan is then connected to the perforated pipe to draw radon from beneath the plastic. This system collects the radon as it comes up from the soil, preventing it from entering the crawl space. The collected radon can then be exhausted harmlessly outdoors.

Chapter 4: Crawl Space Homes

BEFORE ATTEMPTING ANY WORK IN THIS SECTION, BE AWARE OF THE FOLLOWING:

1. You will be spreading plastic in a crawl space. Is there enough working room for you to crawl through this area? Can you get to all of the walls? If not, STOP. You may not want to attempt this work yourself, but rather hire a professional radon mitigator.

2. Solvent-containing caulks will be used to seal the plastic sheeting. ***If you, or other occupants of the home are sensitive to these chemicals - do not attempt this repair***. You must ventilate the crawl space area during the installation to reduce the buildup of fumes from the caulk. This can be done with a window fan. For additional ventilation, you can also run your depressurization piping (described in Chapter 7) into the crawl space area and turn it on.

3. Take proper precautions to protect hands, knees, and eyes. Crawl spaces can have a lot of sharp rocks and construction debris in them. Wear durable coveralls, kneepads, gloves, and goggles (see Chapter 10 and chart below).

4. Take proper precautions to ensure that you are not exposed to other crawl space dangers. Crawl spaces often are the homes of spiders, snakes, and rodents.

5. Crawl spaces are often sprayed with pesticides. Wear proper respiratory protection when working in these areas. Wash hands and face thoroughly after working in these areas, before eating, drinking, or any time you notice any skin or respiratory irritation.

6. **If your home has asbestos materials in the crawl space, DO NOT ATTEMPT THIS REPAIR**. Furnace ductwork and heating pipes are often run through crawl spaces. These can be wrapped in insulation containing asbestos. This material is easily damaged and forms a dust in the air, and if inhaled, can result in serious health problems. If this is the case in your home, contact a professional who is familiar with the proper precautions that must be taken to protect your health and the health of their workers.

    <u>**How to determine if asbestos is a potential problem**</u>: Asbestos wrapped ducts may look like cloth wrapped on sheet metal duct work or a cloth wrap insulation on hot water piping. The insulation on the heat piping may also look like corrugated cardboard. If your crawl space has any material that looks like this, the chances are very good that it is asbestos, and some has fallen on the dirt floor of the crawl space. If you are unsure, it is best to hire an inspector who is trained and certified in asbestos analysis.

7. Do not enter your crawl space if there is evidence of mice. Call your local health department about protection against contacting Hantavirus.

8. While ventilating and working in the crawl space, dust will be created. A dust mask is a requirement for this job (see respiratory protection discussion in Chapter 10).

☮ Tools and safety items you will need:

Goggles		Ventilation Fan		Utility Knife	
Leather Gloves		Trouble Lights		Duct Tape	
Sturdy Coveralls		Knee Pads		Caulk Gun	
Hat		Helper		Polyurethane Caulk	
Dust Mask		Smoke Stick		Flashlight	

Protecting Your Home from Radon

Planning the Sub-Membrane System

This section will focus on the work that will occur in the crawl space. The depressurization system needed to complete the system is described in Chapter 7.

Please refer to the flow chart preceding Chapter 1 to decide if additional areas of the house will need to be repaired to fully reduce radon levels.

Planning Step 1:

Measure the dimensions of the crawl space.

The following is a summary of the planning process that will be described in greater detail with an example for illustration.

Make a drawing: Make a sketch of the crawl space. Be sure to note all of the turns of the walls, the length of the walls and the location of any interior support posts that may be sitting on concrete pads. If there are concrete pads on the floor of the crawl space, measure the location of the pads and their dimensions (all four sides) and include them on your sketch.

Estimating the plastic needed: Once you have completed a sketch of the crawl space, you can estimate the amount of plastic sheeting and caulk you will need. The plastic sheeting will be laid down to cover the entire dirt floor surface of the crawl space area. When installed properly, at least 12 inches of plastic will run up the foundation walls of the crawl space. Seams need to overlap by at least 12 inches. Caulking will be used to seal the edges to the walls and also to seal all of the seams. Duct tape will be used to temporarily hold the overlapped edges of the seams together until the caulk sets up. There are also specialty tapes made by the manufacturers of the plastic sheeting that can seal seams. If you use tape, be certain it is compatible.

Type of plastic sheeting to buy: The type of plastic that is recommended is white, high density, 3-4 mil thick, cross laminated polyethylene. It can be most economically purchased in large 20-foot by 100-foot rolls.

Important: The plastic must be strong enough not to tear while installing it in the crawl space. Another important consideration is long-term durability as you, or others, crawl over the membrane. This could happen during future maintenance work on the home in the crawl space (e.g.: furnace repair, plumbing maintenance, etc.).

It is also recommended that fire retardant plastic be used.

Other Considerations: Some crawl spaces have deep trenches or uneven surfaces. You must allow for enough plastic to cover the sides and bottom of the trenches when you install the plastic sheeting. When the system is turned on, the plastic will be drawn down to the soil and conform to the irregular surfaces. The plastic acts like plastic vacuum packaging you might see on dried foods in the grocery store.

Important: Allow enough plastic so when the depressurization system is turned on and the plastic is drawn down, it will not be pulled away from the walls.

Chapter 4: Crawl Space Homes

Planning Step 2:
Determine how much plastic will be needed.

Determine the best way to lay the plastic on the crawl space surface. The sketch below shows a sample crawl space. Notice there are concrete support pads in the middle of the floor. These pads will have support posts sitting on them that support the house above. You cannot remove these support posts in order to slide the plastic over the pads. Therefore, you will have to fit the plastic around them.

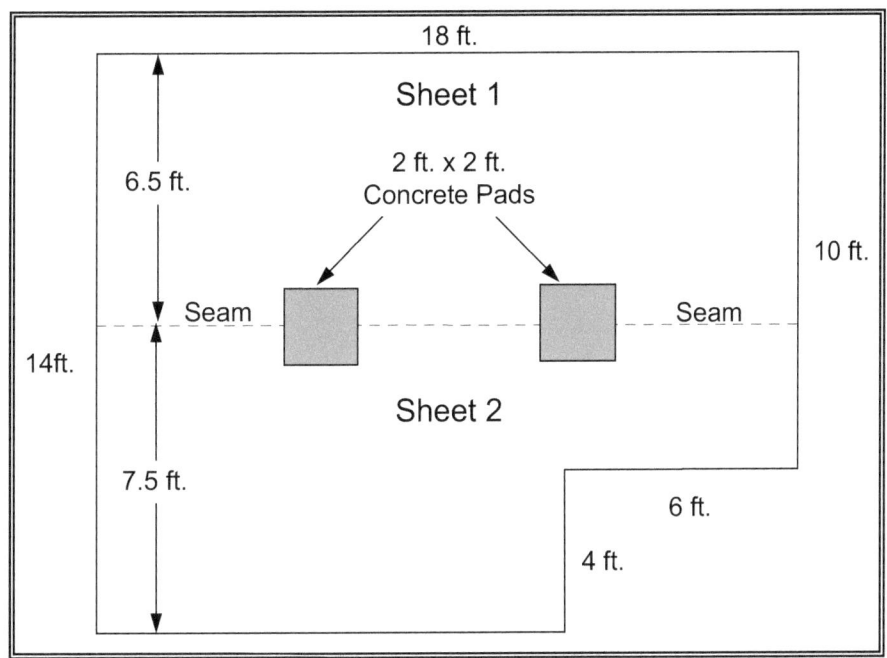

Note: Whenever an obstruction exists, such as the concrete pads shown above, it is best to plan a seam at the obstruction.

A seam line is shown on the above sketch as a dashed line going from left to right. This means that two sheets of plastic, sheet 1 and sheet 2, can be cut prior to installation. The two sheets should overlap at least 12 inches along the seam. Overlapping at the column line will make fitting the plastic around the pads much easier.

The following details are also needed to finalize the measurement of the plastic sheeting:

- Add at least 1 foot to both length and width of the sheeting for each foundation wall that the plastic will be sealed to.

- Add at least 1 foot of length or width to one of the sheets for each seam.

- Remember to add extra length if there are trenches or irregularities in the crawl space floor.

Sheet	Wall Measurement	+ Wall Seal	+ Wall Seal	+ Seam	= Total
Sheet 1 Length (feet)	18	1	1	0	20
Sheet 1 Width (feet)	6.5	1	0	1	8.5
Sheet 2 Length (feet)	18	1	1	0	20
Sheet 2 Width (feet)	7.5	1	0	(Added to sheet 1)	8.5

Protecting Your Home from Radon

Planning Step 3:

Plan how to cut the plastic.

To use the least amount of plastic and get the best results from the sub-membrane depressurization system, the picture below shows how the two sheets of plastic sheeting will be cut. It is best to cut the plastic prior to putting the plastic in the crawl space. Using a 20-foot-wide roll, a length of 20 feet would be cut from the roll and then re-cut into two 10 by 20-foot strips. If you buy the plastic sheeting in a 10-foot roll, two 20-foot-long strips would be cut from the roll.

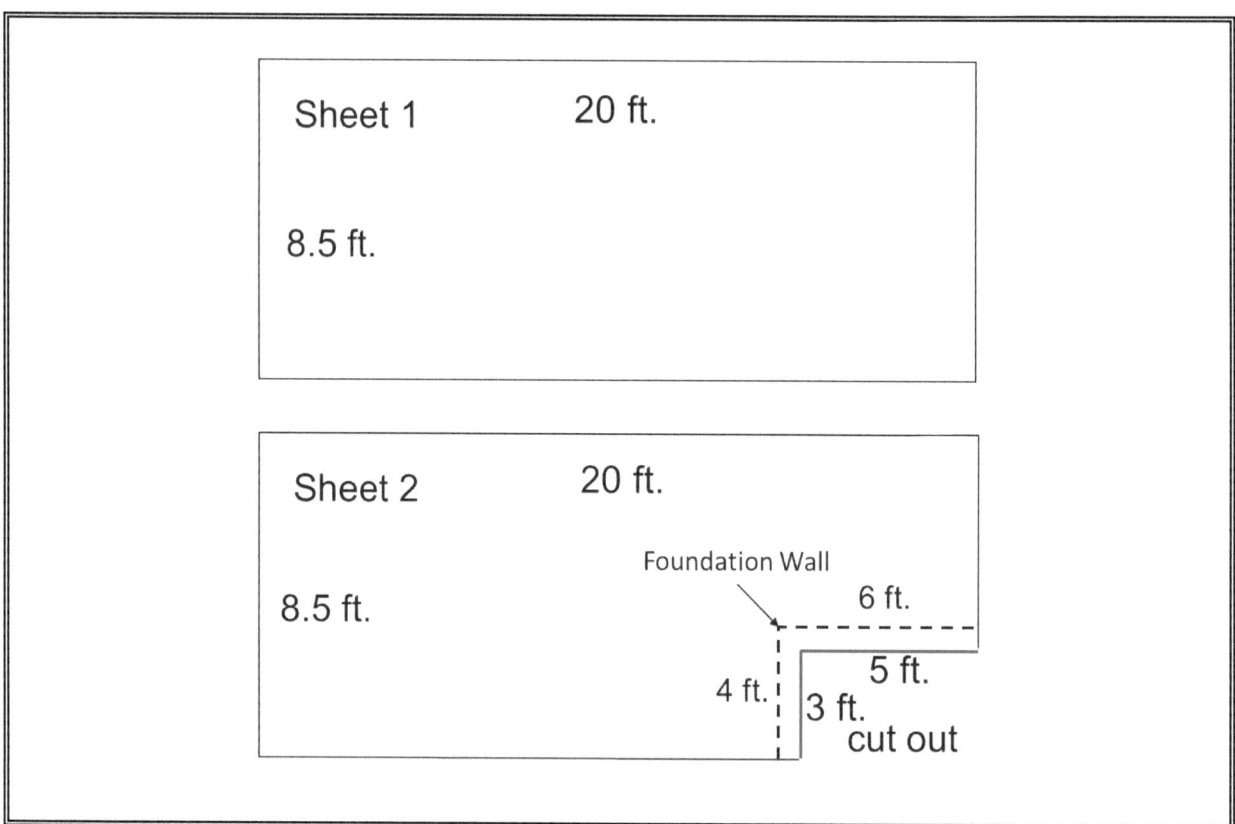

Note: In the example above the width of a single sheet was determined to be 8.5 feet. If you cut the plastic into 10-foot-wide strips this allows for a greater than the suggested 12 inch overlap at the seams. Remember that the minimum overlap is 12 inches - more is okay.

Note that a cut out has been shown for an indentation in the foundation.

How to make the cut-out:

1. Measure from the edge of the plastic closest to the indentation.
2. Make sure to add at least 1 foot of excess plastic to allow for sealing the plastic to the foundation walls.

*In the example above, you would measure 5 feet from the right edge and 3 feet from the bottom edge to accommodate the 6 ft. x 4 ft. wall.

Interior walls:

Some crawl spaces have concrete walls inside of them to support the weight of the home. Treat internal foundation walls exactly the same as an exterior wall. Cut plastic in these areas wide enough and long enough to seal the edges of the plastic at least one foot up on these walls.

Chapter 4: Crawl Space Homes

Planning Step 4:
Plan how much caulk and duct tape will be needed.

The sheeting will be sealed to the walls and at seams with caulk. Duct tape will be used to temporarily hold the plastic sheeting in place until the caulk hardens.

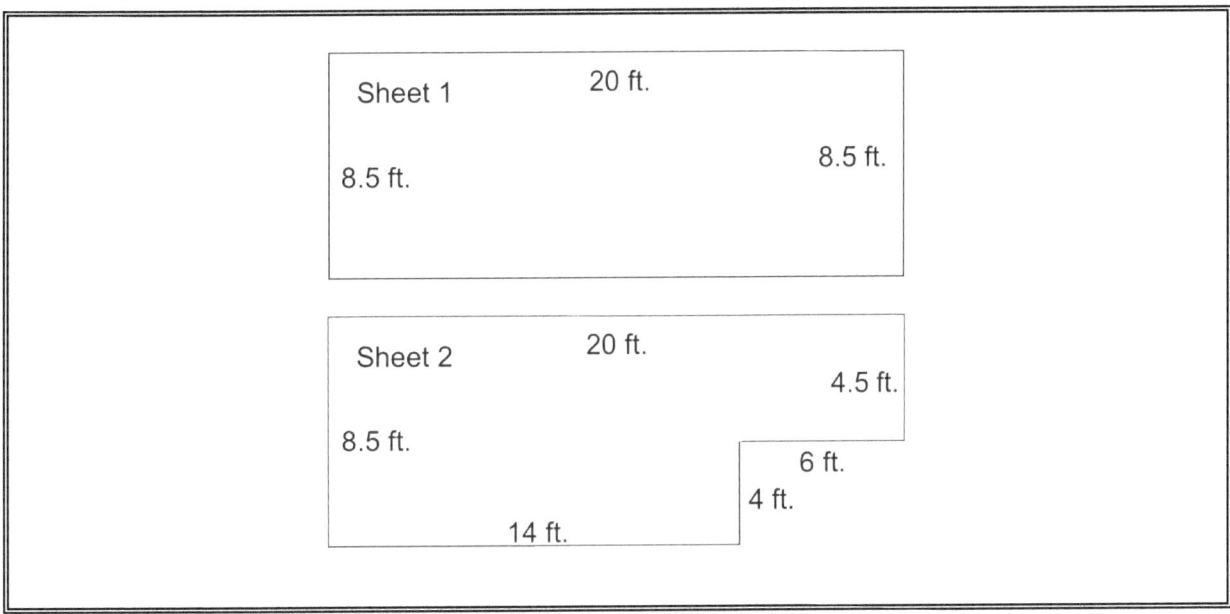

Sealing should be done at:

1. **Edges.** Wherever the plastic will come in contact with a foundation wall of the crawl space.
2. **Internal foundation walls.** If there are concrete walls that run through the inside of the crawl space, the plastic will also need to be sealed to these walls.
3. **Concrete pads.** Wherever the plastic comes in contact with a concrete pad on the floor of the crawl space.
4. **Seams.** Wherever two sheets of plastic come together, the overlapped seam must be sealed with caulk and duct tape run along the free edge to hold it in place temporarily.
    - Polyurethane caulking (or other adhesive approved by manufacturer that also adheres to concrete), which can be applied with a caulking gun. A good rule of thumb for estimating the amount of polyurethane caulk needed is:
        - One 11-ounce tube of polyurethane caulk for 8 feet of joint, seam or edge seal.

Using the previous example and assuming that the concrete pads are 1 ft. by 1 ft.

Foundation Walls	Internal walls	Pad perimeter	Seams	Total feet
8.5+20+8.5+8.5+4.5+6+4+14 =74	+0	+2 pads x4 =+8	+20	= 102

102 ft of sealing will be needed in this example. To get the number of tubes of caulk:

Divide the total feet by 8, or:

102 / 8 = 12.75

Buy at least two more tubes of caulk than needed, or in this example buy 15 tubes of polyurethane caulk. You will also need approximately 150 feet of cloth backed duct tape or construction tape.

Planning Step 5:

Plan the perforated soil gas collection pipe.

A length of corrugated and perforated 3-inch (75mm) pipe will be laid on the crawl space floor prior to installation of the plastic sheeting. This perforated pipe is commonly used as flexible, perforated drain tile around a foundation (ADS is a brand name of a common manufacturer). The perforated pipe will eventually be connected to the depressurization system through a vertical riser of PVC or ABS pipe per the detail shown later in this chapter.

The perforated pipe is laid directly on the soil with a single length of pipe running the length of the crawl space. If the crawl area is divided into sections, there will need to be a length of pipe beneath the plastic sheeting in each section of the crawl space (see next planning step).

It does not matter where the pipe is laid beneath the plastic. It does not need to run through the center of the covered area. It can be run along the wall if desired. You should plan to run it through areas to which you would not need access for routine house maintenance. This minimizes stepping on the pipe and potentially damaging the plastic sheeting that will be laid over it.

Planning Step 6:

Plan the depressurization piping system. *(See Chapter 7)*

A depressurization piping system will need to be installed to collect the radon from beneath the plastic sheeting. This piping system and its fan are described in detail in Chapter 7. The depressurization piping system will connect to a perforated pipe that will be laid on the crawl space floor before the plastic sheeting is installed. As a preview, the depressurization piping will meet the following criteria:

- Pipe above plastic sheeting should be schedule 40 PVC or ABS pipe.
- Piping should be sloped back down to the suction point, which, in this case, is the point that the piping connects to the plastic sheeting.
- The depressurization fan should be mounted vertically in the piping system.
- The discharge of the system (where the radon will be exhausted) should be at a location that will not allow the exhausted gases to re-enter the house.
- The piping system should be labeled.
- The fan should be low-voltage, class 2, installed by homeowner, or 120 volts hard wired according to codes.
- There should be a mechanical performance indicator installed.
- Piping that is routed through unheated spaces in cold climates will need to be insulated.
- When piping is routed from the interior of a home and into a garage via a wall that separates the house from the garage through a garage wall, a fire barrier must be used to maintain the fire rating of the wall. The penetration should also be sealed to prevent air leakage. The same requirement also applies if you are routing through a fire rated ceiling.

Chapter 4: Crawl Space Homes

Planning Step 7:

Planning the depressurization piping system if the crawl space is in sections.

Some crawl spaces have internal concrete foundation walls for supporting the home. If this is the case with your home, you will have to treat each section of the crawl space as a mini-crawl space system.

Each section will have its own piece of plastic sheeting sealed to the concrete walls.

Each section will have a separate suction point riser that is tied to a common depressurization system (see figure below).

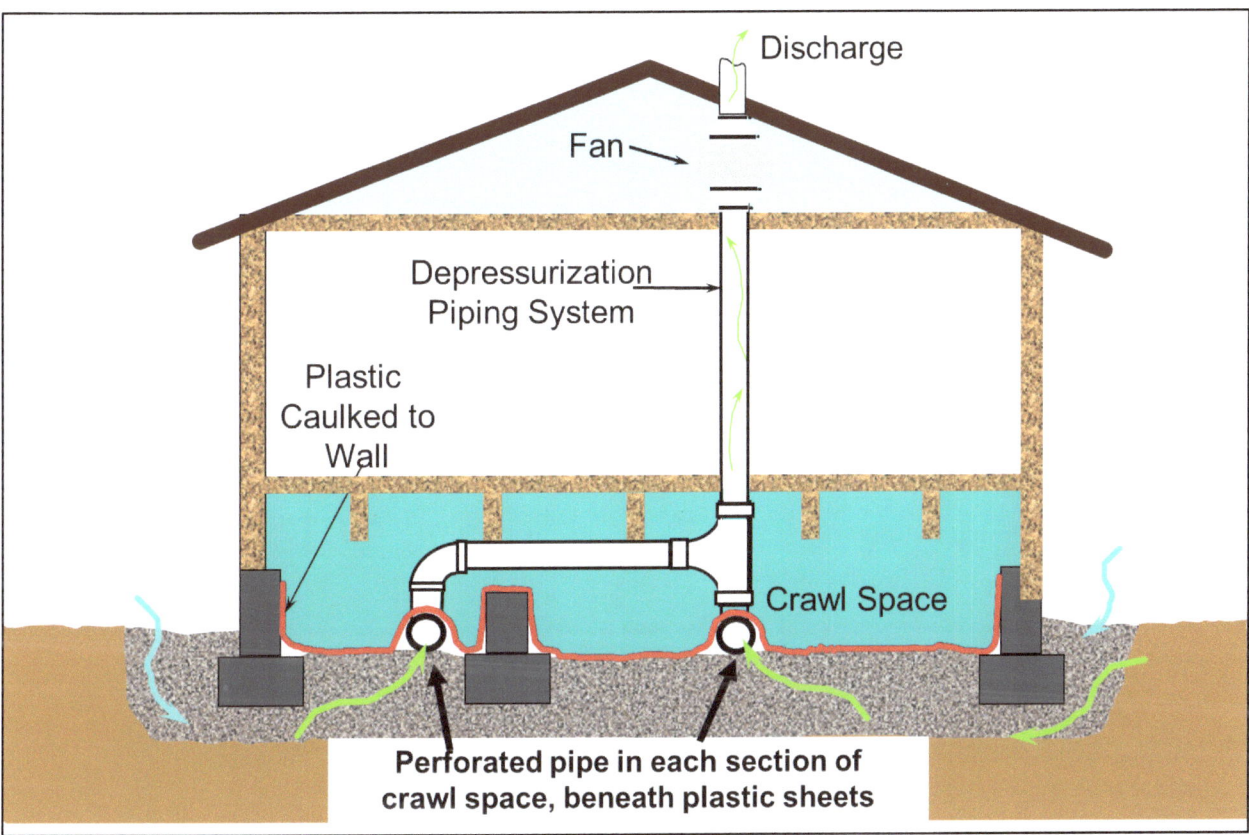

Each of the risers can be connected to a common length of schedule 40 PVC or ABS piping that is then routed to a single fan. This piece of pipe is referred to as a "header" with tees or elbows installed to connect it to each suction point. This header can be supported from the floor joists or on top of the intermediate foundation walls.

Planning Step 8:

Making the connection to the perforated piping.

As described earlier, a length of perforated pipe will be laid on the crawl space dirt before the plastic is installed. Depressurization piping will be attached later to this perforated piping. If the system riser is located in the center of a crawl space, the perforated pipe is cut and a tee is installed (the illustration below shows how this is done). If the suction-piping riser is to be at one end of the crawl space, a PVC or ABS elbow would be used instead of a tee.

Note: If your crawl space is separated by foundation walls, more than one riser is needed.

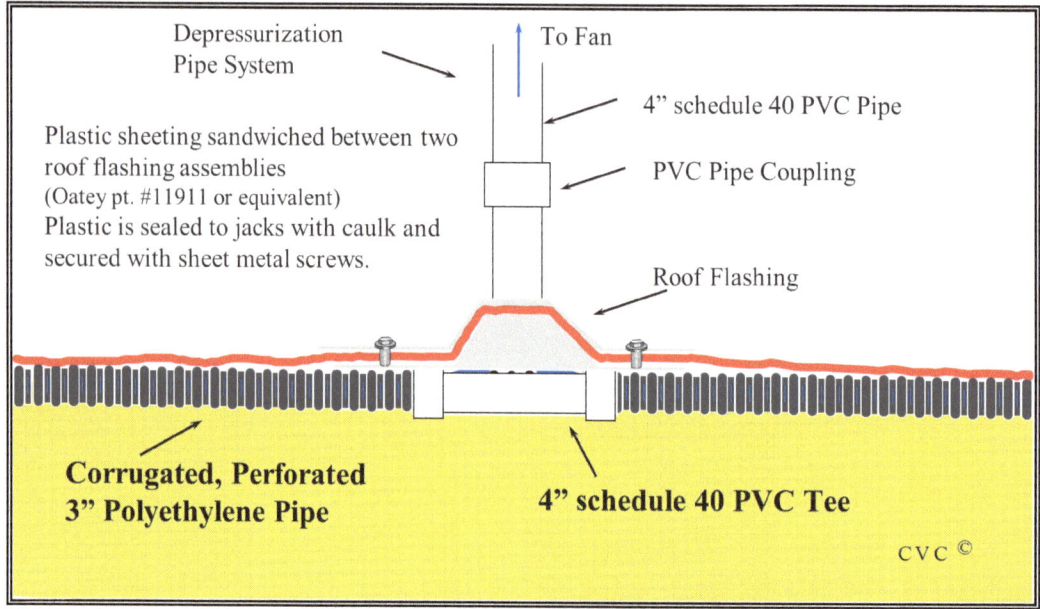

To achieve a tight seal at the point where the suction pipe passes through the sheeting, the use of roof jacks (pipe flashing) with neoprene collars (standard plumbing vent flashing) is very effective. These roof jacks are approximately 12 inches by 12 inches square with a round opening in the middle. This round opening has a flexible neoprene donut or gasket that will slide down around the vent pipe. The neoprene gasket makes the seal around the pipe.

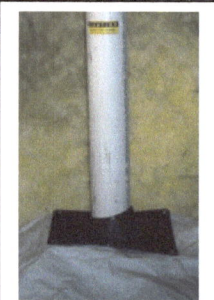

Riser Sealed to Sheeting with Pipe Flashing

Two roof jacks are used to accomplish the seal for each suction riser. One is installed on the riser pipe below the plastic sheeting. The other roof jack is placed on the riser pipe above the plastic sheeting. This allows the sheeting to be sandwiched between the two flat portions of the roof jacks. A round hole is simply cut in the sheeting for the riser to pass through, and a circle of caulking is applied to both the top of the lower roof jack plate and the bottom of the upper roof jack plate. When the two plates are compressed and screwed together, a very tight seal is achieved. In addition to a little caulk, you will need the following materials for each suction point connection:

Item:	Quantity
Polyethylene roof jack for 4-inch pipe	2
4-inch PVC or ABS elbow or tee	1
12-inch-long section of 4-inch PVC or ABS pipe	1
4-inch PVC or ABS coupling	1
# 8 x 3/4-inch sheet metal screws	4
3-inch corrugated and perforated pipe (ADS) long enough to run length of crawl space	

Chapter 4: Crawl Space Homes

Installing the Sub-Membrane System

In this section, step by step instructions will be given for the installation of this system. Read this entire section along with the previous section regarding the planning of the system before proceeding. ***Read Chapter 10 on safety before starting.***

Installation Step 1:

    Assemble equipment and materials.

The following is a checklist of equipment and materials that you will need to have before starting.

Area	Item	🕐
Safety		
	Goggles / safety glasses	
	Dust mask	
	Leather gloves	
	Knee pads	
	First aid kit	
	Ventilation fan	
	Assistant	
	Flashlight	
	Trouble lights	
	Heavy coveralls	
	Hat (Bump cap, skull cap, or heavy baseball cap) to protect head hitting floor joists	
Material	Plastic sheeting-4 mil, high density cross-laminated polyethylene is preferred	
	Duct tape	
	Sheet metal screws	
	caulk	
	corrugated pipe	
	roof jacks	
	Depressurization system piping and fan system (see Chapter 7)	
	4 x 4 x 4 PVC Tee	
	12-inch length of 4-inch (100 mm) PVC or ABS pipe	
	PVC or ABS primer and glue (use appropriate glue for the type of pipe you use)	
Tools	Rake	
	Shovel	
	Utility knife and razor blades	
	Caulking gun	
	Tool bucket	
	Drill	
	Trash can	
	Rags	
	Extension cords	
	Screwdriver	
	Flashlight	
	Smoke stick (see page 4-23 and Chapter 8)	
	Wire brush	

© Copyright 2023 • Center for Environmental Research and Technology, Inc.

Protecting Your Home from Radon

Installation Step 2:

    Set up safety equipment.

DO NOT BEGIN THIS WORK IF:

- **ASBESTOS IS FOUND IN THE CRAWL SPACE**
- **CHEMICAL SPRAYS HAVE BEEN USED, OR**
- **MICE INHABIT THE CRAWL SPACE.**

IF FOUND, CEASE ALL WORK AND CONTACT A PROFESSIONAL!

The first step in this project will be to ensure adequate ventilation during the work.

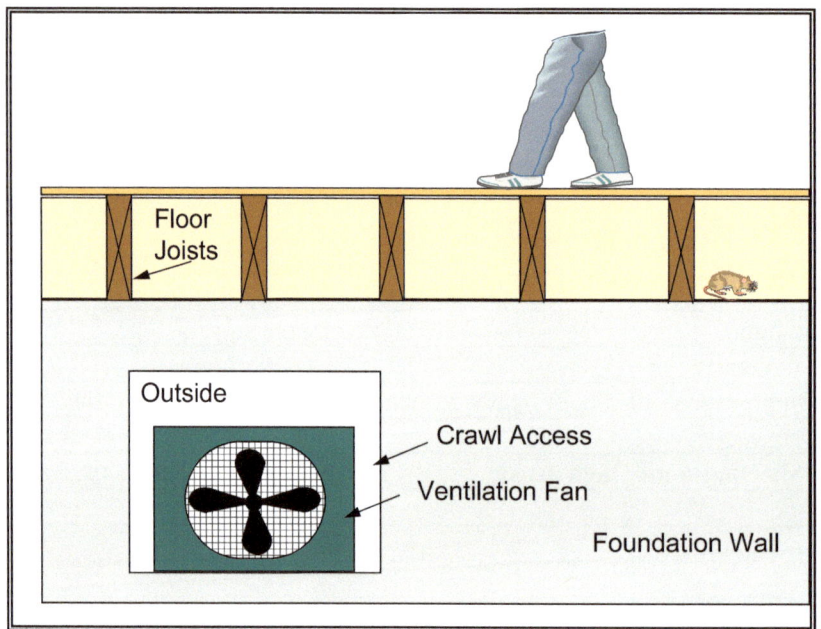

- A powered fan, as shown above, can sit in front of the crawl space access for good ventilation of the crawl space.

- A window fan can be used in place of a powered fan to ventilate the crawl space.

- MAKE SURE ALL OF THE CRAWL SPACE VENTS ARE OPEN TO ENSURE GOOD CROSS FLOW OF AIR.

- Set fans up so they draw air from the crawl space and exhaust fumes and dusts to outside of the home.

Window Fan Providing Fresh Air in Crawlspace While Working

Prepared Homeowner

Protective Clothing

Crawl spaces are notorious for having sharp objects such as old boards with nails, glass, sharp rocks, and construction debris. You should also protect your head and eyes from wires and nails that can protrude down from the sub-flooring.

© Copyright 2023 • Center for Environmental Research and Technology, Inc.

Chapter 4: Crawl Space Homes

Installation Step 3:

Prepare the crawl space floor.

- Remove stored items from the crawl space.
- Remove loose construction debris from the crawl space floor.
- Remove broken glass and other sharp objects.
- Remove large rocks from the crawl space area or dig a pit in the crawl space and put them into it. Cover the pit over with loose dirt.
- Rake the floor to collect small sharp objects and dispose of them.

It is not necessary to remove all pebbles and rocks. The plastic sheeting that is suggested for use is very strong and is resistant to puncture. However, if you plan to access the crawl space often or if you plan to use it as storage in the future, it would be wise to protect the plastic from the rocks beneath it. Protect the plastic in frequently used areas by laying roofing felt (tar paper) on the dirt before you lay the plastic sheeting down. If you plan to store items on top of the plastic, may want to lay carpet scraps over the plastic in these areas in addition to the roofing felt below the plastic to protect it.

Installation Step 4:

Lay out perforated pipe.

Cut the length of corrugated pipe needed to run the length of the crawl space.

Perforated pipe on crawlspace floor

- Lay the pipe in areas away from crawl space access openings.
- The pipe does not have to run the exact length of the crawl space. It can be cut back a few feet from each end of the crawl space.
- If your system suction piping riser is to be at one end of the crawl space, run the pipe to that point where you will connect it to a 4-inch (100 mm) PVC OR ABS elbow riser (see next installation step).
- If your system suction piping riser will be more centrally located, then cut the length of pipe into two pieces. Lay the two sections in the crawl space so two ends of the pipe can be connected to either side of a 4-inch (100 mm) PVC OR ABS tee. The location of this tee should be where the suction system riser will be.
- If your crawl space is broken into sections (as would be the case with internal foundation walls) each crawl space will need a separate system of perforated pipe and suction system riser.

Installation Step 5:

Make riser connection to perforated pipe.

At the point in the perforated pipe where the suction system riser is to be located, make either of the connections depicted below.

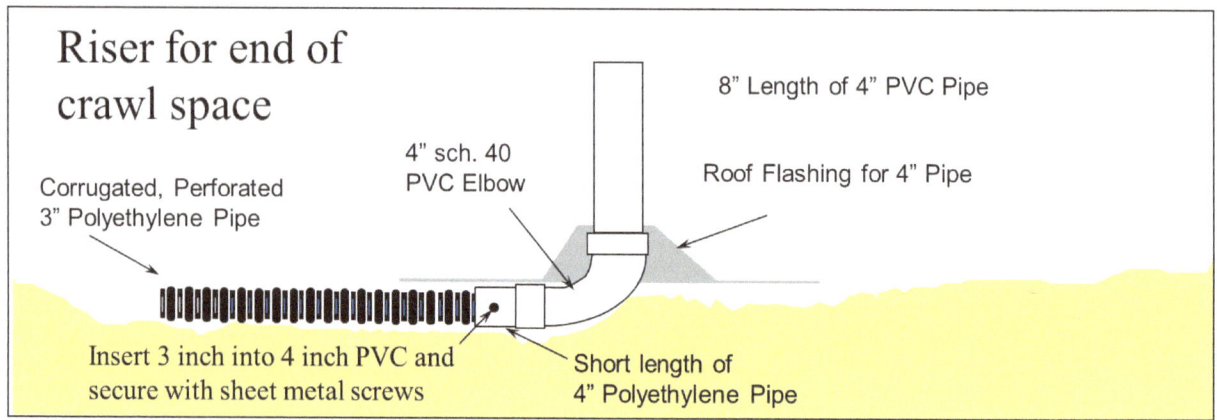

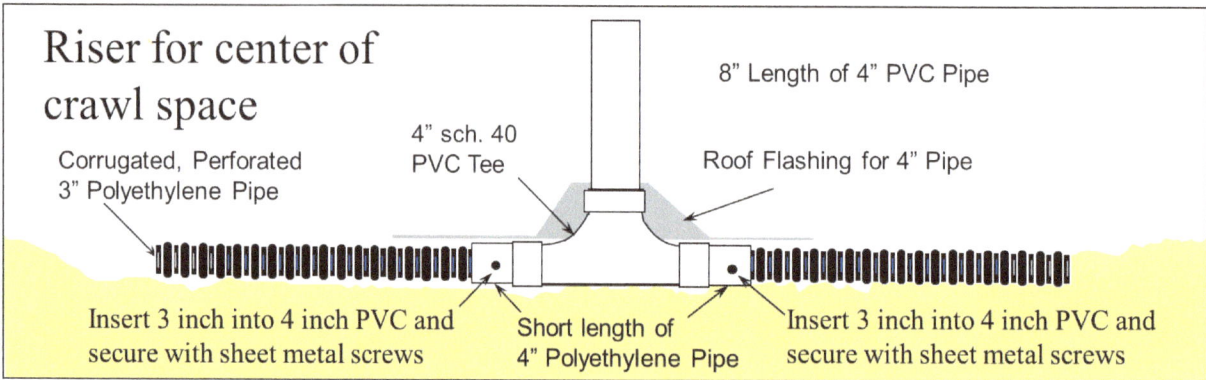

If the perforated pipe is extending only in one direction from the suction piping, use the upper illustration.

If the perforated pipe is to be laid in two opposite directions from the riser point, use the lower illustration.

- If using the upper illustration, glue an eight-inch length of 4-inch diameter PVC or ABS riser pipe into one end of the elbow. If using the lower illustration, glue an 8-inch length of 4-inch diameter PVC or ABS riser into the vertical portion of the tee. The piece of pipe will later be connected to the depressurization system and should not be less than eight inches long. Use proper primer and glue to make this connection. AVOID SKIN AND EYE CONTACT WITH GLUE.

- Connect the perforated pipe to the end of the elbow as in the upper illustration or to both ends of the tee as in the lower illustration. A 3-inch ADS pipe will fit snugly inside of the 4-inch (100 mm) elbow or tee. The ends of the corrugated pipe should be pushed in 2 inches and secured with three sheet metal screws for each connection. The sheet metal screws should be run through the outside of the PVC or ABS fitting and into the ADS pipe to securely hold it into the fitting. Attach with either a drill or screwdriver or use a nut driver on a variable speed electric drill. It is not important to glue this joint since it will be beneath the plastic sheeting.

- Slide the roof jack down over the short length of pipe so its seal is on top.

Chapter 4: Crawl Space Homes

Installation Step 6:
Cut and spread plastic out on floor.

Refer back to the sketch that you made during the planning stage of this chapter. Lay the plastic out on a flat surface like a garage floor or on the lawn. Carefully measure the plastic and cut it to the dimensions that you had planned. ***Remember the old rule: Measure twice and cut once.***

- Use a measuring tape.
- A chalk line is useful in making straight lines for cutting.
- Cut the plastic with a sharp knife or scissors.
- The plastic can be oversized but not undersized. You can trim it once it is installed.

After you have cut the sheets, roll them up and take them into the crawl space. Roll them out in the fashion you plan to install the sheets.

- Remember you will need about 12 inches to go up each wall for a good seal.
- Remember you will need about 12 inches of overlap where the sheets meet to form a seam.
- Spread sheeting under plumbing pipes and ductwork that may be in the crawl space.
- Set rocks or bricks on the plastic to stabilize it while you spread it out and work on it.

Protecting Your Home from Radon

Installation Step 7:

Preparing the walls for sealing.

The key to any seal is how well you prepare the surface. The polyurethane caulk recommended in this manual is very durable, provided it has been applied to a relatively clean surface. Other adhesives such as specialty, double-sided tape may also be used if recommended and approved by the polyethylene manufacturer for this use.

- Brush the surface of the concrete walls where the plastic will contact for sealing. The key is to remove the loose surface dirt. Brush an area of the wall approximately 6 inches above the dirt level. Remember you will next run a thick bead of caulk along this surface. Brush where you think you will be running this bead of caulk.

- You can prep all of the walls at one time, or you can brush a portion and then caulk the plastic to it in order to minimize your movement on the plastic.

- If the walls are damp, this is of no consequence. The polyurethane will adhere to damp (not wet!) concrete walls.

Chapter 4: Crawl Space Homes

Installation Step 8:

Sealing the plastic in place.

Caution: Before proceeding with this step:

- Be sure you have read the manufacturer's safety data sheet for the caulk and are familiar with the properties of this material.
- Be sure your ventilation fan is operating. Some people are sensitive to the fumes from the solvents that are in these caulks. A chemical resistant respirator may be appropriate if you are sensitive or cannot get good ventilation.
- Do not wear a respirator unless you have the pulmonary capacity to breathe through it when you exert yourself.
- See Chapter 10 on safety.

To seal the sheeting to the walls of the crawl space, a thick bead of polyurethane caulk is applied directly onto the surface of the concrete. A hand powered caulking gun works well for application.

- Apply a single continuous bead of caulk on the surface of the concrete about 6 inches up on the wall. The bead should be about 1/2 inch wide. Remember, one tube should run approximately 8 feet. **DON'T SKIMP !**

- As soon as possible (less than 20 minutes) after applying the caulk, press the plastic onto the caulk and smooth the plastic firmly along the entire length of the bead of caulk. Set a rock or a brick on the plastic to keep it from shifting as you move around so it doesn't get pulled off the wall.

- In corners, apply a liberal amount to the wall and the back side of the plastic and fold it into the corner (see Installation Step 11).

Apply ~ ½ inch wide bead of caulk

Press plastic sheeting into place

© Copyright 2023 • Center for Environmental Research and Technology, Inc.

Protecting Your Home from Radon

Installation Step 9:

Temporarily securing the edges of the plastic.

Because it takes a few days for the caulk to fully cure, and you will be crawling around on the plastic, it is a good idea to secure the plastic where you have sealed it.

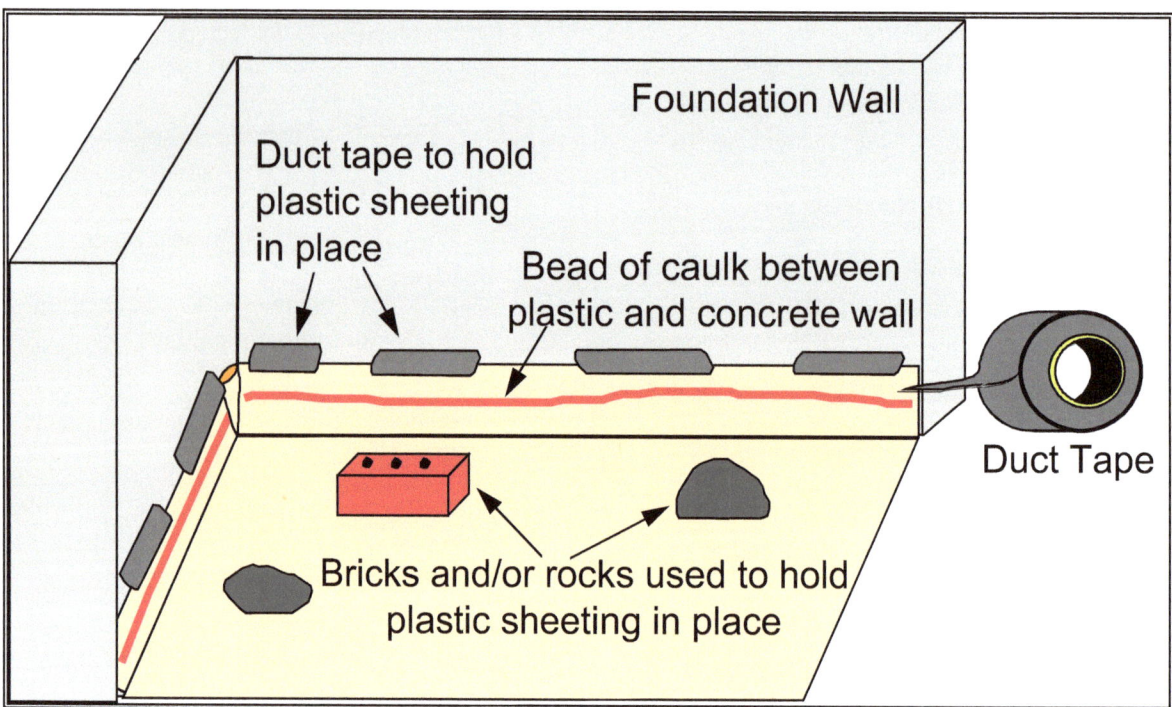

- This can be done by taping free edge of plastic sheeting to the wall with a high-quality duct tape.
- It is also a good idea to set a rock or brick on the plastic near the concrete wall.
- If the plastic is accidentally pulled off, you can always re-glue it to the wall.
- While securing plastic in place, this is a good time to see if you have put a continuous bead of caulk behind the plastic. If not, pull the plastic back and re-caulk it.
- If you have used the plastic and caulk recommended in this manual, you should be able to see the bead of caulk through the plastic.
- Run your hand along the plastic over the bead of caulk and press the plastic on, pushing the plastic onto the caulk on the wall to ensure a good seal.

Chapter 4: Crawl Space Homes

Installation Step 10:

Fitting around plumbing pipes and pads.

One of the difficult parts of installing the plastic sheeting is sealing around obstacles on the crawl space floor. Typical obstructions found are vertical plumbing pipes and concrete pads that are under house support posts.

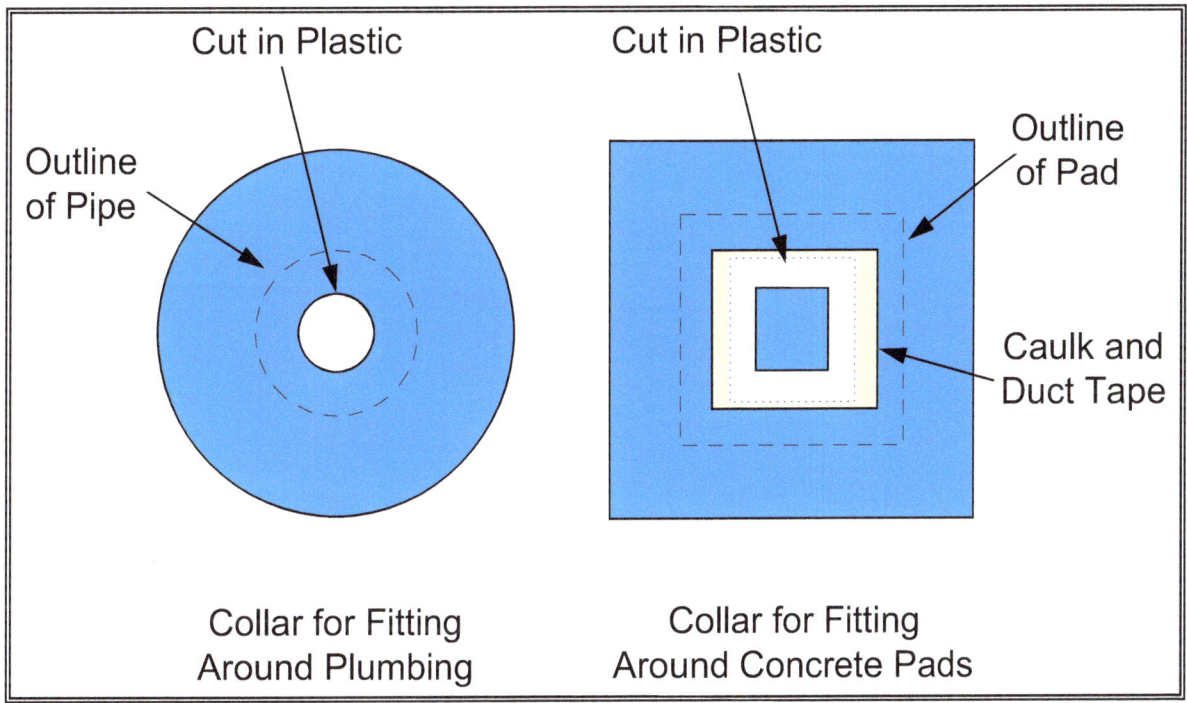

Fitting around vertical pipes:

The cut-out shown on the left side of the figure above would be made for sealing around a plumbing pipe that rises up from the crawl space floor. This circular cut-out is approximately 2 feet in diameter. A round hole cut in the center of the plastic should be at least two inches smaller than the diameter of the pipe you are going to seal around (the outline of the pipe is shown as a dashed line in above left figure). A cut is made from the center hole to the outside edge of the collar. This will allow you to slip the collar around the pipe. Run a 1/2-inch bead of caulk around the surface of the pipe at the point where you are going to seal it to the collar. Open the collar and place the inner circle around the pipe and wrap duct tape around it several times to hold the collar tightly against the caulk. Run a bead of caulk along the cut in the collar, overlap the two edges, press together and cover with duct tape. You should cut the main sheet of plastic so it can be placed around the pipe. The collar should preferably be below the main sheet of plastic. Run a 1/2-inch bead of caulk in a circle on the face of the collar and press the main sheet of plastic onto the caulk. Seal the slit in the main sheet as you would a seam. This method will provide an excellent seal.

Fitting around pads:

The collar shown on the right-hand side of the figure above is for concrete pads (the outline of the concrete pad is shown as a dashed line). Wire brush and apply a continuous 1/2-inch bead of caulk around the top surface of the pad. Fit the rectangular collar around the support post, laying the plastic on the caulk on top of the pad. Press the plastic onto the caulk to form a seal. Apply caulk to the cut on the collar and tape it. Tape the free inside edge of the collar to the concrete. You should cut the main sheet of plastic so it can be placed around the pad and post. The collar preferably should be below the main sheet of plastic. Run a 1/2-inch bead of caulk in a circle on the face of the collar and press the main sheet of plastic onto the caulk. Seal the slit in the main sheet as you would any seam.

© Copyright 2023 • Center for Environmental Research and Technology, Inc.

Protecting Your Home from Radon

Installation Step 11:

Fitting plastic into corners.

Sealing the plastic into corners is important for obtaining a good seal. This is especially true for areas of the crawl space that are the closest to the perforated gas collection pipe. Sealing corners is similar to wrapping gifts.

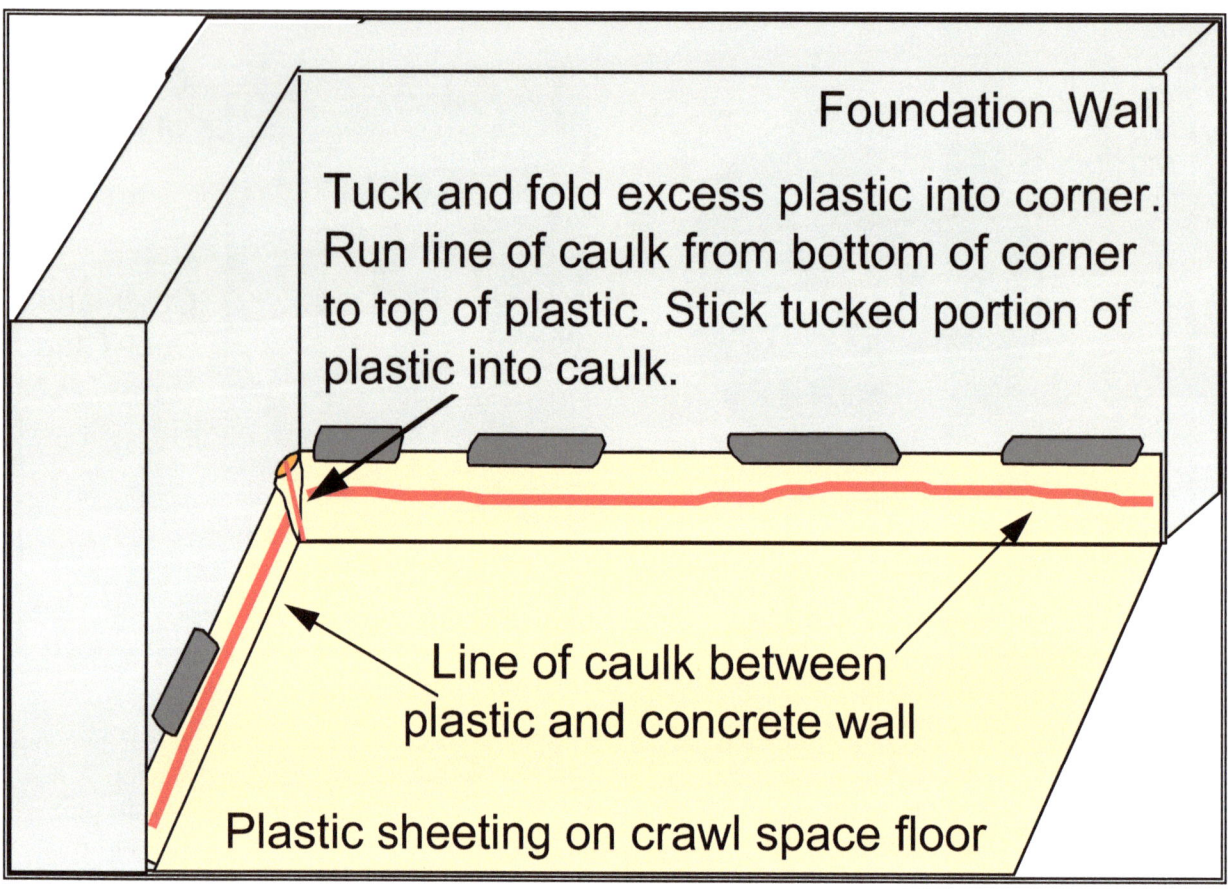

Run a ½-inch bead of caulk along the walls for sealing the edges of the plastic. Run this bead into and around the corner. While pushing the plastic into the corner at the base of the wall, press the edges of the plastic into the caulk on the walls and corner. This should leave a triangular shaped flap extending out from the corner. Run a bead of caulk on the exterior surface of the plastic, on one side of the corner and press this tuck onto it. Open the flap of the tuck and squirt some caulk into it and press it closed.

Tape the free edges of the plastic to the walls and set rocks or bricks on the plastic to hold it in place until the entire installation is completed.

Chapter 4: Crawl Space Homes

Installation Step 12:

Sealing seams.

After the plastic has been fit and sealed onto the walls, into the corners and around posts, it is time to seal the seams.

IT IS CRITICAL YOU DO NOT PULL THE PLASTIC TIGHT TOWARDS THE SEAM. LEAVE IT LOOSE WITH SEVERAL INCHES OF EXCESS IN THE PLASTIC.

IF YOU MAKE A TIGHT FIT, THE PLASTIC WILL BE PULLED AWAY FROM THE WALLS WHEN THE DEPRESSURIZATION SYSTEM IS TURNED ON.

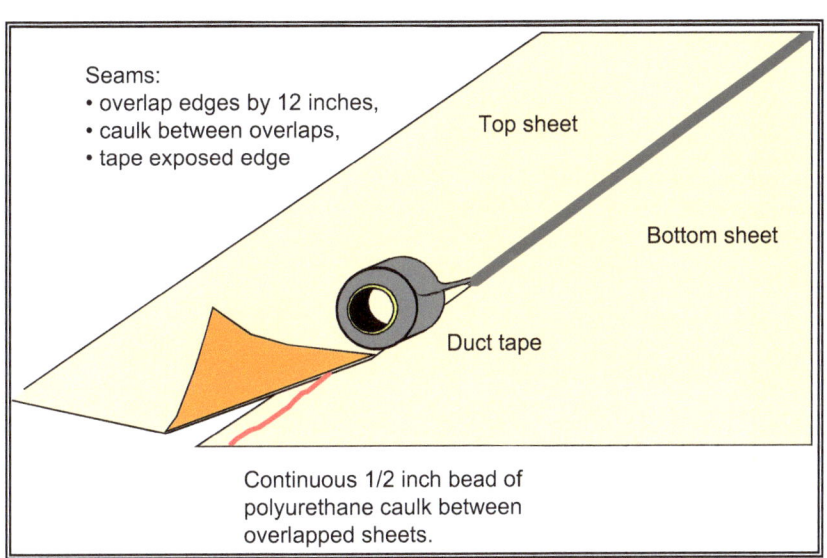

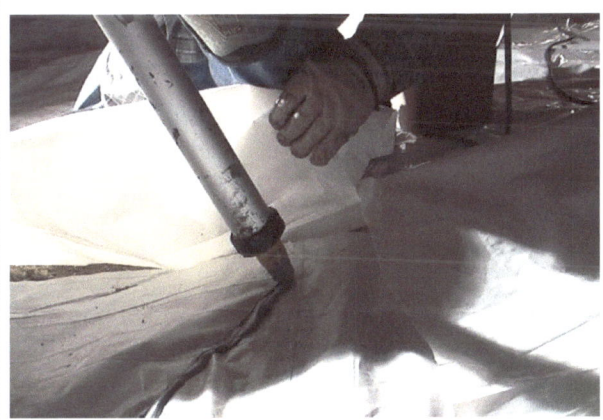

Apply polyurethane caulk at seam, overlap by 12 inches, and press top sheet into caulk.

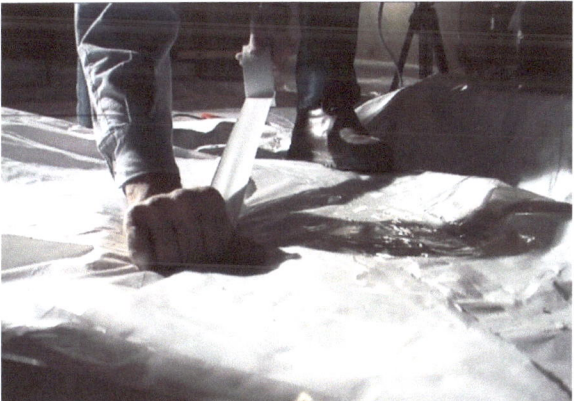

Apply tape at edges to hold poly in place until caulk cures.

The seam seal is made by overlapping two edges by at least 12 inches. Apply a 1/2-inch-wide bead of caulk on top of the sheet of plastic that will be on the bottom of the overlap. Lay the overlapping sheet on top of the bottom sheet. Using your hand, press down on the top sheet along the bead of caulk. You should be able to see through the plastic in order to see you have a continuous bead of caulk. Using cloth backed duct tape or construction tape, secure the free edge of the top sheet to the bottom sheet. This will hold the seam until the caulk sets up.

Protecting Your Home from Radon

The bead of caulk does not have to be straight as long as it is continuous - don't skip sections. The bead should not be closer than 3 inches from either edge of the seam or it will squirt out and make a mess when you press the two sheets together.

Installation Step 13:

    Finish connection at riser pipe.

Return to the location where the riser attached to the perforated pipe comes through the plastic. Note that the 4-inch PVC or ABS riser should be protruding through a 6-inch circular hole in the plastic sheeting.

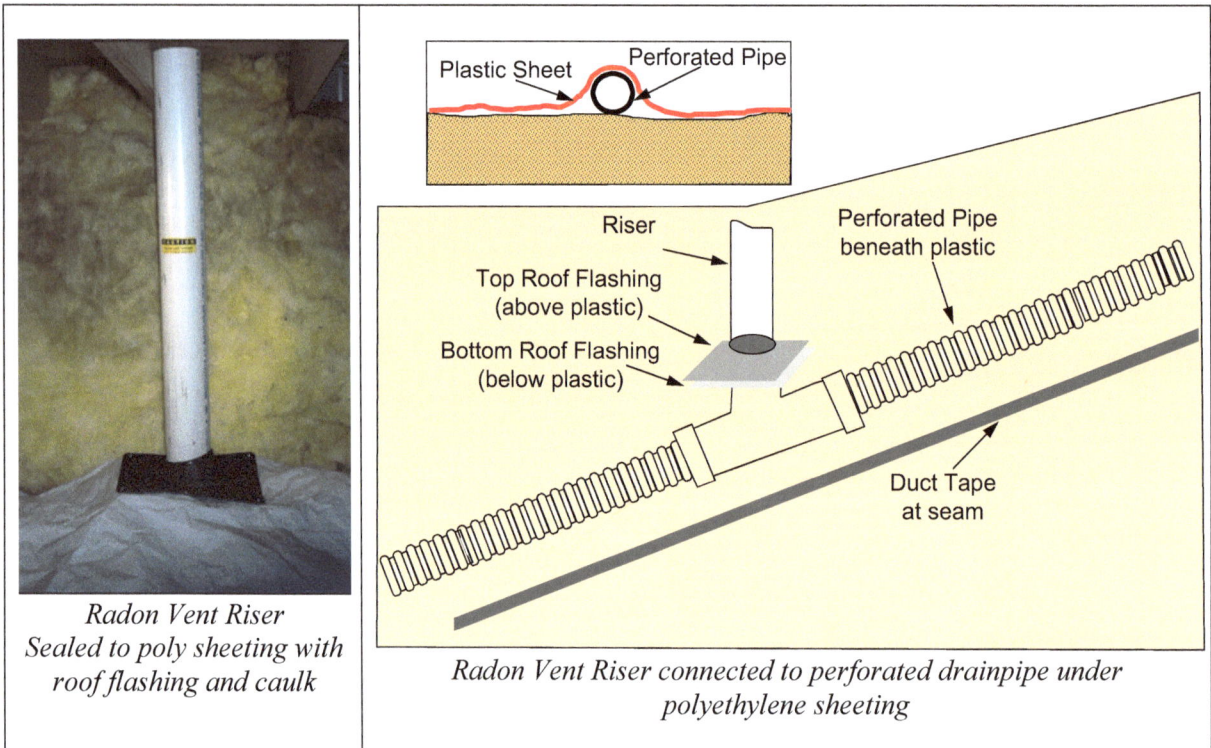

Radon Vent Riser Sealed to poly sheeting with roof flashing and caulk

Radon Vent Riser connected to perforated drainpipe under polyethylene sheeting

- Apply a 1/2-inch-wide circle of caulk to the surface of the plastic around the 6-inch hole.
- Slide the second roof flashing down over the 4-inch PVC or ABS riser pipe and press the plate portion of the roof jack onto the caulking.
- Using four 1-inch #8 self-tapping sheet metal screws, secure the top roof jack to the bottom roof jack beneath the plastic. Drill the four screws in so that they will penetrate through the caulking that was applied to the plastic sheeting. Tightening the screws will draw the plates together and sandwich the plastic in between. The caulk will set up and create a good seal at this critical point.
- Connect the depressurization piping system to the riser by using a 4-inch (100 mm) PVC or ABS pipe coupling (see Chapter 7).

Chapter 4: Crawl Space Homes

Installation Step 14:

Checking for leaks with system fully installed and on.

After the system has been turned on, a suction will be created beneath the plastic. This vacuum catches radon and other soil gases that would have otherwise entered the crawl space and eventually entered the home. The better the vacuum is, the better the radon reduction will be. A better vacuum can be produced by finding and sealing leaks in the plastic at seams, edge seals and at locations where the plastic was sealed around obstructions.

Overhead View of where polyethylene sheeting is attached to wall

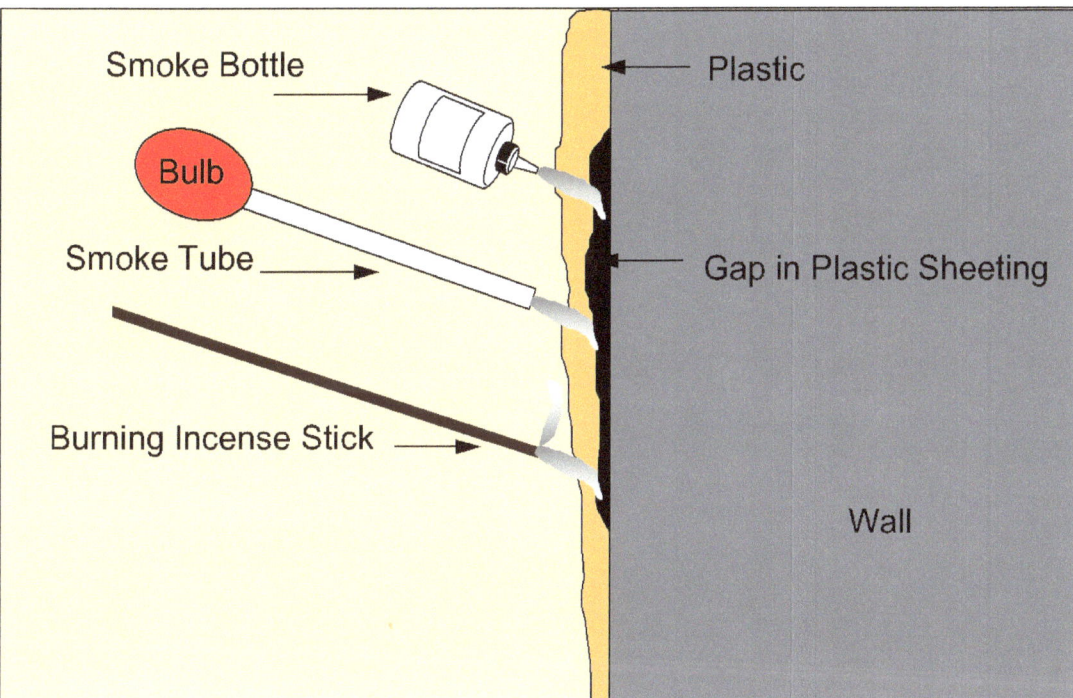

Sometimes you can hear air being drawn down through a leak. However, it is best to use some type of smoke generator to detect air being drawn down below the plastic. The picture above shows three different types of smoke generators that can be used for this purpose. A flashlight should be used to help see the direction that the smoke moves. If it goes down through an opening, use some caulk to reseal the opening until smoke is no longer seen flowing through the opening.

Burning Incense Stick: An incense stick or a "punk" can be purchased that, when lit with a match, burns slowly, and produces a light smoke. This can be held close to a seam to see if a leak is causing the smoke to be drawn down. If so, re-seal the seam with caulk. Because the smoke is warm, it will want to rise on its own, therefore it is as not as sensitive for finding leaks as other devices. To compensate for this, put the burning end as close to the opening as possible and shine a flashlight on the smoke and look for small wisps of smoke being drawn down.

Smoke Bottles or Tubes: These are devices that can be ordered from radon catalog supply houses or from a heating and ventilating equipment supplier. They are filled with a fine powder that when squeezed from the bottle will float in the direction of air flow. These devices are typically more sensitive than the incense stick and more likely to find leaks. Use a flashlight with these devices as well.

For this application the incense stick is more than satisfactory.

Installation Step 15:

Labeling and maintenance.

After you have spent what was probably an incredibly entertaining weekend of crawling through the underbelly of your house, it would be a shame if one of your family members or a workman in the future inadvertently damaged the plastic sheeting. A label should be placed near or on the crawl space access door to warn people not to cut or remove this plastic sheeting. There may be times; however, that access may be needed beneath the plastic. This could occur if a plumber would need to work on piping beneath the home.

> ## Radon Mitigation System
>
> **Do not damage plastic on floor of crawl space.**
>
> If plastic must be cut or removed for maintenance purposes, turn off fan located in ___*location*___, by flipping switch for fan located in ___*room*___, or breaker # ___*number*___ in circuit panel.
>
> If plastic is damaged, repair with polyurethane caulk and/or duct tape. Turn system on after repairs are made.

Access beneath the plastic is not a problem, providing the system is temporarily turned off. Turning the system off prevents the loss of a large amount of interior air, which could cause backdrafting of combustion appliances (see Safety Chapter 10). After the necessary work is done, the plastic can be folded back together and re-caulked and taped. It is a good idea to make straight cuts in the plastic when this is done and to save left over plastic for such an event.

If small holes are made in the plastic, this is not a serious problem. It only means that the system will have to move a slightly larger amount of air. These small leaks can be easily fixed with a piece of duct tape placed over the top of the puncture.

If the crawl space is to be used for storage, it is a good idea to lay down a rug or scrap of carpet in these areas to prevent accidental punctures. The plastic recommended for use is actually very durable and the small punctures will need very little attention. It is the large rips and cuts that are of concern.

An example label is shown above that will help you and future homeowners maintain the quality of your work. This can be made up on a piece of paper and glued to the access door, or directly on the plastic sheeting where a person would enter the crawlspace.

Don't forget to label all visible sections of the depressurization system piping.

Chapter 5

How to Make Use of Existing Water Drainage Systems to Reduce Radon

How to Make Use of a Sump System

Planning the Sump Depressurization System

Installing the Sump Depressurization Systems

Planning the Exterior Drain Depressurization System

Installing the Exterior Drain Depressurization System

Protecting Your Home from Radon

CHAPTER 5 - HOW TO MAKE USE OF EXISTING WATER DRAINAGE SYSTEMS TO REDUCE RADON

This chapter deals with how to use the water drainage system that *may* have been installed during the construction of your home, to reduce radon. Radon reduction systems that capture radon by creating a vacuum on the drainage system itself have proven to be very effective in reducing radon.

How to Make Use of a Sump System

The diagram below shows a water drainage system that was installed on a home with a basement. During the construction of the home, a perforated pipe was placed at the bottom of the trench made when the footings of the home were poured. This perforated drainpipe forms a partial loop around the foundation and collects rainwater that seeps into the soil above it. The drain is connected to a pipe routed to a sump inside the home. This sump could be made out of concrete, steel, plastic, or simply be a hole in the concrete floor. A pump that will remove the water into the storm sewer system is normally found in these sumps.

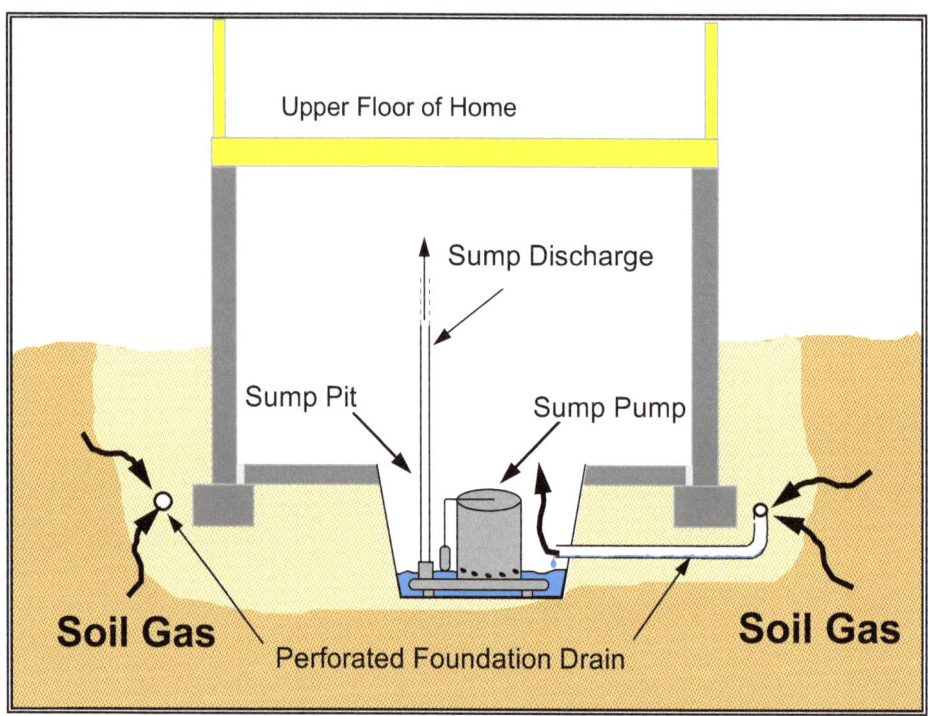

These drainage systems were installed so water could easily reach the drainage collection pipes. This factor allows radon, as a gas created in the soil, to also reach these same collection pipes. The natural vacuum that the house exerts on the soil causes a significant amount of radon to enter the home through the collection pipes, into the sump and then into the home itself. Merely sealing off the sump with a sealed lid is <u>not</u> a reliable solution. However, if a vacuum was applied to this same lid and the entering radon is collected and exhausted outside, a very reliable mitigation system would result. This method is referred to as "**sump depressurization**." How this is done depends upon the type of drainage system that was installed in your home. Depressurization of exterior foundation drains tile not attached to a sump works equally well and is described later in this chapter.

Important: To utilize this approach you must have had a drainage system installed on your home during its construction. Not all homes have them. If you do not have a drainage system, other techniques like sub-slab depressurization are more cost-effective than installing a new drainage system. Also, if you have a crawl space you should deal with that area first or simultaneously (see flow chart preceding Chapter 1.)

How a Depressurization System Can Use an Existing Drainage System to Reduce Radon

The picture below shows how a depressurization system is used to collect radon from a drainage system and exhaust it harmlessly outside the home. Refer to the illustration on the previous page where the radon was shown to enter the home through the perforated water collection piping. By creating a vacuum on the sump, you not only catch radon at a major entry point, but you can also catch it at other places in the soil via the vacuum created on the entire drainage system. The system shown below is more specifically referred to as "**sump depressurization**."

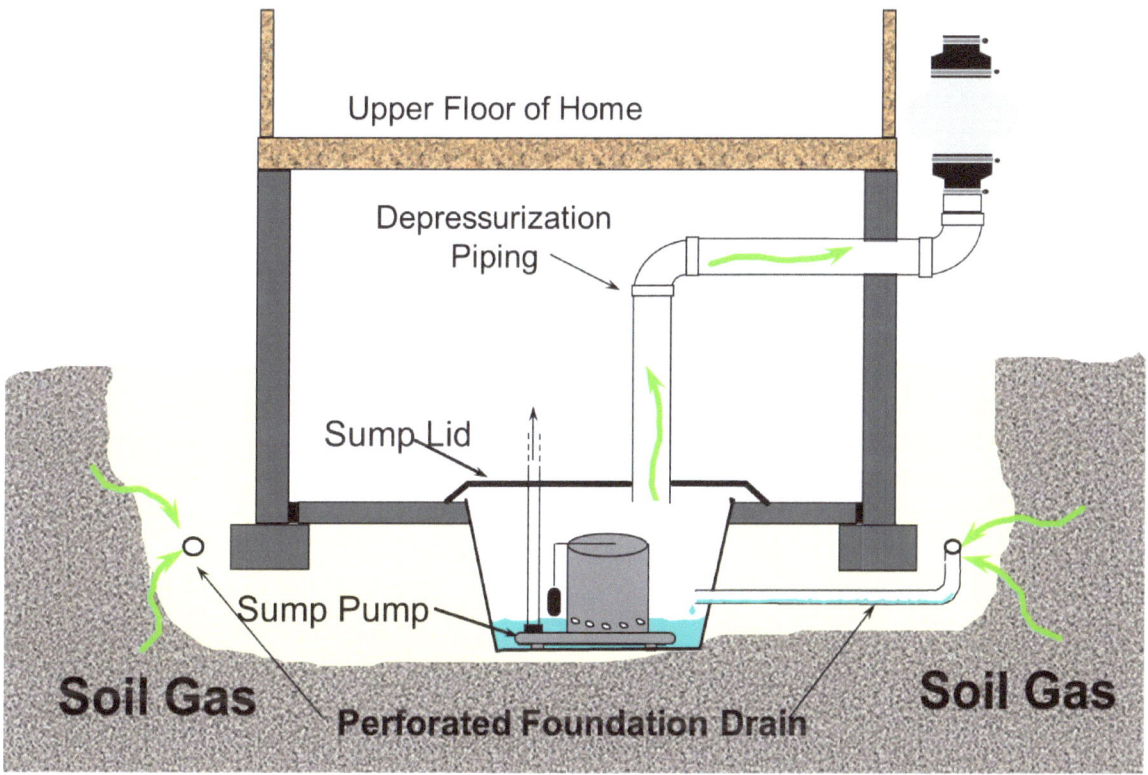

The sump depressurization system shown above was installed by first installing a cover or lid over the sump. This lid was placed on the concrete floor around the sump. It was also sealed to the floor to prevent air leakage. The depressurization system piping was attached to the lid and then routed to the depressurization fan. The fan creates a vacuum on the sump.

When a vacuum is created on the sump, a vacuum is also created on the drainage piping that is connected to the sump. Because the drainage collection system in this illustration is a perforated pipe looped completely around the foundation of the home, a large radon capture area is created. This explains the excellent reductions that are generally seen with these types of systems.

Note: In this example, the fan is located outside the house. It could also have been located in the attic of the home. *The routing of the depressurization system is detailed in Chapter 7 and should be read as part of the overall design of these systems.*

Protecting Your Home from Radon

Planning the Drainage Depressurization System

The discussion in this chapter will concentrate on how connections are made to the various types of drainage systems commonly found in homes. The depressurization system that will collect the radon from the drainage system and exhaust it outside is described in Chapter 7.

Please refer to the flow chart preceding Chapter 1 to determine if additional portions of the house will also need to be repaired to adequately reduce radon levels.

Planning Step 1:

Deciding what kind of drainage system was installed on your home.

Most homes that are constructed in areas of high rainfall or are built on hillsides where ground water could flow into the home are constructed with some means for reducing the entry of rainwater into the home. This is done by two basic methods:

1. **Sumps.** Water is routed to a sump or holding tank where a pump is used to pump the water to a storm drain system. A diagram of this type of system was shown on the previous page. Water is often routed to a sump, located inside of the home, by means of water collection pipes that are either in the ground outside the home or are in the soil underneath the concrete slab. If you look down into the sump basket and see pipes penetrating the side of the basket, this is probably the type you have (see illustration in Planning Step 2).

   Sometimes the water flows through gravel that has been laid beneath the concrete slab to get to the sump. In this case, the sump basket has perforations in its side where the water can easily flow into the basket for collection (see illustration in Planning Step 2).

2. **French Drains or Perimeter Drains.** These are systems where perforated pipes have been installed in a bed of clean gravel either around the outside of the foundation or around the inside of the foundation. These are the same types of pipes that can be found in conjunction with sump systems. However, the difference here is that rather than going to a sump, they have a length of pipe that is routed away from the house that allows the water to be drained away from the house. The drainage away from the house generally happens by three different methods:

   a. **Daylight Drain Discharge.** This is typically seen on homes that are constructed on a hillside. One or two pipes are connected to the perforated water drainage pipe and slope away from the house to a point where the pipe or pipes exit the hillside. This allows the collected water to drain down the hillside away from the house.

   b. **Dry Well.** In this case a pipe is connected to the foundation drainpipe and routed away from the house to a hole that has been dug and filled with rocks or gravel. Water collected in these holes can easily drain into the water table below. This is more common with older homes.

   c. **Storm Sewers or Interceptors.** This is where the perimeter foundation drain is connected to large pipes designed to collect ground water from several homes in a neighborhood. These large pipes may be connected to the storm drain system where the storm water is collected and diverted away from the subdivision. They may also be connected to large underground pipes that run off a hillside where the storm water from the subdivision is drained away.

Important: *If the drainage system of your home is connected to a storm sewer or an interceptor, this technique will not work.* You will not be able to achieve a sufficient vacuum due to the large amount of air in these underground collection systems. You will need to employ the method(s) described in Chapter 6 (slabs and basements). If you do not know if your drainage system is connected to one of these systems, ask your builder or call your local building department.

Chapter 5: Using Drainage Systems

Before you begin this work -- BE AWARE:

- These drainage systems were originally installed for the purpose of preventing drainage water from entering your home. They were not installed for future use as a radon reduction system. If done properly, the drainage system can be used very effectively for radon reduction while still being able to divert water from the home.

- The important thing to remember is that **you cannot modify the drainage system in a fashion that will not allow it to function as a water drainage system, or not allow for maintenance.** Some key elements are as follows:

    - Lids placed over sumps should be sealed with gaskets and mechanical fasteners, rather than caulks to allow for future access to the pump beneath it.

    - If a pump is located in the sump, it cannot be removed. This is especially true if a pedestal type pump is installed in your sump. If you have a pedestal style water pump, it will need to be replaced with a submersible type.

    - If your house has a perimeter foundation drain that drains off a hillside (daylight drain discharge), you cannot seal off these drains in order to improve the vacuum on the radon reduction system. "P" traps or other types of water trap seals are not appropriate since they can become filled with silt and restrict the normal flow of water away from the home. Special check valves have been designed for this purpose and are discussed later.

    - The type of fan used to create the vacuum for the radon reduction system should not exceed a maximum suction pressure of 1 ½ inches of water column. The typical radon fan described in Chapter 7 is appropriate for this application, since it is capable of moving the amounts of air needed with these systems while not creating too large a vacuum that would affect the natural gravity flow of the water drainage. The use of higher vacuum capability fans could prevent proper water drainage away from the house.

Each of these concerns and how to deal with them will be detailed in the balance of this chapter.

Protecting Your Home from Radon

Planning Step 2:

Determine the style of sump you have.

The diagram below shows four types of sumps that are often found in the lowest floor of a home. Sumps are usually located in the corner of a slab. In newer homes, they are typically made out of black plastic and are set into the aggregate prior to the concrete being poured up to them. They vary from 18 to 30 inches in diameter.

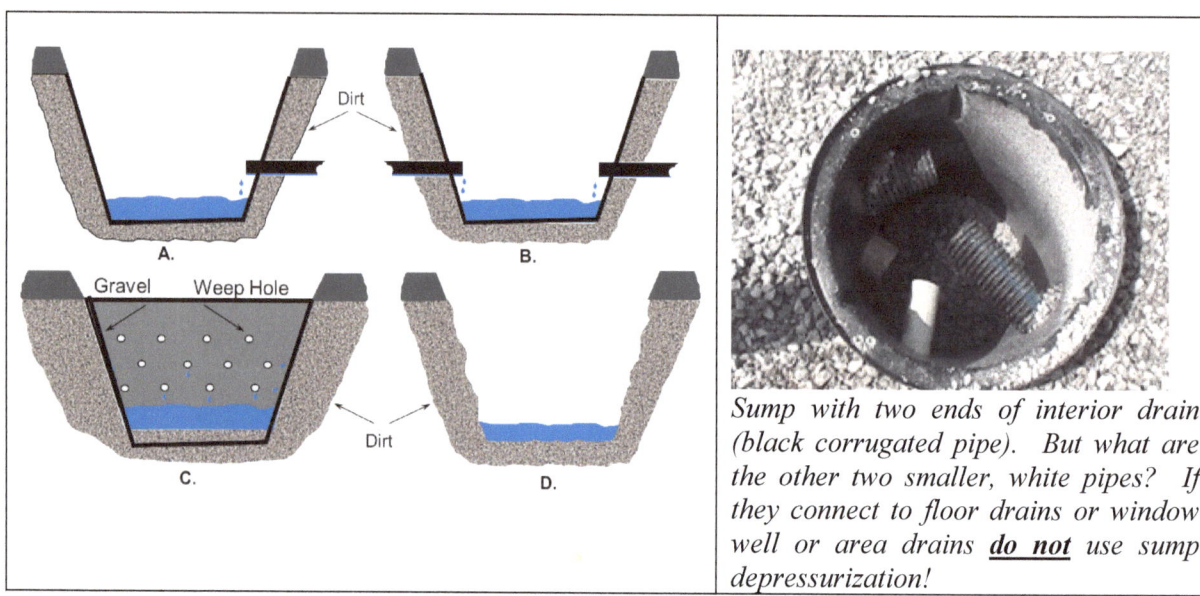

*Sump with two ends of interior drain (black corrugated pipe). But what are the other two smaller, white pipes? If they connect to floor drains or window well or area drains **do not** use sump depressurization!*

First: Look down into the sump with a flashlight to see if there are one or two drainpipes entering the side of the sump. If there is only one pipe entering the sump (*illustration A*), then it is probable there is a loop of perforated drainage pipe running around the outside of the foundation with a single leg running to the sump. This will allow for the depressurization system to be attached either to a lid placed on the sump or alternatively, to the perforated pipe outside the foundation as described in the exterior drain system later in this chapter.

If there are two pipes entering the sump pit (*illustration B*), it is likely there is a loop of pipe beneath the slab inside of the foundation wall. The significance of this is you must attach the depressurization system directly to the lid placed over the sump. You do not have the option to connect to a drainage pipe outside the home.

If your sump does not have any pipes entering it, but rather has holes through its sides (*illustration C*), or is an open pit (*illustration D*), you have a sump that has no perforated piping connected to it. In this case you can assume the sump was set through a layer of gravel that was placed on the soil prior to the concrete slab being poured. This means the depressurization system would be connected to a lid placed over the sump. The depressurization system will extract the radon from the gravel layer through the holes in the side of the sump. Alternatively, you could put a lid on the sump, but connect your radon system through the concrete slab as discussed in Chapter 6.

Second: Determine if there are any pipes other than those for ground water drainage entering the sump. Examples of this would be floor drains, wastewater from laundry machines, or pipes connected to hollow block drainage systems. If this situation exists within your sump, a depressurization will draw a significant amount of air from the inside of the home. **_This will not only hurt the efficiency of the radon reduction, but more importantly could cause the combustion appliances to backdraft and cause poisonous carbon monoxide to enter the home_**. If this is the case in your home, you need to use the sub-slab depressurization methods described in Chapter 6.

Chapter 5: Using Drainage Systems

Decision Point

> If you have a sump style drainage system, continue with this section.
> If you have an exterior style drainage system, you may want to go to the exterior drain section of this chapter. It is important to note that you may have a combination of sump and exterior drain so that both sections of this chapter will need to be understood.

Planning Step 3:

Sumps: Determine what type of sump pump you have and whether it needs to be replaced.

Determine whether you have a submersible pump or a pedestal style pump. The importance of this is to determine how the lid will fit over the sump hole and still allow the piping and electrical cord to enter and exit through the lid.

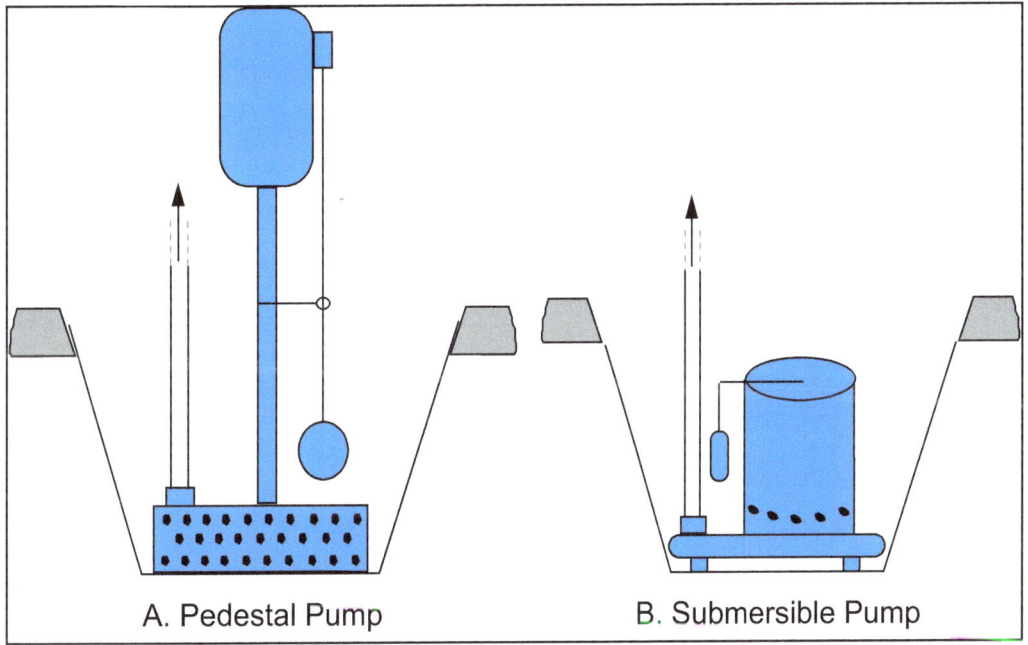

Illustration A depicts a **pedestal style pump**. This pump has an electrical motor elevated well above the sump hole. There is a rotating shaft that is connected to the actual water pump located down in the sump pit. It will be impossible to install a lid that will properly seal around the shaft or shaft casing. *You will need to replace this pump with a submersible type.* Purchase the new pump first or obtain sufficient information on the one you plan to purchase to determine pipe size openings for the lid.

Illustration B depicts a **submersible pump**. These low-profile pumps have both the electrical motor and the water pump packaged in a single unit. They are called submersible because they are sufficiently sealed to where they can be set slightly off the bottom of the sump and not be damaged by the accumulated water. These are desirable because the only penetrations that need to go through the lid are for the electrical cord and the discharge piping.

In obtaining a sump pump, it is recommended it be equipped with an air bleed port on the discharge piping to avoid an air lock situation.

Protecting Your Home from Radon

Planning Step 4:

Sumps: Determining how plumbing will have to be revised to accommodate lid.

Since a lid will be placed over the entire sump hole, the plumbing will need to pass through the lid. If you purchase a prefabricated sump lid for radon reduction, you will have to ensure your sump pump piping will pass through the precut openings provided in the lid. If you decide to make your own lid, or the size or configuration of your sump does not allow for the use of a prefabricated lid, you will still need to plan the penetrations.

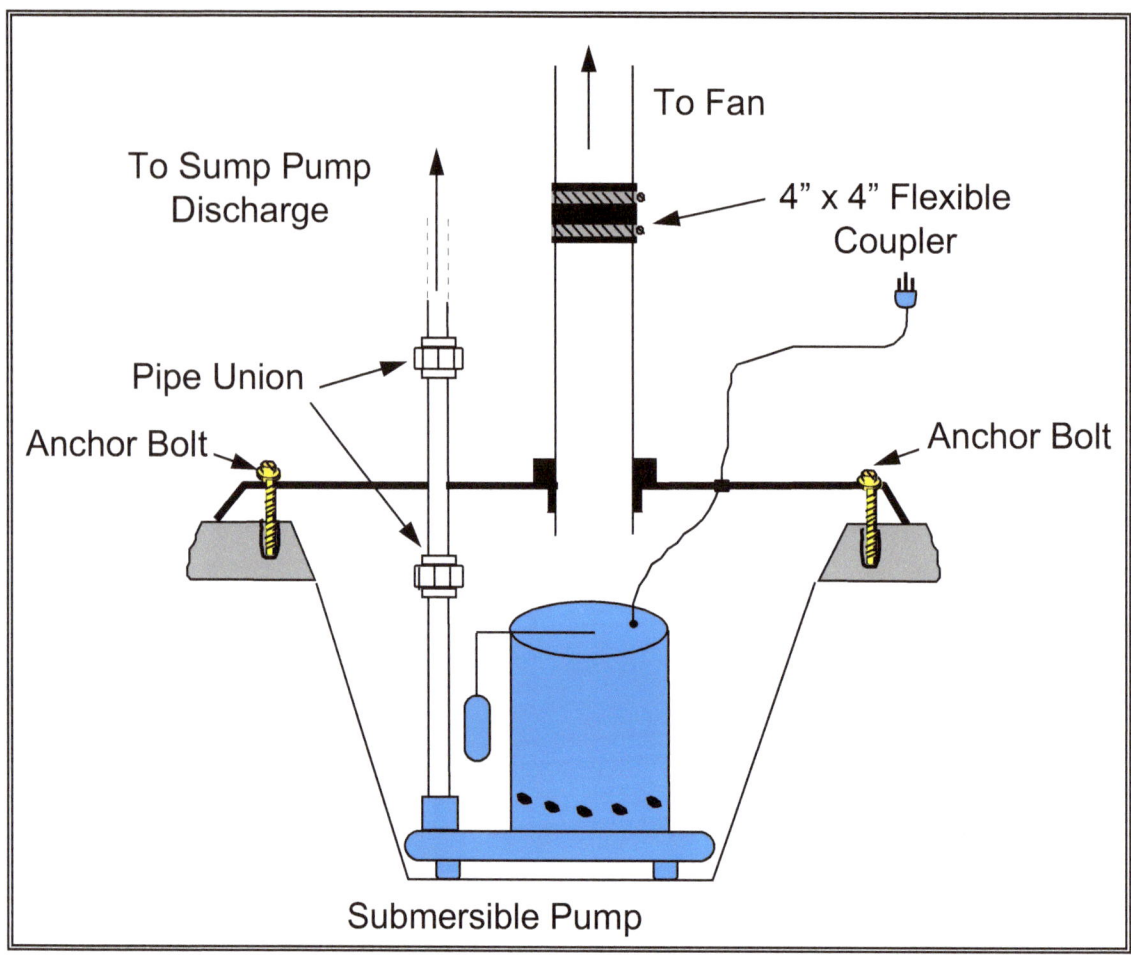

The illustration above shows the piping running through the sump lid. Note that a union has been installed on the water discharge piping above and below the lid. A union is a device for connecting two straight lengths of pipe with wrenches. The union on the discharge piping of the sump is important because this allows the piping to be disconnected from the lid. Then the lid can be disconnected from the concrete floor and slid up far enough to allow access to the lower union. Once access is obtained to the lower union, it can be disconnected, and the lid moved out of the way to allow access to the sump pump. Unions can be commonly found at any plumbing or building supply store.

The necessary vacuum seal is accomplished between the lid and the straight section of pipe with rubber seals that can also be obtained at plumbing or building supply stores. The use of the rubber seal allows the lid to slide up and down on the pipe for easy removal and access to the pump below.

If you are not comfortable with installing the unions on the pump discharge piping, it may be wise to purchase the lid and hire a plumber to make these modifications.

Planning Step 5:
Sumps: Determining the lid size and penetration sizes for round sumps.

Step 1: Measure the outside diameter of the sump. This is done by using a measuring tape laid across the sump opening flush with the floor. Measure from edge to edge of the sump opening. Pivot the measuring tape to make sure you come up with the largest measurement. This is the diameter. Your sump lid will need to be a minimum of 3 inches larger in diameter than the diameter of the sump opening. This will allow for the sump lid to attach to the concrete around the sump. For example, if the diameter of the sump is measured to be 18 inches, the lid will need to be 21 inches or larger to allow for a minimum 1 ½-inch overlap all around the opening.

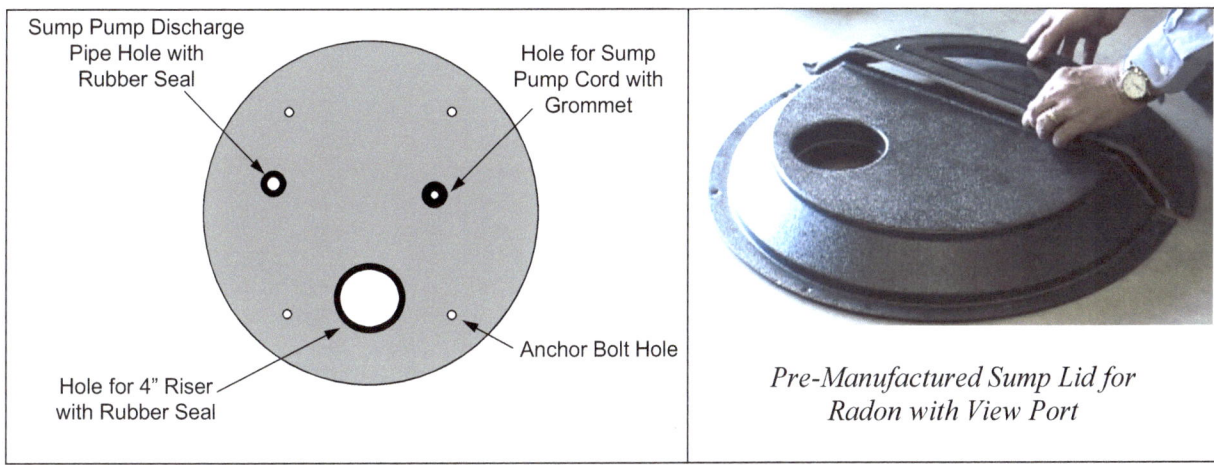

Pre-Manufactured Sump Lid for Radon with View Port

Step 2: Measure the outside diameter of the discharge piping of the submersible pump. Do this by holding the measuring tape up against the pipe and at a right angle to it. Consult the following chart to determine the proper size of pipe.

If outside diameter of pipe is (in inches):	Then pipe size (schedule 40) is (in inches):
7/8	½
1 1/16	¾
1 5/16	1
1 11/16	1 ¼
1 15/16	1 ½
2 3/8	2
2 7/8	2 ½
3 ½	3

Step 3: Fill out the following table. Contact a radon equipment supplier and provide this information to them. Many plumbing or building supply houses also have access to these covers as well.

Minimum lid diameter (actual measurement plus 3 inches)	
Sump pump piping hole diameter	
Depressurization piping hole size	4 ½ to 5 inches (for 4-inch or 100mm pipe)
Electrical cord for sump pump hole size:	1 ½ to 2 inches with rubber seal for standard cord

Protecting Your Home from Radon

Planning Step 6

Sumps: Making your own lid.

You may not be able to find a prefabricated lid for your sump hole. This can happen if your sump is rectangular rather than circular. In this case you will need to make your own lid and obtain the appropriate plumbing connection. Also, if you are installing a sub-slab system as described in Chapter 6 you will still need to have a cover over an open sump, otherwise there will be too much leakage at the sump.

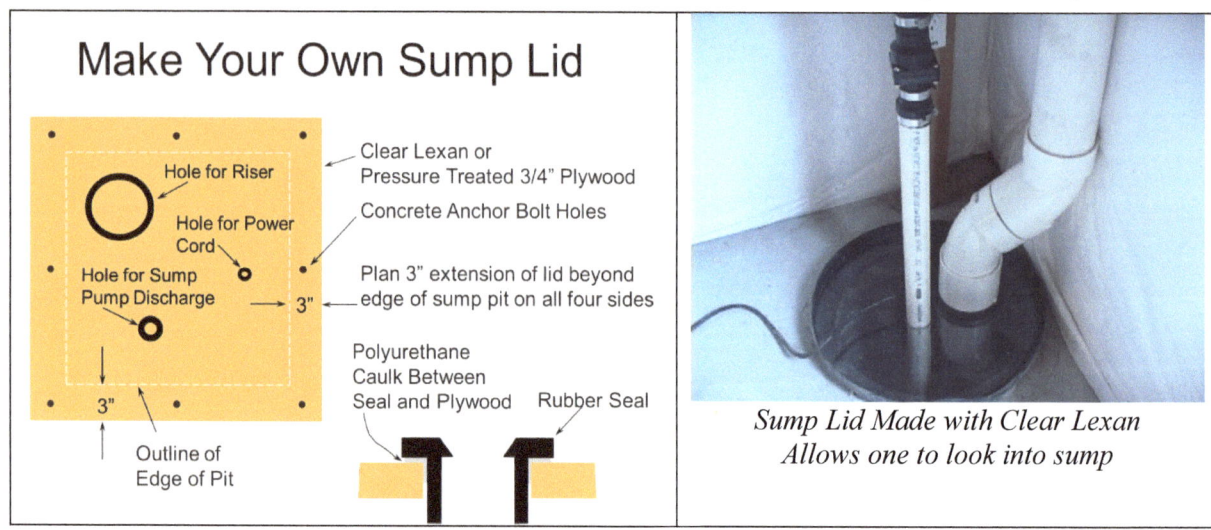

Sump Lid Made with Clear Lexan Allows one to look into sump

Making a rectangular sump lid:

Step 1.   Measure the dimensions of the sump hole. Your homemade lid will need to be at least 3 inches wider on *each* side of the sump opening. Measure the sump pump piping diameter (see Planning Step 5).

Step 2.   On a piece of paper, layout the dimensions of the lid. Don't forget to add 3 inches for the overlap on each side. Lay out where the penetrations for the piping and electrical cord should be. Plan a hole for the 4-inch (100 mm) schedule 40 PVC or ABS depressurization pipe.

Step 3.   Purchase appropriately sized rubber seals for each of the lid penetrations from a plumbing or building supply store. Uniseal® is a brand name commonly used for this purpose. A ½" thick bead of silicone caulk will be run under the lip of the seal and then pushed into place (see Chapter 8 on sealing). The hole cut in your lid will be a function of the outside diameter of the rubber seal, but probably will require a 5-inch hole.

Step 4.   Purchase the lid material. The lid material that you purchase must be of suitable strength to support a 250-pound person who might stand on top of it. ¼ inch clear plastic such as Lexan is often used for this purpose. A clear lid allows one to look down into the sump.

One could also use ¾ inch pressure treated plywood. If using plywood and the opening the lid will cover is greater than 2 feet, the lid should be reinforced by attaching 2 x 2-inch wooden boards screwed to the bottom side of the lid. Place braces on 12-inch centers, making sure these braces do not sit on the concrete, so when the lid is set down the braces fit up to the inside edge of the sump without interference.

Chapter 5: Using Drainage Systems

Planning Step 7:

Determine what slab openings will need to be caulked and sealed.
(Refer to Chapter 8 for more on sealing slab openings).

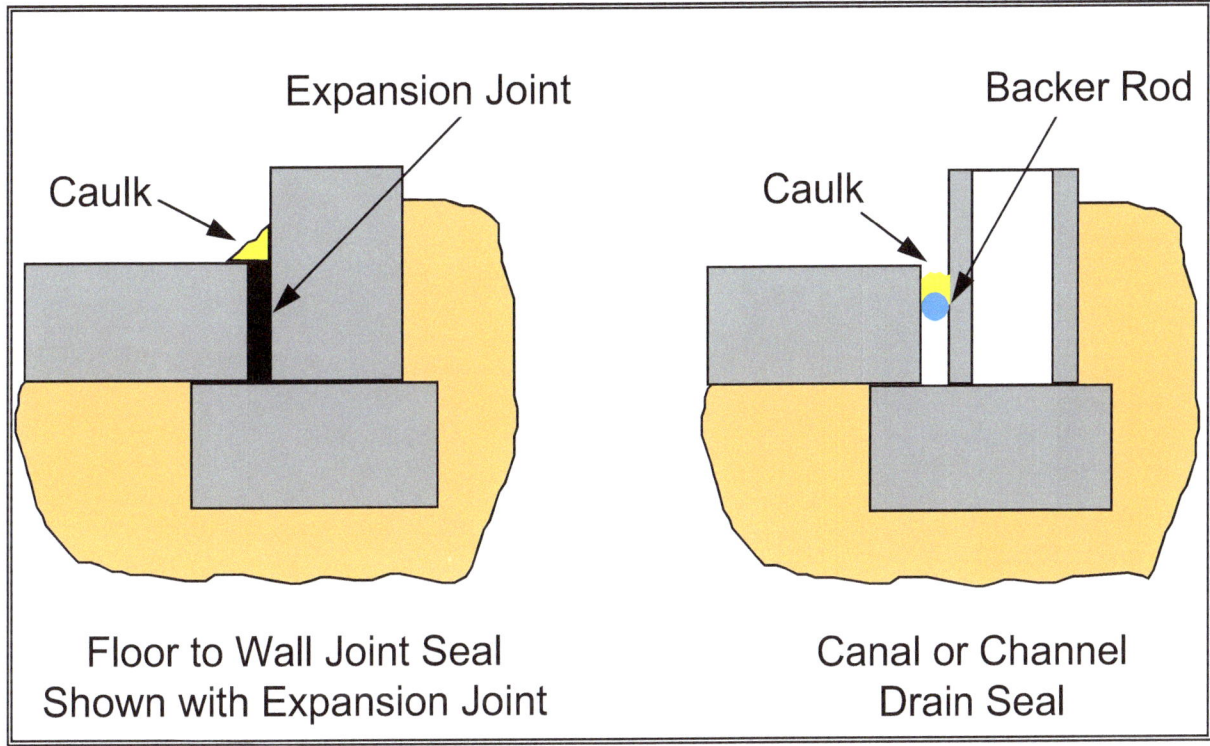

Floor-to-Wall Joints

Because sumps are often located in corners and near outside walls, special attention needs to be paid to sealing the floor-to-wall joints, especially the ones nearest the sump itself.

The floor-to-wall joint area could be just a simple crack (cold joint) between the floor and the wall. If so, this should be wire brushed and caulked with polyurethane caulk as described in Chapter 8. Use the guidance detailed in that chapter as to the amount of caulking that will be needed.

Be sure to follow the ventilation and safety precautions when using this caulking as detailed in Chapters 8 and 10.

Canal or Channel Drain

The floor-to-wall joint area could also be what is referred to as a "canal drain." These are wide channels in the concrete floor (typically 2 inches wide) that run along the outside edge of the basement floor. These are intended to collect drainage water which then seeps into the gravel under the slab. These cannot be completely sealed without impacting the home's drainage system. They need to be filled with a backer rod that is squeezed halfway down into the channel (see illustration B above). Caulking is then applied on top of the backer rod. Although this is described in more detail in Chapter 8, it is important to plan for this and to make sure that the pathway to the sump for the collected drainage water is not disrupted.

Be sure to follow the ventilation and safety precautions when using this caulking as detailed in Chapters 8 and 10.

Planning Step 8:

Planning the depressurization piping system connection to the sump lid.

The most appropriate size and type of depressurization system pipe to be used for this method is 4-inch (100 mm), schedule 40 PVC or ABS. The connection of the piping to the lid should be made by inserting a minimum 24-inch length of 4-inch pipe through the rubber seal on the lid. This riser should be inserted approximately 4 inches down through the lid. The rubber seal should fit snugly around the outside edge of the pipe.

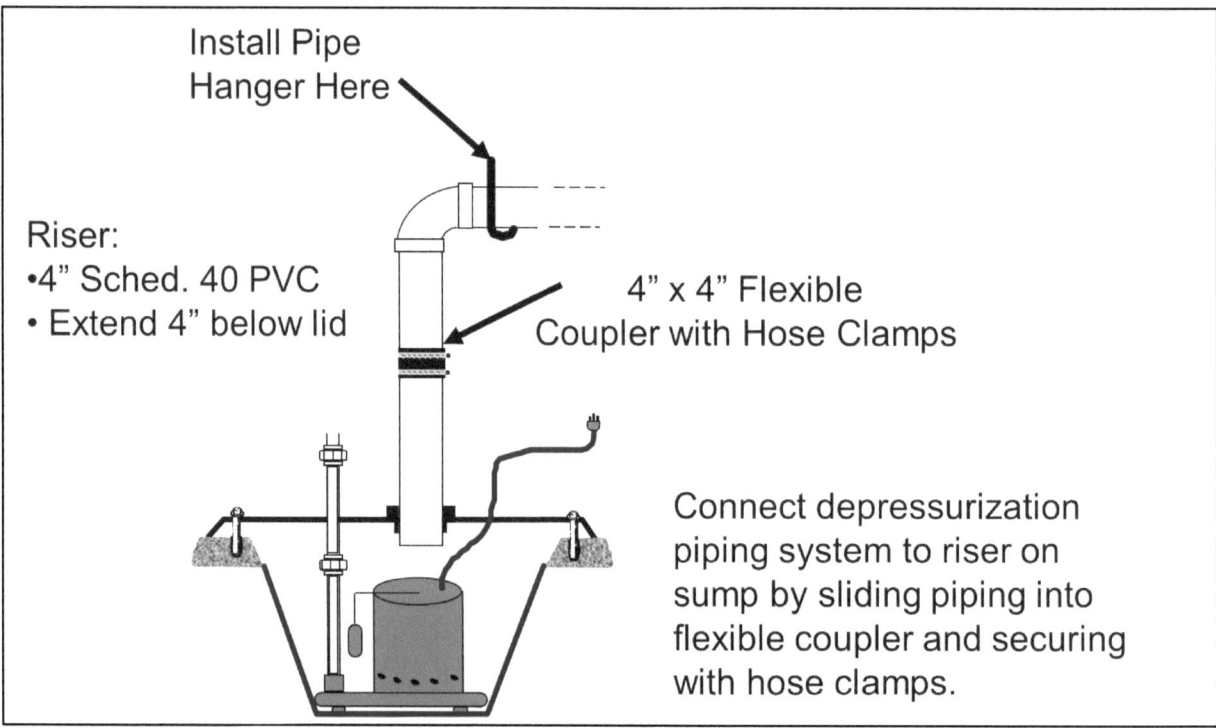

The depressurization piping system described in Chapter 7 will connect to this riser with a 4-inch (100mm) rubber or neoprene hose clamp style coupler. This coupler is designed to slip over the outside of the two pipes that are butted together. A seal on either end is accomplished with hose clamps that tighten the flexible neoprene onto the pipe. These couplers can be purchased from most plumbing supply stores and the radon equipment supply houses. The purpose of using a connector here, as opposed to gluing the piping together, is so this connection can be loosened, and the sump lid removed for maintenance purposes.

Planning Step 9:

Planning the depressurization system piping. *(Also See Chapter 7)*

A depressurization piping system will need to be installed to collect the radon from the sump. This piping system and fan are described in detail in Chapter 7. The depressurization piping system will connect to the 24-inch long, 4-inch PVC or ABS riser on the lid with the flexible pipe coupling described in the previous step. As a preview, the depressurization piping system should follow the criteria listed below:

- Pipe should be schedule 40 PVC or ABS pipe.
- Piping should be sloped back to the sump to allow condensed water to flow back to the sump.
- The depressurization fan should be mounted vertically in the piping system to allow condensate to drain back into sump.
- The discharge of the system should be at a proper location to reduce potential for re-entrainment back in through building openings.
- The piping system should be labeled.
- The fan should be either low-voltage, class 2, installed by homeowner or 120 volts hard wired by an electrician.
- There should be a mechanical performance indicator (such as a u-tube manometer and audible alarm) installed.
- Piping routed through unheated spaces in cold climates should be insulated.
- When piping is routed through a garage wall or a fire rated wall, the wall should be maintained as an airtight wall and a fire stop used.

Installing the Sump Depressurization Systems

This section is devoted to the installation of a depressurization system that will be attached to a sump inside the house. Read this section along with Chapter 7 on Depressurization Systems, Chapter 10 on Safety, and Chapter 8 on Caulking and Sealing before proceeding with this work. You should also read the "Finishing Touches" section at the end of this chapter. If you are attaching the depressurization system to an exterior drain, you can skip to that section of this chapter.

Step 1:

Assemble Equipment and Materials

The following is a checklist of equipment and material that you will need to gather before starting:

Area	Item	√
Safety	Goggles/safety glasses	
	Dust mask	
	Leather gloves	
	First aid kit	
	Ventilation fan	
	Flashlight	
	Coveralls or old clothing	
Material	**Prefabricated Sump Lid Materials**	
	Prefabricated lid with rubber seals	
	Four 1 inch long by ¼ inch concrete anchor bolts and anchors (should be supplied with lid)	
	Home-Made Lid	
	¼ inch Lexan or ¾ inch plywood	
	Marine grade paint and brush	
	Four 1 ½ in. long by ¼ inch concrete anchor bolts and anchors	
	Rubber seals for pipe and electrical penetrations	
	Other Materials:	
	1 tube of silicone caulking	
	4 inch (100 mm) flexible pipe coupling	
	Two pipe unions of appropriate size for sump pump piping	
	Necessary piping for retrofitting the sump pump piping	
	Polyurethane caulking for sealing concrete openings (see Chapter 8)	
Tools	Electric drill or hammer drill	
	Carbide tipped drill bit, sized for concrete anchors	
	Caulking gun	
	Rags	
	Trash can	
	Extension cords	
	Wire brush	
	Wrench for concrete anchor bolts	
	Smoke stick (see Chapter 8)	

Step 2. Clean the sump. This may be your last chance to remove the debris which has accumulated in the sump over the years. For some reason these areas seem to be the final resting place for super balls and small toys from the local hamburger stand. After you put on the lid you will not want to remove it to fix a sump pump clogged by these. Scoop this stuff up and dispose of it. Wire brush the top of the concrete around the sump that your lid will contact. *Watch out for spiders!*

Modifying the plumbing system:

Discuss this modification with a knowledgeable person at a plumbing supply store or hire a plumber to do this work. **Refer back to the illustration in Planning Step 4.**

Step 3. If you have a pedestal style pump - remove it and replace it with a new submersible pump.

Step 4. Cut the sump discharge piping at the location where you plan to install the upper piping union.

Step 5. Remove the sump pump and cut the discharge piping approximately 3 inches above the discharge port of the pump and install the lower piping union.

Step 6. Insert the appropriate length of sump pump piping through the seal in the lid you either bought or had made. Install the matching parts of the unions on the two ends of this pipe after it has been inserted. Use the appropriate pipe cement as recommended by your plumbing supply store if PVC or ABS pipe is used. If metal pipe was originally installed either have the pipe ends threaded for steel pipe or replace this section with schedule 40 PVC or ABS pipe rated for at least 125-pound pressure service.

Step 7. Align the lid up over the pump so the stub of pipe runs through the lid and lines up with both the discharge of the sump pump and the rest of the sump piping. Take a pencil and insert it through each of the holes on the side of the lid to mark on the concrete the locations for the anchor bolts.

Step 8. Set the lid off to the side and drill holes in the concrete slab using a carbide tipped concrete drill bit or a hammer drill. Use the bit size recommended on the packaging of the concrete anchors you purchased. Vacuum out the concrete dust and the surface of the concrete that the lid will set on.

Step 9. Remove the rubber seal in the lid for the electrical service cord. This seal should have a split in it. Route the plug end of the cord up through the hole in the lid. Place the split rubber seal around the cord and reinsert into the hole in the cover. Pull the desired length of cord up through the rubber seal.

Step 10. Set the lid back in place and connect the sump pump piping. Tightly fasten the lid to the concrete with the anchor bolts.

Step 11. Plug in the pump and run water into the sump with a garden hose inserted through the large hole that will be used for the depressurization piping. The sump pump should turn on and begin pumping this water away. Check for water leaks at your two union connections. If they leak, remake the joints. If not, proceed to the next step.

Protecting Your Home from Radon

Connecting the depressurization system to the sump lid.

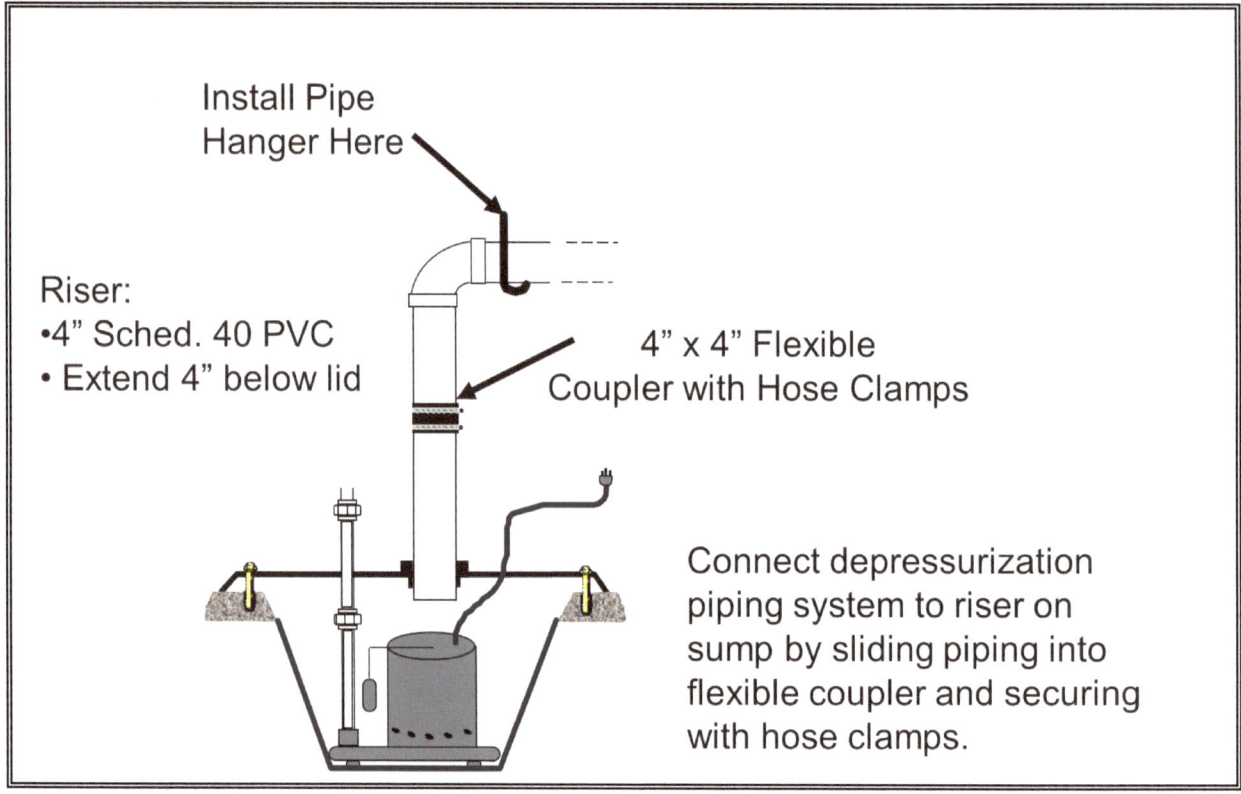

Radon Pipe Pushed through Uniseal in Lid

Step 12. Insert the riser (4 inches in diameter, with a minimum 12-inch-long PVC or ABS pipe) through the large rubber seal in the lid. The pipe may need to be lubricated with some soapy water to help fit it through the rubber seal. The pipe should extend at least 4 inches down through the sump lid. Measure the vertical distance from the lid up to the top of the riser pipe and write this dimension down.

Step 13. Install the depressurization piping system per the methods described in Chapter 7. Plan to run the depressurization piping down towards the riser on the lid so the end of the depressurization piping stops 1 ½ inches above the top of the sump riser, with the measurement made in step 12 above.

Step 14. Take the 4-inch flexible rubber coupling and apply a soapy solution to the inside surface, if necessary. Loosen the hose clamps fully. Slide one end of the coupling over the end of the depressurization system piping. Slide it up about 3 inches on the pipe. Line the riser pipe up with the depressurization piping and pull up on the riser so it is about 1 inch from the open end of the depressurization piping. Slide the rubber coupling down over the riser and position it on the riser and the depressurization piping so the hose clamps will tighten up on each pipe to make a good airtight connection.

Step 15. Turn the system on and check for leaks and have the draft of your combustion flues checked.

Step 16. Turn to "Finishing Touches" at the end of this chapter for labeling and other helpful hints.

Chapter 5: Using Drainage Systems

Sump Installation Step 17:

Check for leaks with system installed and turned on.

After the system has been turned on, suction will be created in the sump and, in turn, in the soil under and around the home. This vacuum catches the radon and other soil gas that would have otherwise entered the home. The better the vacuum -- the better the radon reduction. Finding and sealing leaks around the lid and at the pipe penetrations can produce a better vacuum. You should also check the floor-to-wall joints and other slab joints at this time (see Chapter 8 on sealing floor cracks and joints).

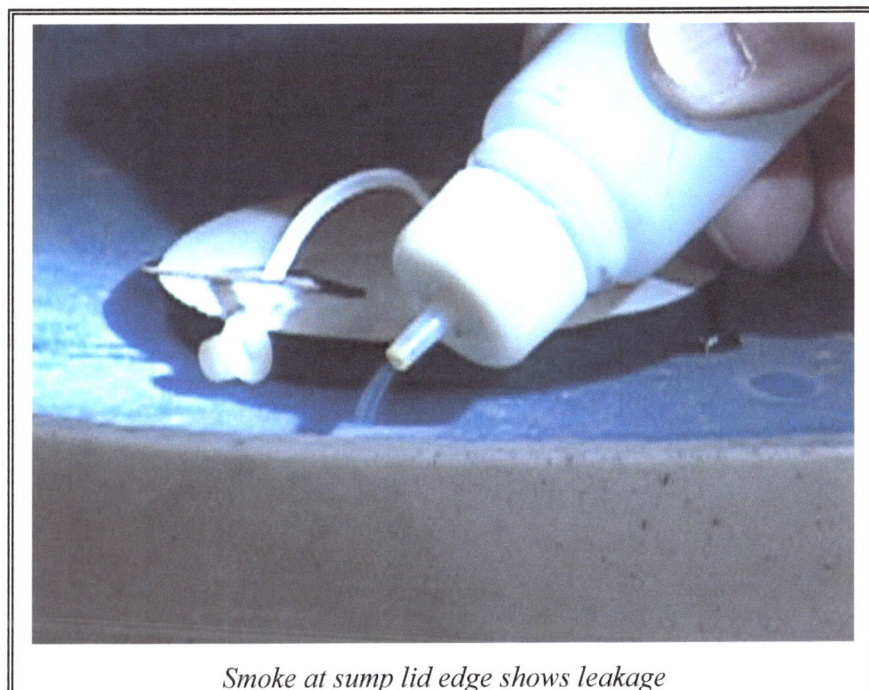
Smoke at sump lid edge shows leakage

Sometimes you can find a leak by hearing the air being drawn down through it. However, it is best to use some type of smoke generator to detect air being drawn down through the leak. The picture on the left shows smoke being drawn down through a leak in a sump lid. A flashlight should be used to help see the direction that the smoke moves.

If smoke goes down through an opening, use some caulk to reseal the opening until smoke is no longer flowing down. If the leak is at the sump lid, use gaskets or silicone caulk rather than polyurethane. Silicone will allow for future access to the plumbing system, whereas polyurethane will not. You should, however, use polyurethane caulk if the leak is between the floor and the side of the sump basket as well as for concrete cracks and floor-to-wall joint areas as described in Chapter 8.

Burning Incense Stick: An incense stick or a "punk" can be purchased and when lit, it burns slowly and produces a light smoke. This can be held close to a suspected leak area to see if the smoke is drawn down. If so, seal the leak with caulk. Because the punk's smoke is warm, it will want to rise on its own. Therefore, it is not as sensitive for finding leaks as the other devices. To compensate for this, put the burning end as close to the opening as possible and shine a flashlight on the smoke and look for small wisps of smoke being drawn down into the crack or opening.

Smoke Bottles: These are devices that can be ordered from radon catalog supply houses or from a heating and ventilating equipment supplier. They are filled with a fine powder that when squeezed from the bottle will float in the direction of air flow. These devices are typically more sensitive than the incense stick and more likely to find leaks. Use a flashlight with these devices as well.

For this application the incense stick is satisfactory.

Planning the Exterior Drain Depressurization System

If you have determined that you have an exterior drainage water collection system from the information provided earlier in this chapter, this section will assist you in how to attach a depressurization system to the exterior drain.

Planning Step 1:

    Understanding exterior drain tile systems.

This technique is used where perforated pipes have been installed for water collection either around the outside or the inside of a foundation. These are the same types of pipes that can be found in conjunction with sump systems. However, the difference is that rather than going to a sump, they have a leg of pipe that is routed away from the house. This allows the water to be drained away from the house rather than being collected in a sump and mechanically pumped away.

The perforated drainpipe can be a corrugated 3-inch or 4-inch flexible black polyethylene pipe. It could also be a 3-inch or 4-inch rigid PVC or ABS pipe with holes drilled in it. Regardless of the type of pipe, they are generally laid in a gravel bed just below and beside the bottom of the foundation footing. (This would have been installed during the construction of the home and is not something that would be specifically installed for radon reduction.) If you do not have an internal or external drainage system, refer to other methods described in this book.

Generally, there are three different methods for draining water away from the house:

    A. **Daylight Drain Discharge.** This is typically seen on homes constructed on a hillside. One or two pipes are connected to the perforated water drainage pipe and slope away from the house to a point where the pipe or pipes exit the hillside. This allows the collected water to drain down the hillside away from the house.

    B. **Dry Well.** In this case, a pipe is connected to the foundation drainpipe and routed away from the house to a hole that has been dug and filled with rocks or gravel. Water collected in these holes can easily drain into the water table below. This is more common with older homes. They are also referred to as simple French Drains or Rock Pits.

    C. **Storm Sewers or Interceptors.** This is where the perimeter foundation drain is connected to large pipes that are designed to collect ground water from several homes in a neighborhood. These large pipes may be connected to the storm drain system where the storm water is collected and diverted away from the subdivision. They may also be connected to large underground pipes that run off a hillside where the storm water from the subdivision is drained away.

Important: *If the drainage system of your home is connected to a storm sewer or an interceptor, this technique will not work.* You will not be able to achieve a sufficient vacuum due to the large amount of air in these underground collection systems. You will need to use the techniques described in Chapter 6. If you do not know if your drainage system is connected to one of these systems, ask your builder or call your local building department.

Chapter 5: Using Drainage Systems

Before you begin this work BE AWARE:

- These drainage systems were originally installed for the purpose of preventing drainage water from entering your home. They were not installed for future use as a radon reduction system. If done properly, the drainage system can be used very effectively for radon reduction while still being able to divert water from the home.

- The important thing to remember is that **you cannot modify the drainage system in a fashion that will not allow it to function as a water drainage system, or not allow for maintenance.** Some key elements are as follows:
    - If you have an exterior drain that has been routed to an interior sump you have the choice of creating a vacuum on the drainage system by connecting the depressurization system to either a sump lid or directly to the exterior drainpipe itself.

Regardless of which method is used for connecting to the system, if the drain is connected to an interior sump the sump pit must be sealed with a lid. Failure to do so may not only affect radon reduction <u>but could cause combustion appliance backdrafting and carbon monoxide poisoning</u>.

- A perimeter foundation drain that drains off a hillside (discharge) may have openings that will need to be sealed to accomplish the desired vacuum. If done correctly, you can close them off without affecting the ability of your drainage system to work properly. "P" traps are not appropriate since they fill with silt and, over time, will restrict the normal flow of water away from the home. Special traps have been designed for this purpose and are described later.

- The type of fan used to create the vacuum for the radon reduction system should not exceed a maximum suction pressure of 1 ½ inches of water column. The typical radon fan described in Chapter 7 on depressurization systems is appropriate for this application, since it has the capability to move the large amounts of air needed with these systems, while not creating so much vacuum to affect the natural gravity flow of the water drainage. The use of higher vacuum capability fans could prevent proper water drainage away from the house.

Each of these concerns, and how to deal with them, will be detailed in the balance of this section.

Protecting Your Home from Radon

Planning Step 2:

Determine if you have a drain discharge.

Drain discharges are where water, which is collected by the exterior foundation drain, can drain by gravity off a hillside. They are often found on homes that have been built into a hillside as the illustration below shows. These drain discharges have open ends of a perforated piping system. These pipes often stick out the hillside. They are generally 3 or 4 inches in diameter and made out of black corrugated pipe or white PVC pipe.

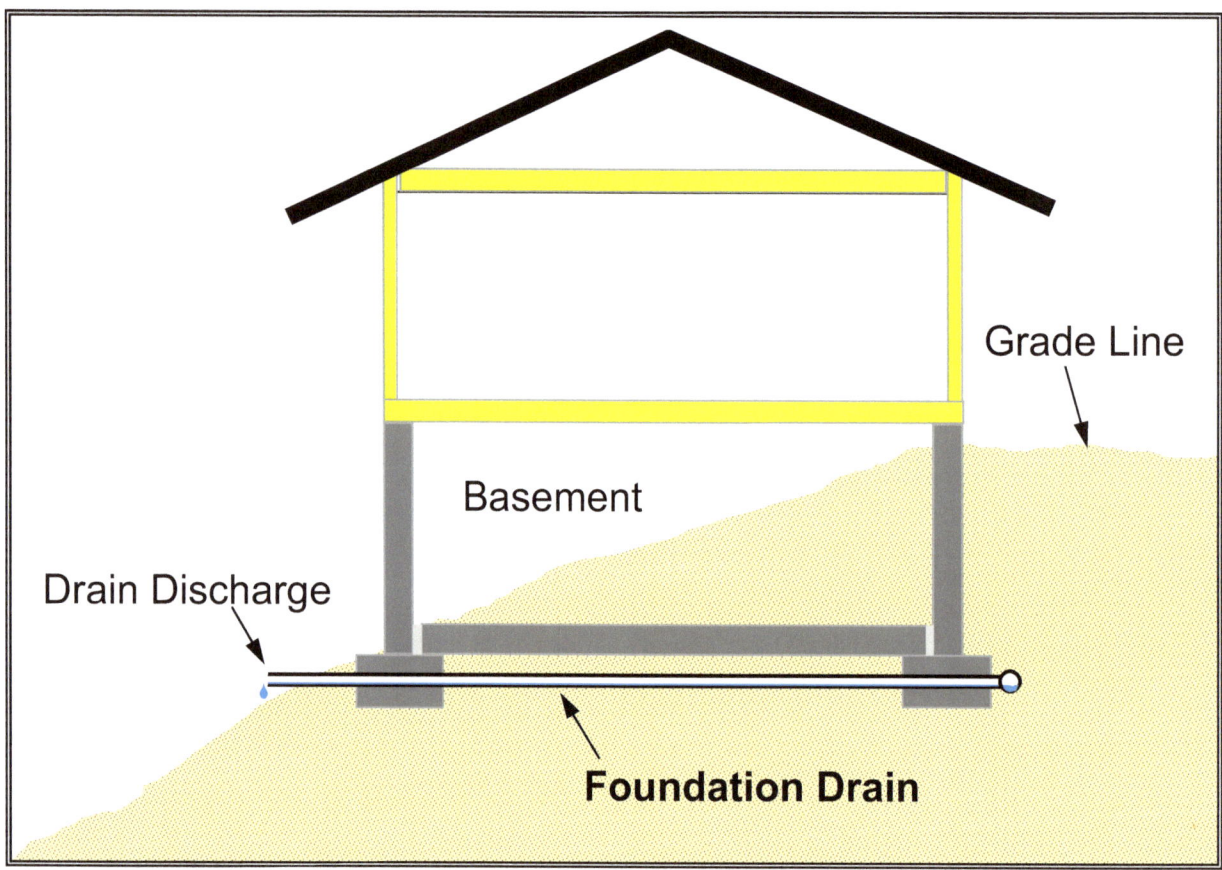

Sometimes the builder will connect the same type of corrugated pipe to the downspouts of the gutter and run them off the hillside as well. You may find several pipes coming out of the side of the hill. If this is the case, you will have to figure out which one is which.

1. Count the number of downspouts that have pipes connected to them that also go down below the ground.

2. Count the number of pipes that come out of the back of the hillside.

If the number of pipes coming out of the hillside is 1 or 2 more than the number of downspouts, you probably have that number of drain discharges rather than a dry well. Now the trick is to determine which is which.

Your local building department may also have information that was submitted by the home builder when a building permit was obtained. This can include helpful information on your drainage system.

Chapter 5: Using Drainage Systems

Planning Step 3:

    Identifying the drain discharges.

It is important to find the drain discharges in order to achieve a proper vacuum. Exterior foundation drains that go to daylight discharges are generally installed one of two ways:

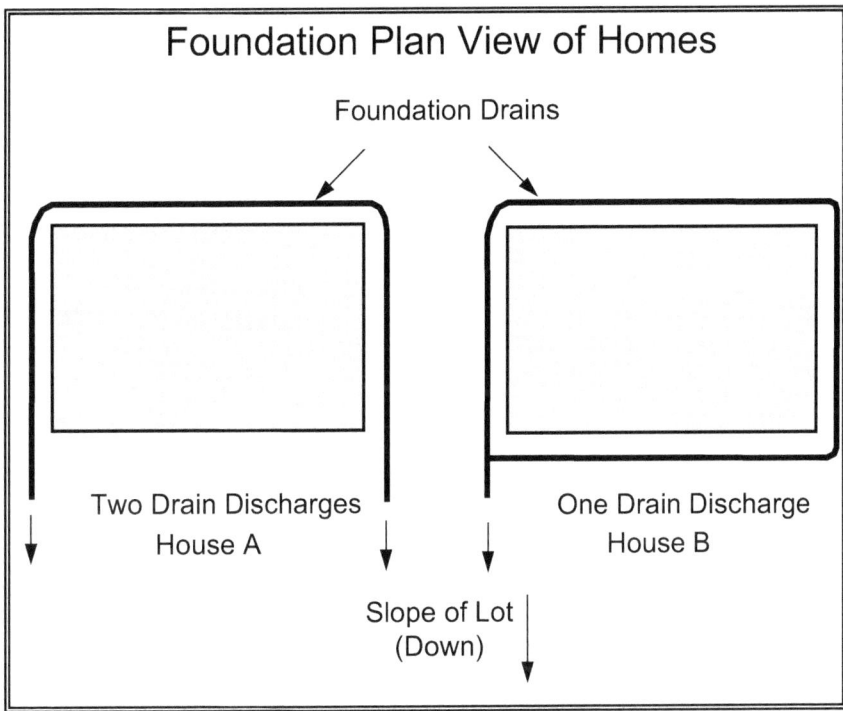

1. They can be laid around the foundation on three sides in the shape of a horseshoe (*House A*). The side that would not have a drainpipe along it would be on the side of the house, where the elevation of the ground is the lowest. In this case there are two drain discharges that would extend out from the hillside. These can generally be found coming off two corners of the home directly toward the low side of the lot.

2. A continuous loop of foundation pipe can also run around the house (*House B*). In this case there is only one drain discharge coming off the house. This drain discharge generally will be off one corner of the home and run directly toward the lowest point of the lot. Look for a pipe at this location.

If your downspouts have pipes attached to them for drainage, as described previously, you will need to:

1. Look at each of the downspout pipes and draw a direct mental line from where it penetrates the ground to the hillside. Chances are you will find a pipe penetration there. This is the downspout. Repeat this for all of the downspouts.

2. If you find one or two pipes coming off the corners of the house that cannot be accounted for (after eliminating all of the downspout pipes), you have found the drain discharge(s).

At this stage, note the number of drain discharges that you think you have. This will be confirmed either by the next step or when you actually install the system. Measure the diameter of the drain discharge ends to determine the pipe size of the drainpipe. It should be either 3 or 4 inches in diameter.

Protecting Your Home from Radon

Planning Step 4:

Confirming you have an exterior foundation drain.

The sure-fire method to confirm the existence of the exterior drain and the location of at least one drain discharge is to dig down and find it. This might seem like a lot of work in the planning stage, but if you dig it correctly, and have allotted sufficient time to do so, you can make the radon system connection and fill the hole back in at the same time.

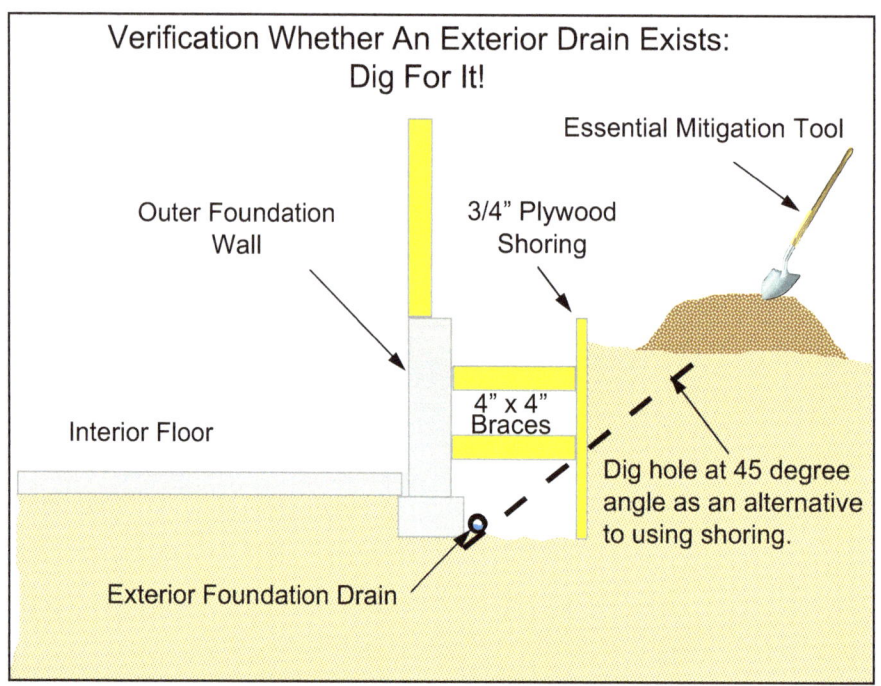

Before you dig the hole, plan how you intend to run the depressurization piping system. Typically, depressurization systems attached to exterior foundation drains are run totally outside the house. Pick a location on a side of the house that would be an appropriate spot for the depressurization fan and piping to be located (see Chapter 7). Do not pick a location on the downhill side of the house since the drain may be in a horseshoe shape rather than a loop. Don't pick a spot outside a garage wall either since drains are generally not routed around garage foundations. ***Before digging, read Installation Steps 2 and 3 of this section.*** Note: If you don't find a drain, you can still use the hole for a sub-footer suction system - See Chapter 6.

Once the foundation drain is exposed, you can get its exact size. You can also cut a small hole into it and insert a garden hose. Turn it on and look for water coming out of an open end of a pipe. Let the water run fully open for several minutes. The end of the drain could also be covered over by dirt and rocks. In this case, you may see a wet spot. If you do not see any evidence of water, and you have checked with the local building department to make sure you are not connected to a storm sewer or an interceptor, you can assume that either the drain discharge runs to a dry well in the ground or it is well covered over. In this case, you won't need to seal it. Methods for sealing exposed drain discharges will be discussed later.

<u>*Important:*</u>   *When you dig the hole you must provide shoring to keep the hole from caving in or dig a much larger hole, so the sides are at a 45-degree angle. You must take these precautions especially if the hole is greater than 3 feet deep. Don't ignore this. People have suffocated to death when dirt has caved in on them. Also, when you dig the hole, it should not be left open for someone to fall into. Cover it with a sheet of plywood and rope it off and encircle it with yellow and black barrier tape that you can find at most hardware stores.*

Chapter 5: Using Drainage Systems

Planning Step 5:

Planning the riser connection.

One of the critical parts of this system is the connection of the riser to the exterior drainpipe. Basically, you have two options:

Option 1 - Saddle Connection.

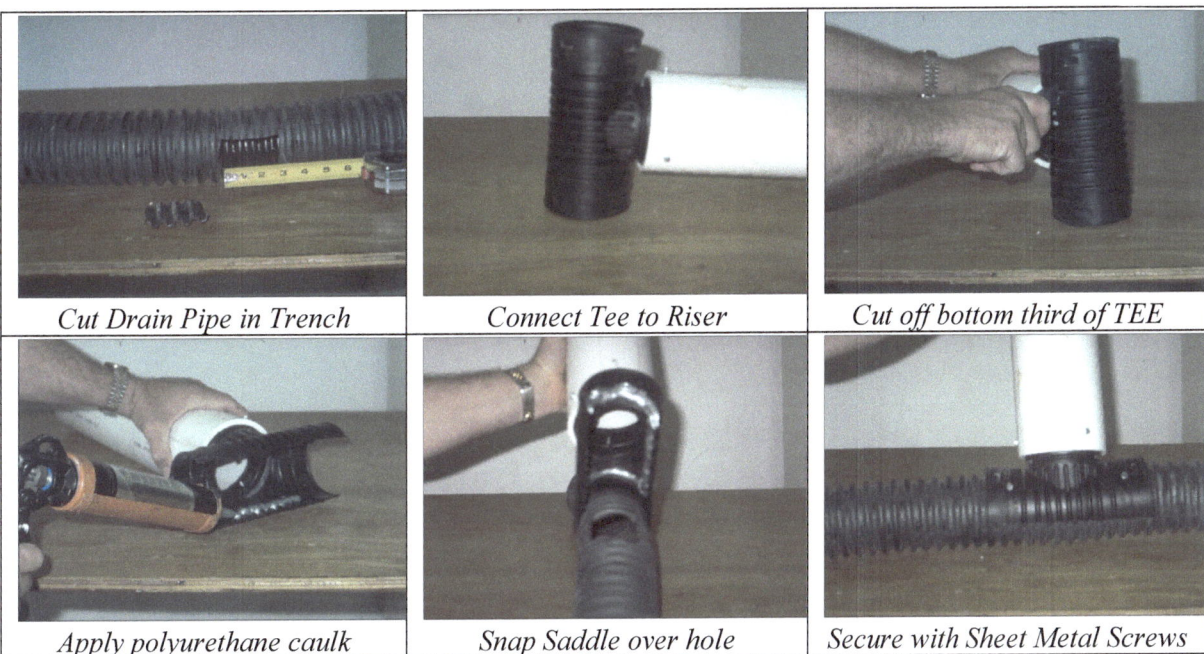

| Cut Drain Pipe in Trench | Connect Tee to Riser | Cut off bottom third of TEE |
| Apply polyurethane caulk | Snap Saddle over hole | Secure with Sheet Metal Screws |

The sequence above shows an easy method for attaching the system riser to the drainpipe. You can purchase a "tee" that is made for flexible and corrugated piping systems from your local plumbing or building supply house. This type of tee is made by ADS or may be referred to as a "weeping tile fitting". If you cut off the bottom third of the straight section of the tee, you end up with a saddle that will snap over the existing drainpipe. This allows for an easier connection than cutting out a section of the existing pipe and inserting a tee. This riser connection can be made during the planning stage if you dig down to the drain to verify its existence, or later when you plan to install the entire system.

Note: If you plan to make the connection before finishing the system, make sure you read the portion of the installation steps that covers backfilling the hole. Also, if you plan to leave the riser open to the atmosphere for a while, be sure to tape over the discharge to keep out debris. The connection can be carried out as follows:

Step 1. Cut off the lower third of the "Tee" fitting to create a saddle.

Step 2. Cut the appropriate length of riser. This riser should be 4-inch diameter schedule 40 PVC or ABS pipe. The length of the riser should be long enough to extend from the exterior foundation drain vertically, to about 2 feet above grade.

Step 3. Apply a ½-inch wide bead of polyurethane caulk around the outside surface of the throat of the saddle. Slide this up into the end of the riser and screw three ¼-inch by 1-inch-long self-tapping sheet metal screws to hold the saddle securely in place. A variable speed drill with a nut driver works well for this. If you do not have one, insert the un-caulked saddle into the pipe and pre-drill three pilot holes through both the riser and the top of the saddle. Then caulk it and screw the assembly together.

Step 4. Cut a 2 ½-inch diameter hole in the top of the exterior drainpipe with a utility knife. This hole should be at the location where the riser is going to connect to the drain.

Step 5. Apply a ½-inch wide bead of caulk continuously around the underside of the saddle (see figure above).

Step 6. Carefully set the saddle onto the drainpipe with the riser located directly over the top of the hole that was cut in the previous step. Push down on the riser and snap it into place. Using four self-tapping sheet metal screws, ¼-inch by 1-inch, screw the sides of the saddle into the drain. Having a person hold this vertical while it is screwed into place is very helpful. Also, if you do not have the variable speed drill and nut driver as described in Step 3, you will need to place the riser on the drain before caulking the underside of the saddle, and pre-drill the holes. After this is done, caulk the underside of the saddle, snap into place and screw the two pieces together.

This method of attachment can be used for flexible and corrugated pipe as well as plastic pipe drain systems. This method has the advantage of not requiring the drainpipe to be cut entirely into two pieces to allow for the insertion of a tee fitting.

Option 2 - Inserted Tee. Another method for securing the riser to the drain would be to actually cut a full section out of the drainpipe and insert a tee. Subsequently, the riser can be glued into the top opening of the tee. Methods for gluing pipe are thoroughly described in Chapter 7. It is difficult to move the drainpipe around enough to insert the tee with this method. A great deal of difficulty can be encountered in trying to keep loose dirt and rocks out of the drainpipe. Generally, the first method described with the saddle, results in the cleanest connection.

Important: *Regardless of the method for connecting the riser to the drainpipe, it is important to make sure no gravel or dirt enters the drainpipe or the riser when it is exposed. If debris enters the pipe, it can block the normal flow of drainage water and also prevent the radon system from functioning properly.*

After the connection is made, you can immediately refill the hole. You do not need to wait for the caulk to cure on its own. It will cure underground just as easily as above ground. If there was gravel around the drain when you uncovered it, replace it before you begin refilling the hole.

As you fill in the hole, hold the pipe vertical, stop every 6 inches and tamp the dirt down by stomping on it. Pack the soil thoroughly as the hole is filled to reduce the amount of vacuum lost due to outside air leaking down to the connection point. This will improve the performance of the radon system.

Riser Ready for Fan

Chapter 5: Using Drainage Systems

Planning Step 6:

Location of the depressurization fan.

When you are connecting to an exterior drain, all of the piping and the fan can be outside of the home. This is great as it does not take up any interior space. However, the moisture carried by the system can cause water to condense and freeze in the fan and piping system -- especially in cold climates. Note the fans used are rated for outdoor use, but ice can block the discharge or damage the fan if ice chunks fall into it.

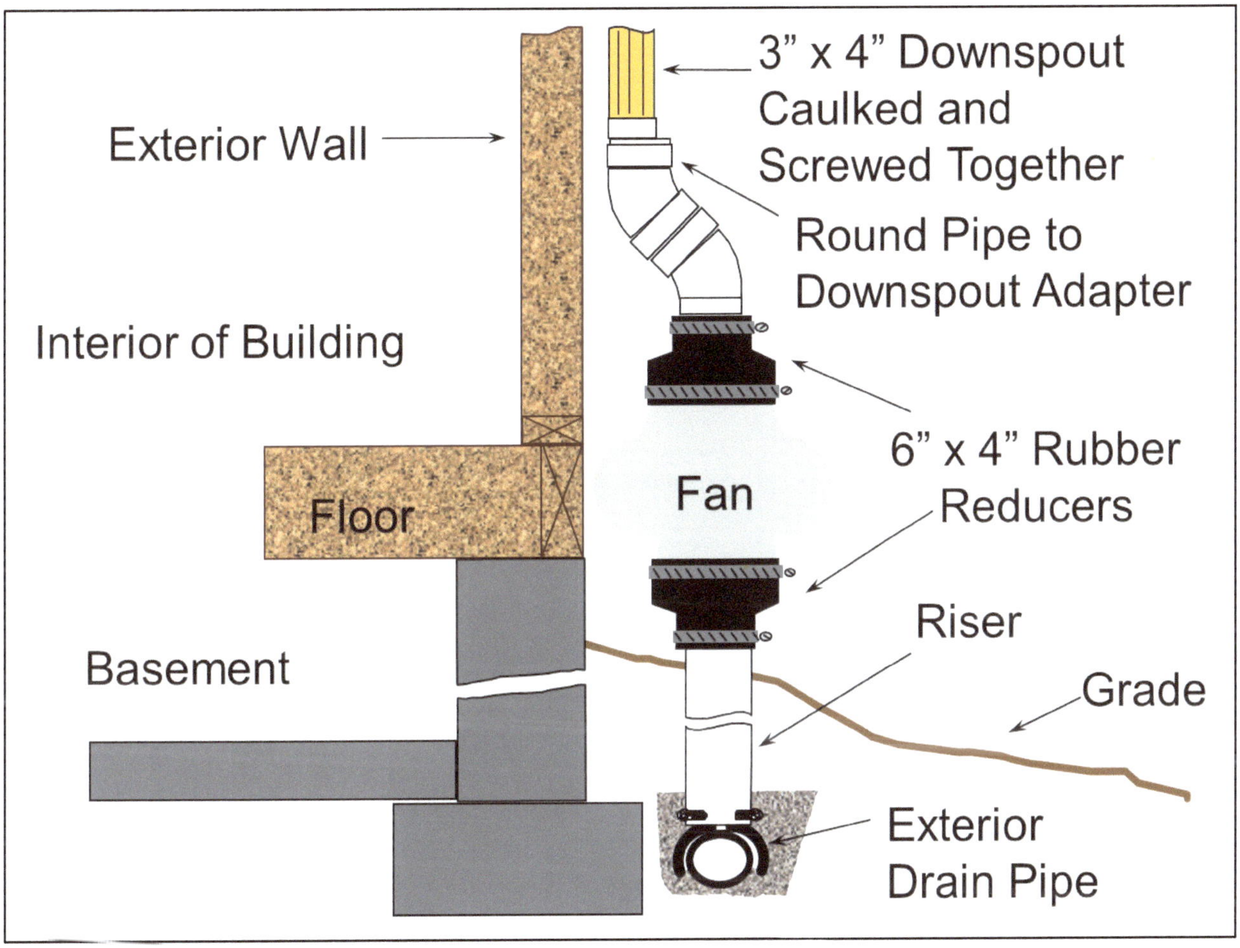

To reduce the impact of this you can:

1. Place the fan and discharge piping on the southern exposure of the home to minimize ice build-up in the fan and piping.

2. Minimize the amount of exposed piping

3. Run a couple pieces of stainless rod through discharge pipe just above fan to prevent ice from falling into fan. The lengths of 3/8 inch all thread will stop the ice chunks and allow the ice to slowly melt. See diagram to the right.

Criss Cross in Pipe Discharge Above Fan

As in all cases, locate the fan so its discharge is away from building openings. (See Chapter 7).

© Copyright 2023 • Center for Environmental Research and Technology, Inc.

Planning Step 7:

Sealing major leak points and the drain discharge ends.

When the depressurization system is connected to the riser (which is in turn attached to the drain system), a vacuum will be created. The stronger the vacuum is, the better the radon reduction will be. Air leakage into the system will cause the vacuum to be less than desirable. Major air leaks to consider are:

- Floor-to-wall joints inside the home.
- Sump holes where the drain does not go to a daylight end but rather drains to a sump inside the home (see the earlier section of this chapter on installing sump pit lids).
- Daylight ends of the drain system-in this case you will need to install check valve(s)

During previous steps of this section, you should have determined the drain discharges for the drain system. You should also have determined the number and size of these pipes.

Note: It is possible that your drain discharges were buried under landscaping, or they alternatively went to a gravel pit under the soil. If your drain discharges are not exposed, you may not need to be concerned with these until after you install the system.

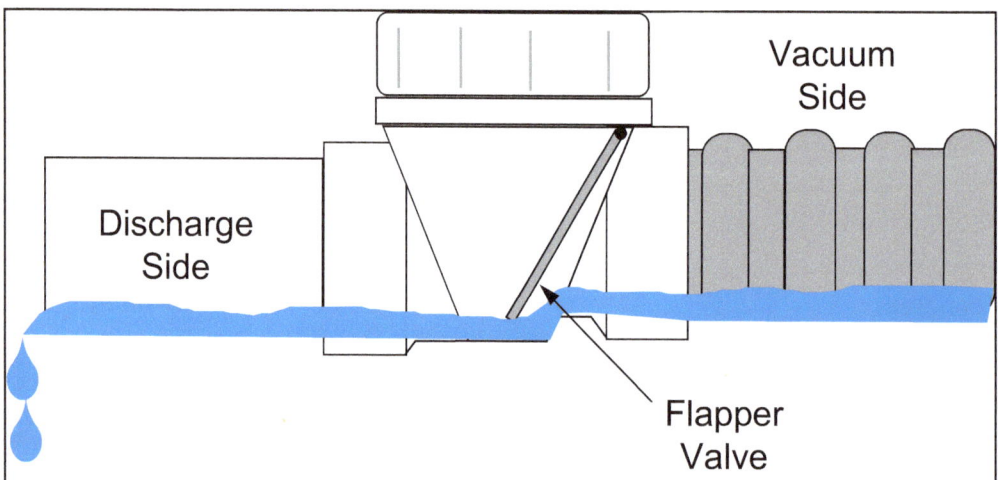

The illustration above shows a commercially available drain discharge check valve often referred to as a backwater valve that can be used for radon reduction. These are designed in different sizes for different sized drain discharge pipes. The design allows the daylight end to be glued and screwed into the daylight ends of the drainpipe. The large area of the flapper, along with the seal, allows for a tight seal when the depressurization system is operating. The angled design of the flapper allows for the full, unobstructed flow of water out of the end of them during rainy periods. Determine the size and number of these that will be needed and order them from a catalog supply house listed in the appendix.

Full throated check valve installed on daylight soak away

Important: *Do not seal off drain discharges or put traps on them that can fill with dirt or rodent nests. These drain discharges must be allowed to drain water freely.*

Chapter 5: Using Drainage Systems

Installing the Exterior Drain Depressurization System

This section is devoted to the installation of a depressurization system that will be attached to an existing, exterior foundation drain. You should read the previous section on planning the exterior drain system along with the first section of this chapter on sump systems. If your drain is connected to an interior sump, the details for sealing these sumps are contained in the sump section of this chapter. Read this section along with the Chapters 7, 8, and 10 on Depressurization Systems, Sealing, and General Safety Precautions before proceeding with this work. You should also read the "Finishing Touches" section at the end of this chapter.

Installation Step 1:

Assemble equipment and materials.

The following is a checklist of equipment and material that you will need to gather before starting:

Area	Item	√
Safety	Goggles/safety glasses	
	Dust mask	
	Leather gloves	
	First aid kit	
	Ventilation fan	
	Flashlight	
	Coveralls or old clothing	
	Helper or observer	
Material	Materials for sealing interior sump - if needed	
	Shoring materials for stabilizing excavation (see Planning Step 4)	
	Piece of plywood, wood stakes, rope, cloth strips for covering hole and warning kids away from hole if it is to be left open for a period of time	
	1 tube of polyurethane caulking	
	1 ADS (weeping tile) tee	
	10-foot length of 4-inch, sch. 40 PVC or ABS pipe (riser)	
	1-inch #8 self-tapping sheet-metal screws (7)	
	Drain - check (backwater valve) for drain discharge ends (see Planning Step 7)	
	Duct tape or cap for temporarily sealing off riser	
	Material needed for depressurization system (see Chapter 7)	
	10 x 10 sheet of plastic or drop cloth	
Tools	Electric drill - cordless or powered	
	Screwdriver or ¼-inch nut driver	
	Caulking gun	
	Rags	
	Sharp utility knife	
	Extension cords	
	Shovel and other digging tools	
	Wire brush	
	PVC saw	
	Smoke stick (see Chapter 8)	

© Copyright 2023 • Center for Environmental Research and Technology, Inc.

Protecting Your Home from Radon

Installation Step 2:

Dig down to the drain.

At the location where you plan to install the riser, lay out a sheet of plastic or a drop cloth on the ground where you can put the excavated dirt. This will make it easier to clean up the loose dirt when you refill the hole. Begin digging the hole with a shovel, pick, etc. *If the hole is going to be deeper than 3 feet, you must make provisions to ensure that the hole does not cave in.* You have two options for preventing the hole from caving in: (see Planning Step 4).

1. Dig a tapered hole as wide as it is deep. This makes the sides of the hole at a 45-degree angle to prevent caving in. You get a bigger hole, but it is certainly a smaller hole than the one that they will bury you in if the hole caves in on you.

2. You can dig a smaller hole than described above, if you use ¾-inch plywood on the sides of the hole and brace them against the side of the house with 4 x 4 pieces of wood toe nailed to the plywood. As you dig deeper, a brace should be located every 2 feet below the grade.

The author will agree that digging a large hole is a lot of work and the use of shoring may save some excavation but working in a hole with wood bracing in the way is not any easier. We recommend following the first method -- dig a large hole!

Important: As you dig, be careful of breaking gas lines, sprinkler lines, and exterior buried conduit that may be located around your home. The existence of these obstructions should not prevent you from digging at these locations as long as caution is exercised so they are not damaged. This is why we do not recommend the use of power digging equipment like backhoes, jackhammers, and powered augers. Another reason for not using this equipment is the potential for damage to the side of the house. Use a shovel and other hand tools.

The drains are generally just below the foundation footing. They will be laid right next to the footing. You may have to dig a little deeper than the top of the footing to find it. You will know when you are getting close when you encounter drain rock (clean gravel) or a fibrous, geotextile cloth. If you run into this cloth uncover the cloth with your hands. *Do not rip the cloth out.* Carefully cut the cloth with a knife and fold the cloth back out of the way.

Geotextile cloth being pulled back from drain rock covering perimeter drain

Once the cloth has been moved out of the way, scoop out the drain rock that is between the cloth and the drainpipe. Place this clean rock in a separate pile or a bucket for later use. As the gravel is removed, the drain should be exposed. Remove a sufficient amount of gravel to allow you to make the riser connection. If you have already assembled the necessary materials for connecting the riser, move onto the next step.

If you have dug down to the drain to confirm its existence and to make the necessary measurements for drain size and discharge location, perform that work now. If you are planning to leave the hole open long enough to obtain the necessary riser connection materials, you should replace the drain rock around the exposed pipe, lay the fiber cloth back over and close it with duct tape (this keeps dirt from getting into the drain). Place a large sheet of ¾-inch plywood over the hole. Place stakes around the opening and run a rope along the stakes and attach the ends to the house. Tie some white strips of cloth to the rope. You can also obtain yellow caution tape at building supply stores. The plywood sheet and warning rope is to warn burglars not to step into the hole at night and sue you.

Chapter 5: Using Drainage Systems

Installation Step 3:

Make the riser connection.

After you have exposed the drain and assembled the necessary parts for the riser connection, refer back to the step-by-step instructions detailed in Planning Step 5 of this section. This would be a good time to have a helper with you to hand things to you and to hold the pipe as you backfill the hole and make the connection. *Be sure to follow the safety instructions on the side of the tube of caulk.*

After making the connection, place the gravel back around the pipe that you removed in the previous step. Lay the geotextile cloth back over the gravel. Seal the two edges of the cloth with some of the polyurethane caulk that you used to make the drain connection. Tape the edges together with duct tape so they will stay in place as you fill the hole.

Backfill the hole with the dirt. Be careful not to disturb the riser connection or the fiber cloth that you repaired. Have your assistant hold the pipe vertically as the hole is filled. As the hole fills up, stop every six inches and stomp on the dirt to compact it. Repeat this filling and compaction process until the hole is filled.

Installation Step 4a:

If your drain goes to a daylight discharge - install the drain discharge checks.

Install the drain checks described in Planning Step 6. Be sure to follow the manufacturers' instructions. Since polyurethane caulks or PVC/ABS glues will be used to make this connection, follow safety procedures provided with the material and the general safety procedures described in the safety section of this manual (see Chapter 10).

When installing these devices, be sure to locate them at the end of the drain discharges. Make sure they are oriented in a manner so when the flapper opens it will rotate upwards to a horizontal position. If needed, put a block or some rocks beneath them for support to insure it is level and will drain freely.

If desired, dig back along the drain discharge pipe into the hillside and cut off a portion of the pipe. Then attach the drain check so the end of it will stick out of the hillside when the dirt is replaced.

It is important to install these checks so water can continue to flow out of them unobstructed and in a location where they will be protected from lawn mowers and where gradual hillside erosion will not cover them over.

Installation Step 4b:

If your drain goes to a sump - a sump cover is needed.

If your drainage system did not have drain discharge but rather was attached to an internal sump, install the sump lid.

Installation Step 5:

Install the depressurization system.

Install the depressurization piping system as planned earlier in this section and as detailed in Chapter 7.

© Copyright 2023 • Center for Environmental Research and Technology, Inc.

Protecting Your Home from Radon

Installation Step 6:

Check for air leaks.

After installing the system, turn it on and check for air leaks. This is done with a smoke stick as is described in Planning Step 3 in Chapter 8 on sealing. Some key areas to check are:

- The drain discharges to see if the flappers are seating well. Some leakage may occur at this point; but if it is a major leak, make sure no dirt is lodged between the flapper and the inside of the trap.
- Check other pipes that come out of the hillside to see if smoke is drawn into them. If so, there is an additional discharge that needs a drain check - install it.
- If you have an interior sump and attached a lid to it, check for leaks around the lid.
- Check the floor-to-wall joints and cracks in the slab of the home. Check around plumbing and electrical penetrations through the interior floor and walls. If smoke is drawn through these openings, seal them per the techniques shown in Chapter 8.

Installation Step 7:

Check flues for backdrafting and install a carbon monoxide detector.

Contact a competent inspector to test these devices. Do not run system until this test has been completed (see Chapter 10).

Finishing Touches

After the sump suction or the exterior foundation system has been installed, run through the following check list to make sure you have done everything:

Item	√
Checked for air leaks at:	
Sump lid	
Sump lid penetrations	
Floor-to-wall joints	
Floor cracks	
Drain discharge	
Checked the drafting of your combustion appliances and installed carbon monoxide alarm. See Safety Chapter 10	
Installed a system performance indicator	
Labeled the piping system at all visible locations	
Installed a system label	
Painted exterior metal parts	
Re-tested the home for radon	

Chapter 5: Using Drainage Systems

Finishing Touches (cont.)

Install at least one system label describing the system.

In at least one location, a label should be placed to tell workers and future homeowners about the system you have installed. This is to ensure radon reductions are maintained and serious health concerns are not encountered if the systems are improperly disconnected for maintenance work. The key concern is if the system is opened up and the depressurization fan is left on. This could cause large amounts of air to be drawn from the house and could cause combustion appliances to backdraft. These labels can be made on paper and glued to an appropriate location or typed on an adhesive backed label.

Here is a sample label for a depressurization system on sumps. This can be used for a sump system as well as an exterior foundation drain system that goes to an interior sump.

> **RADON MITIGATION SYSTEM**
>
> Do not remove sump lid without shutting off system
>
> If lid is to be removed for maintenance purposes, turn off fan located in _____. Disconnect for fan is located in _____. Fan powered from breaker # ____ in electrical breaker panel. After maintenance has been performed, all pipe connections should be remade, sump cover replaced in the manner in which it was found, and fan turned back on.

Below is a sample label for exterior foundation drain depressurization system with daylight discharge. Since this label is outside, you should write it on a plastic label with an indelible marker or glue it inside a sealable plastic envelope and attach it to the fan.

> **RADON MITIGATION SYSTEM FAN**
>
> This fan is connected to the exterior foundation drain.
>
> If work is to be done on the foundation drain, this fan can be shut off by disconnect located _____. The fan is powered from breaker # ____ in the electrical breaker panel.
>
> There are also ____ drain check assemblies located on the hillside on the ____ side of the home. If these are to be temporarily removed for service work, they should be reinstalled after the work has been completed.

Chapter 6

Sub-Slab Depressurization Systems

When do I need to use sub-slab depressurization?

Planning the Sub-Slab Depressurization System

Installing the Sub-Slab Depressurization System

CHAPTER 6 - SUB-SLAB DEPRESSURIZATION SYSTEMS (SSD)

The illustration below shows a sub-slab depressurization system. A hole is cut through the concrete slab. A cavity is formed in the soil beneath the hole. A PVC or ABS pipefitting is set into the hole and attached to the depressurization system. The depressurization system creates a vacuum near the hole, if not entirely under the slab. The vacuum created at the hole under the slab causes radon, as well as other soil gases, to move toward the suction point where it is collected and exhausted safely outside the home. (See Chapter 7 for routing and discharge options).

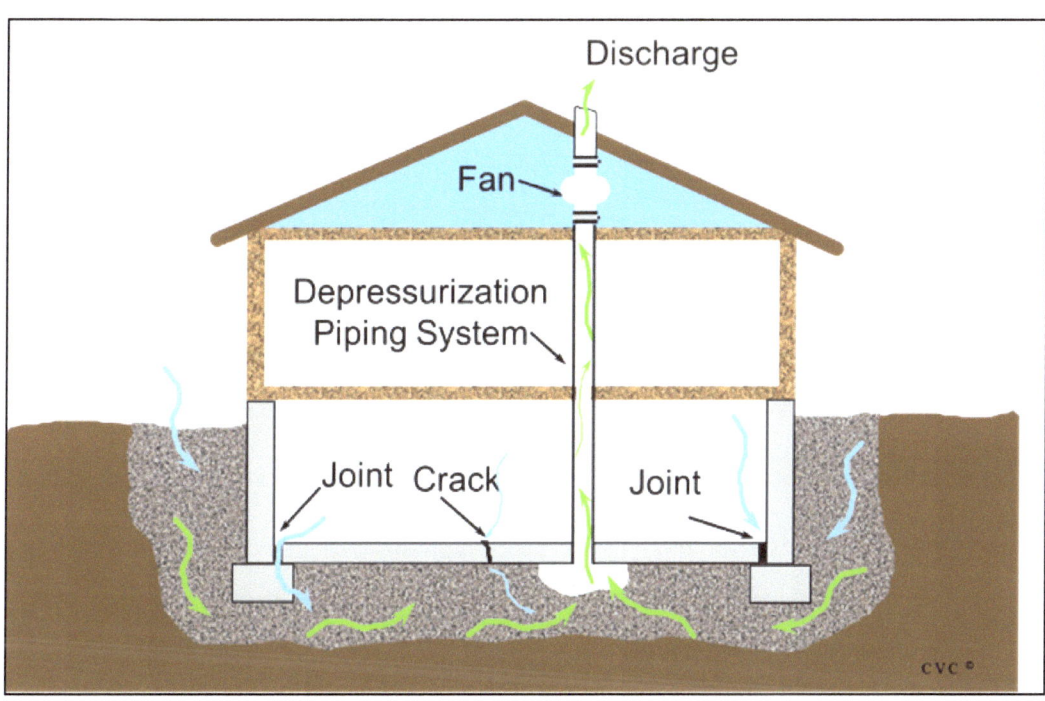

The success of the SSD system depends on how porous the soil is beneath the slab. If the slab was poured on top of gravel or washed rock, the potential for collecting radon from beneath the entire slab is very good. However, in cases where the soil is tightly compacted only a small area of the slab will be under vacuum. In these "tight soil" cases, additional suction points may be needed to adequately reduce the radon. Professional mitigators have methods for estimating the number of suction points before an installation. However, a suitable compromise for the homeowner is to install a system with one suction point. Then perform some tests to see if the system needs to be expanded. One suction point is generally sufficient. Sometimes two suction points are needed, but rarely more than two in a home.

When do I need to use sub-slab depressurization?

Use sub-slab depressurization on homes that have concrete slab floors resting directly on the soil and if they do not have water drainage systems associated with the house. Drainage systems often work better than a single sub-slab depressurization point system. This is because the vacuum created by the drainage system approach extends around several sides of the house or beneath the entire slab itself. However, if your slab was constructed on top of clean aggregate throughout the entire slab, sub slab depressurization will work very well.

If your house is built over a crawl space, this technique will **not** apply. Your home could also have a crawl space and a basement foundation type in which you may need to apply both sub-slab and sub-membrane depressurization systems and connect them to a common depressurization piping system (see Chapter 9).

Protecting Your Home from Radon

Planning the Sub-Slab Depressurization System

This chapter provides information on the location and installation of the actual suction point. The result of the work in this chapter will be a 4-inch PVC or ABS riser from the concrete floor. Before beginning the installation, the safety information in Chapter 10 should be thoroughly reviewed. To complete the system, you will have to install the depressurization piping system described in Chapter 7.

Consult the flow chart preceding Chapter 1 to determine if additional approaches also need to be considered.

Planning Step 1:

Confirming sub-slab depressurization is appropriate or if you need assistance from a professional mitigator.

Sub-slab depressurization systems are used as a first option under the various conditions shown below:

	Question	If NO:	If YES:
1	Is the house built totally over a crawl space?	Proceed with this chapter	Also consult Chapter 4
2	Does the house have both crawl space and concrete slab?	Proceed with this chapter	Also consult Chapters 4 & 9.
3	Is there a sump or an exterior drain system on the home?	Proceed with this chapter	Also consult Chapter 5.
4	Is the native soil permeable? An example would be decomposed granite/gravel.	Go to next question	Proceed with this chapter.
5	Is the native soil impermeable but had gravel placed beneath the slab during construction?	Go to next question	Proceed with this chapter.
6	Is slab setting on clays with no gravel beneath it?	Go to next question	Call a professional radon mitigator.
7	Are you unsure of soil permeability beneath slab?	Proceed with this chapter	Read through the planning steps in this chapter.
8	Do you have ductwork for your forced air furnace or air conditioner beneath the slab?	Proceed with this chapter	Call a professional radon mitigator.
9	Do you have a hydronic heating system (a grid of hot water pipes beneath the slab)?	Proceed with this chapter	Call a professional radon mitigator.
10	Do you have a thermal or solar heating system with ductwork, piping or open spaces that distribute soil air into the home?	Proceed with this chapter	Call a professional radon mitigator.

Note: *Before giving up, read the following planning steps.*

Chapter 6: Slabs and Basements

Planning Step 2:

Determining relative location of a suction point.

The first step is to determine whether you can place the suction points near an outside wall.

Typically, it is best to locate the suction point next to an outside foundation wall. We know this is contrary to common sense that would locate it in the middle of the floor. Better vacuum is typically achieved with a sidewall location because:

1. The soil is generally looser under this portion of the slab.

2. The vacuum is applied to the floor wall joint which is a large radon entry point.

3. The adjacent wall provides a convenient support surface for piping attachment.

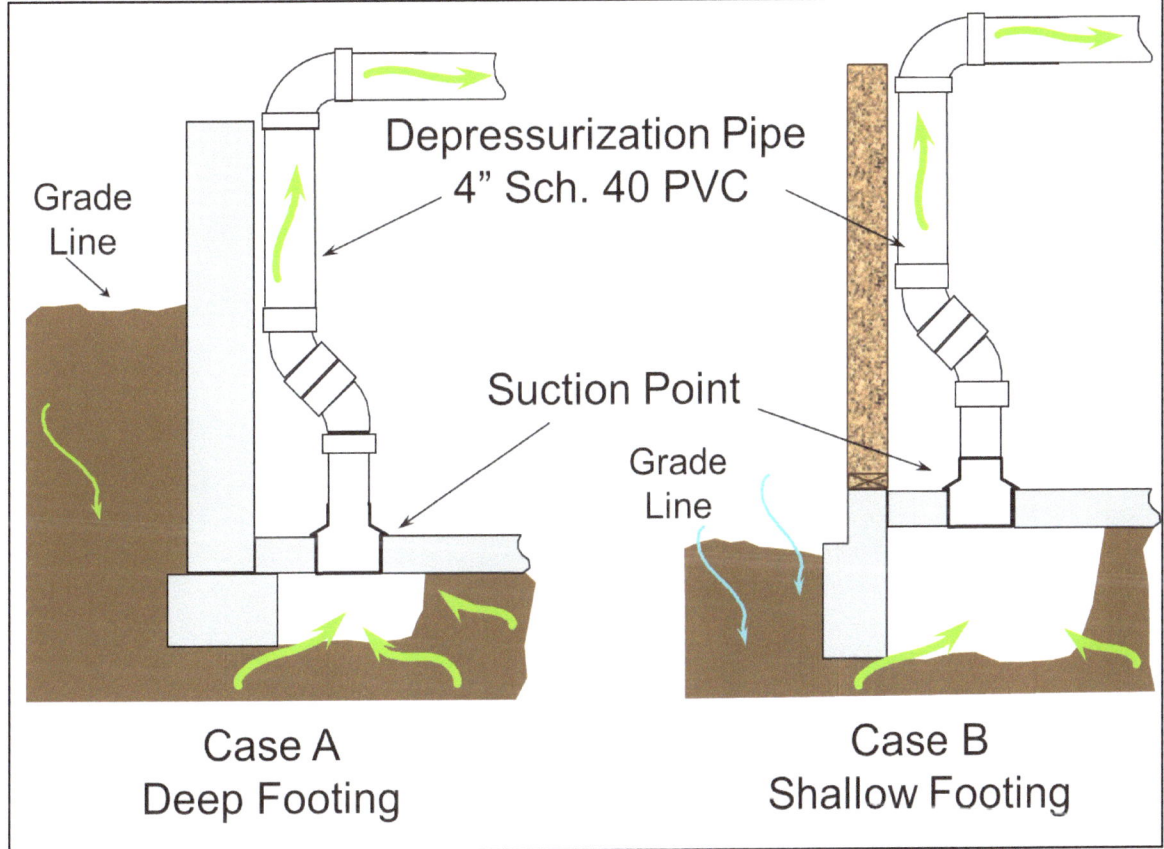

A concern with an outside foundation wall suction point location is if the vacuum will be defeated by outside air being drawn in rather than air from beneath the slab. Refer to the figure above. In *Case A*, the suction point has been installed in a slab of the basement (or a slab on grade home) where the footing is well below grade due to frost codes (2 ½ to 3 feet or more). Most of the air in this situation is being drawn to the suction point from the soil beneath the slab -- this is good. In *Case B*, the shallow footing is close to the surface of the soil. When the footing is close to the surface of the outside grade, a lot of outside air can be drawn in, thereby reducing the sub-slab vacuum and the system's efficiency.

Shallow footings are generally found in parts of the world where frost does not form in the ground (unless earthquake codes call for deep footings). If you have shallow footings, you will need to choose a more centrally located suction point for the most optimal radon reduction. However, for the most part deep footings are found. This is why the suction point is commonly located next to an exterior foundation wall.

© Copyright 2023 • Center for Environmental Research and Technology, Inc.

Planning Step 3:

Avoiding potential problems by eliminating certain suction point locations.

When selecting a suction point, pick a location that is convenient and where the "radon capture zone" (sometimes referred to as "suction field") will extend as far as possible beneath the slab. A large opening in a slab can prevent a vacuum from being extended beyond the opening.

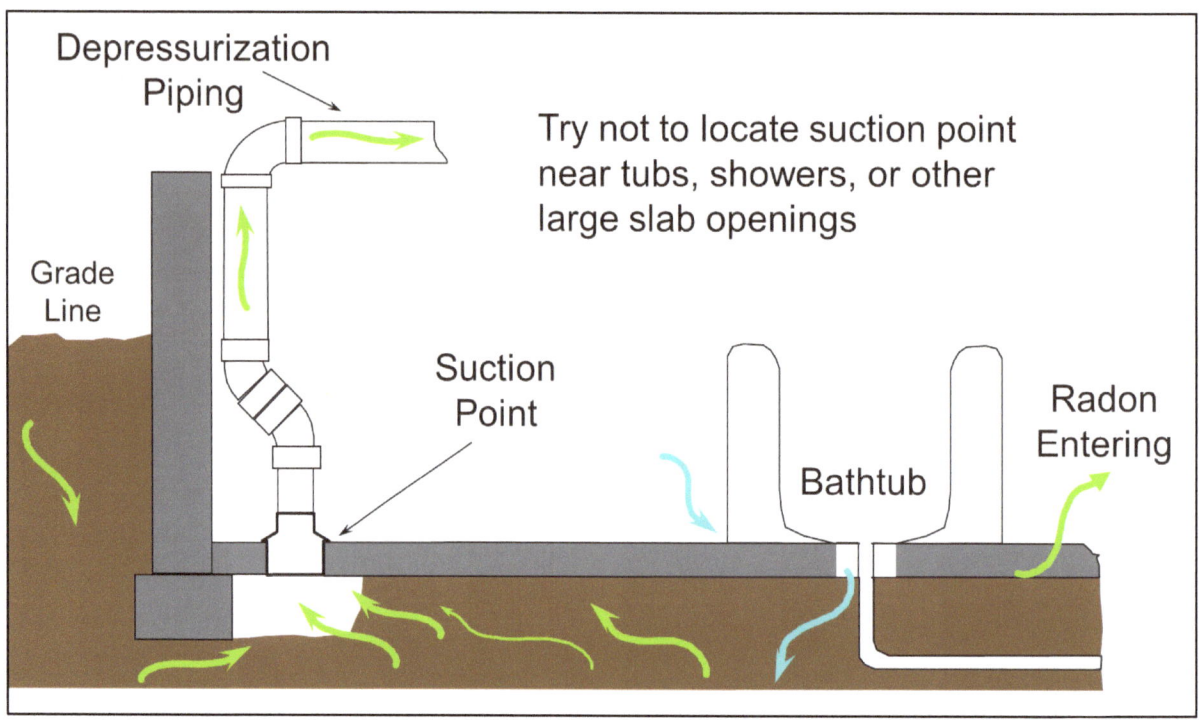

An example of this is shown above where a suction point was located near a bathtub. There is generally a 12-inch by 12-inch opening in the slab beneath the tub for plumbing. A similar opening in the concrete can be found beneath showers, and toilets. When a suction point is very close to these openings, air from inside the room is drawn down through the opening rather than from beneath the slab. This presents two problems:

1. The suction field does not extend beyond the major leak point because room air instead of soil air is being collected. This could require the addition of more suction points to obtain full coverage of the area under the slab; and

2. Excess air is drawn from inside the house. This will increase the potential for backdrafting combustion appliances and increase the heating cost of the home.

Try to select locations for the suction points as far away from these locations as possible. If you must locate a suction point near these large openings, be prepared to get involved with significant sealing efforts.

In selecting a location near an outside wall, the suction point would be near the floor-to-wall joint. These are significant leak points. However, these can be easily sealed if they are accessible. Therefore, try to select an area of the floor where the walls are not firred out and finished. This will allow you to access those critical joints, which are closest to the suction point. An unfinished utility room or laundry room is ideal for this reason.

Chapter 6: Slabs and Basements

Planning Step 4:

Choosing potential suction points.

Although it could be a great conversation piece, running your depressurization system piping through a home is not very attractive. A suction point is generally most effective when placed next to an outside wall, so an unfinished room is often where we try to place suction points.

First, walk through the basement and look for unfinished areas that you do not plan to remodel. At the same time, think of how you might route the depressurization piping either through the house or to the outside. See Chapter 7 on piping systems to help with the planning process.

Pick a suction point using the criteria described in the previous steps. Balance that with the easiest and most direct route for running your depressurization system piping. Once you have selected a suction point where it would be the most convenient to install, you are ready to proceed.

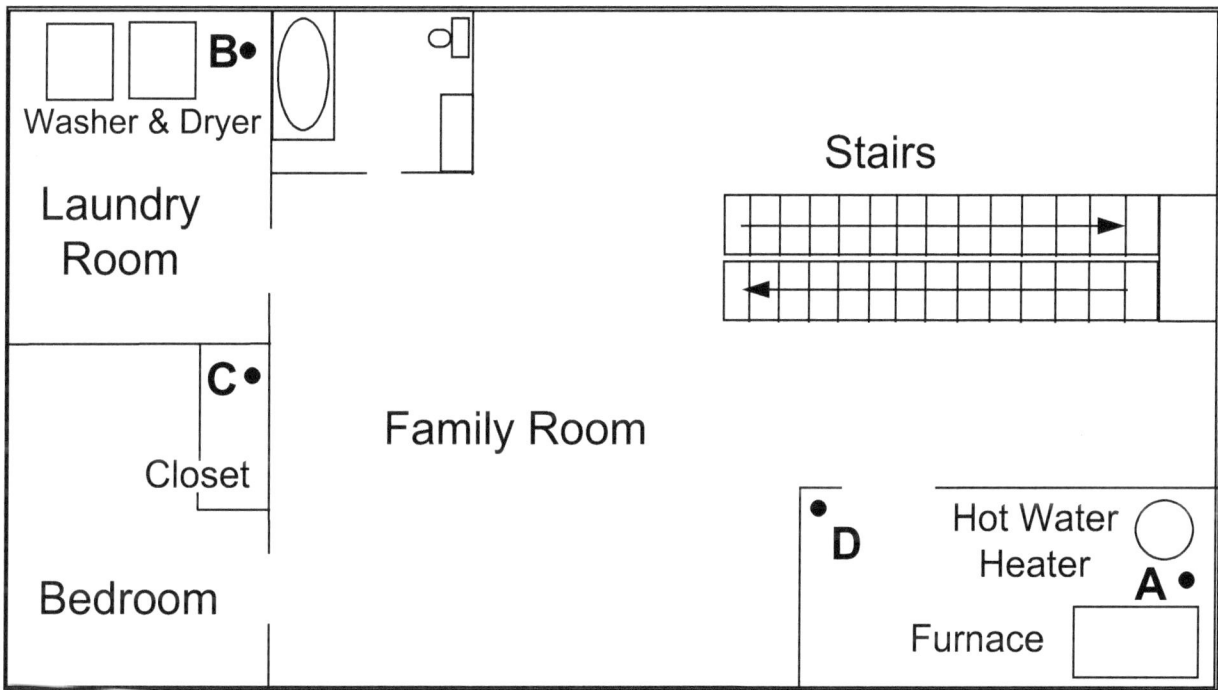

The illustration above provides an example of a basement floor plan. If the footings are deep (over 2 ½ feet below grade), point B in the laundry room or point A in the furnace room would be convenient choices for suction points. However, point A will probably work better than point B because it is further from the bathroom/tub area that likely has a large slab opening beneath the tub. Select point A, in this case as your prime location, and point B as your backup location.

On the other hand, if the footings are very shallow, one might select point C or D since they are more centrally located. Select closets or inside corners of unfinished areas, if possible, to conceal the piping. Because some air noise can be heard through these pipes, try to keep them out of frequently used rooms. If you have shallow footings, select point D as your first suction point location and point C as your back-up choice.

Protecting Your Home from Radon

Planning Step 5:
Obstacles to suction field extension-Multiple Suction Points

One suction point may be able to impact the entire area under the slab if the underlying soil is uniformly permeable. An example of this would be where gravel has been laid completely under the slab when the house was built. Sometimes there can be obstacles to the movement of soil gas beneath the slab, even when the soil is permeable. One common example of an obstacle is when a footing or grade beam runs under the middle of the slab.

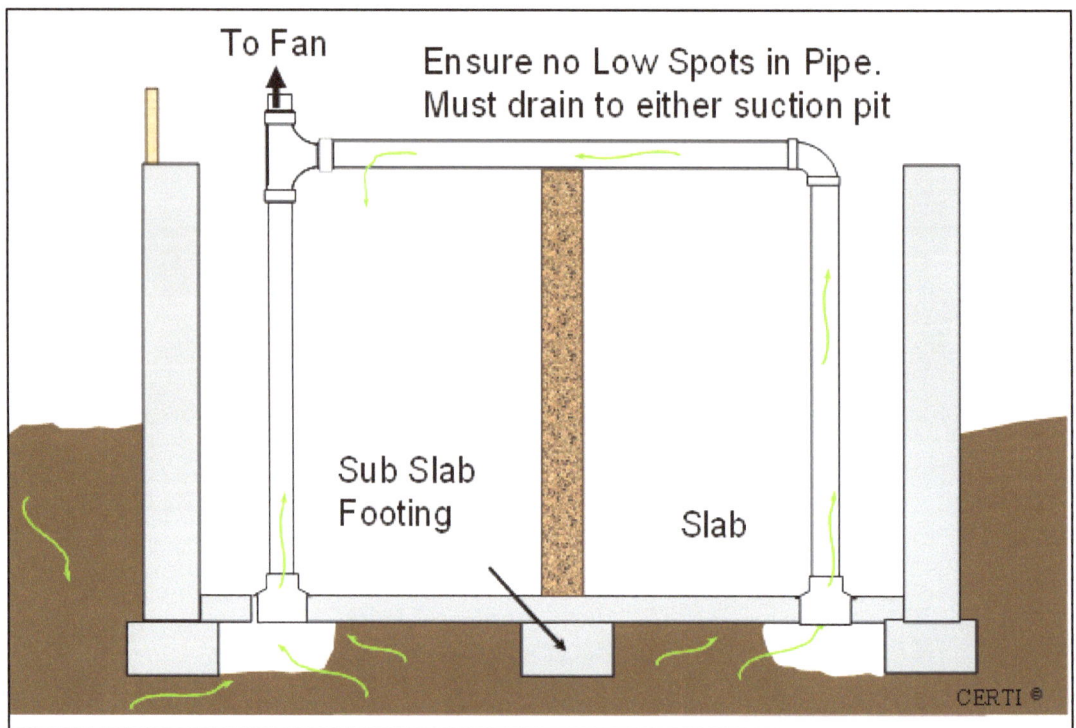

An intermediate foundation footing or grade beam is often run under a slab to support a load-bearing wall (generally running through the center of the room). One way to tell if you have a load-bearing wall is to look at a wall in the center of a room. If the ends of the upper floor joists set on top of this wall, it could be a load-bearing wall with a footing beneath the slab. Sometimes the floor joists are set on a beam held up by support posts that are on small pads beneath the concrete. The small pads will not disrupt the suction field, as a continuous concrete footing running the length of the basement will. One method for overcoming an obstacle (like a continuous intermediate footing) is to place a suction point on both sides of the intermediate footing as shown above.

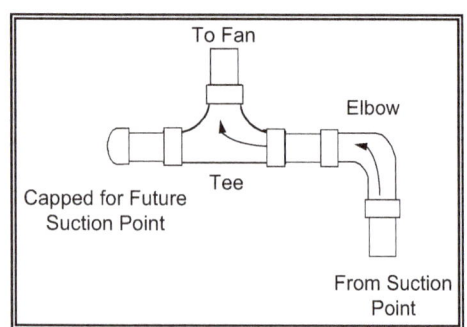

It is always a good idea when locating your primary suction point that a second suction point be planned, which could be attached to the other point as conveniently as possible. Generally, a tee is installed in the piping system at the point where a second suction point could be connected. This tee would be installed with a short length of capped PVC or ABS pipe. The pipe could be cut at a later time for connection to a second suction point, if needed.

As discussed in the following step, a second suction point is not always necessary.

Important: If you add a second suction point be sure to slope the pipe back to either suction point so condensed moisture does not accumulate. Do not create traps or low spots in pipe.

Chapter 6: Slabs and Basements

Planning Step 6:

Suction point location -- using plumbing trenches.

To overcome obstacles and fully extend the suction field under the slab, a trick that many professionals use is to locate a suction point near an existing underground plumbing line. This could be a water pipe or, more commonly, a sewer line. The figure below illustrates this.

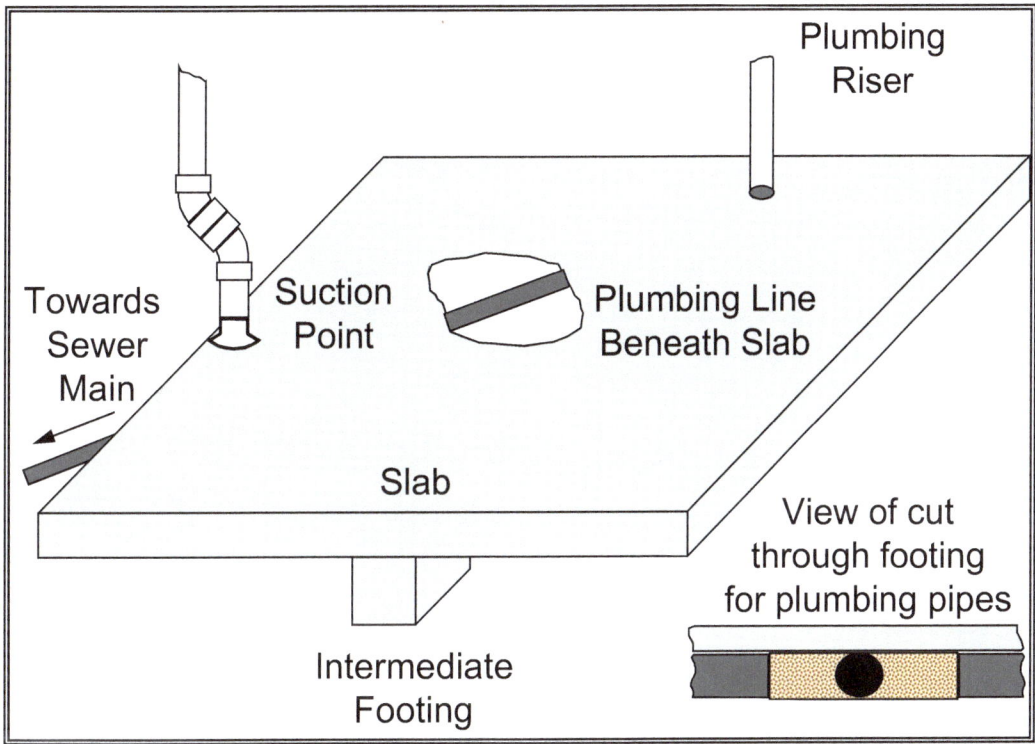

When plumbing is installed before the slab is poured, it is laid in trenches. These trenches are loosely backfilled before the concrete is poured. Also, if there are intermediate foundations for bearing walls, as described in the previous planning step, these plumbing lines and trenches pass underneath or through a notch in the foundation footing. If you create a vacuum along the side of one of these pipes, it is possible to extend the suction field along the trench. This is especially helpful where an intermediate footing would otherwise be an obstacle to the suction field. When this technique is used, the vacuum can often be extended beyond the footing and to the opposite end of the slab since soil air can move along the plumbing trench.

The best way to decide if plumbing trenches will help is to locate the riser on your sewer piping. These risers are generally found in your utility room or furnace room. Note the riser's location. Next, locate where the sewer main is by finding the manholes. (Manholes are typically in the street in front of your house, but in some instances could be in an alley.) Draw a mental line from the point the sewer riser comes through the slab in the basement to where the manhole is. If this cuts across a large portion of the basement slab or if it crosses where you think an intermediate footing for a bearing wall is, this location could be a good primary suction point.

Important: *When you cut through the concrete for the installation of the suction point, do not cut through the concrete directly above the plumbing trench. Rather than drilling directly above the trench, drill down along the side and dig sideways under the slab (by hand) until you reach the pipe. Take your time here because if you break a pipe under the slab, it could be very costly to repair. This will require caution in drilling the concrete but could save you the trouble of making more than one suction point.*

Protecting Your Home from Radon

Planning Step 7:

Planning the suction point location.

The figures below illustrate how the actual suction point core and pit will look when installed next to an exterior wall. A suction point located near an interior wall would be installed similarly. One of the criteria in choosing a suction point is the limitations that the piping system will place on its location. The following discussion provides some details that will help you locate the hole. How to cut the actual hole and install the fitting through the floor will be discussed later in this chapter.

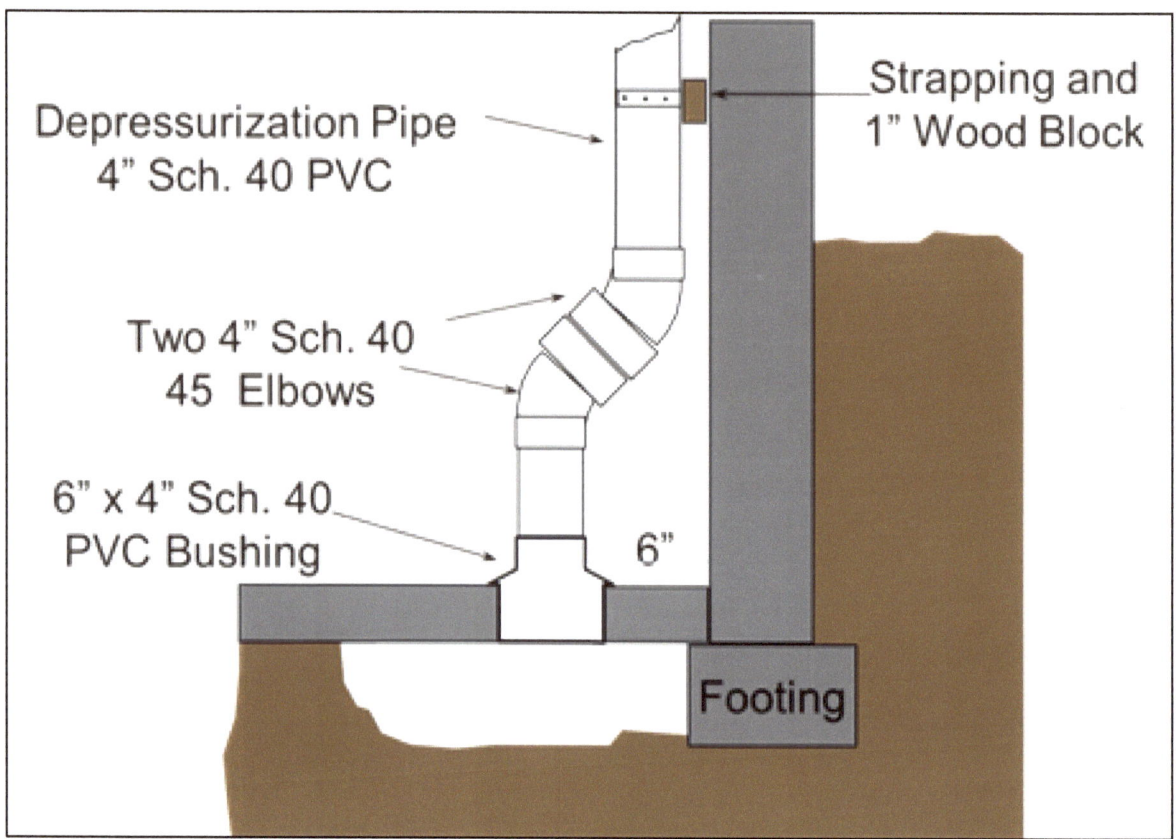

Note that a 1-inch-thick block of wood has been shown between the vertical portion of the depressurization piping and the wall. This will be used to support the piping. See Chapter 7 for more details. The installation detail above shows two 45-degree fittings glued together with a short section of pipe in between them. In this example, the pipe stub between the two 45's is no longer than 3 ½ inches, so the two 45's butt up against each other. With these conditions, the closest edge of the hole will be 6 inches away from the wall. Of course, it can be farther away from the wall if the section of pipe between the elbows is made longer. Note, you may have to extend the distance away from the wall if you have wider than normal footings.

The technique of putting two 45-degree fittings together allows for the pipe to be firmly attached to the wall near the suction point. It also minimizes the amount of lost living space that you will experience.

The purpose of locating the hole this precisely is because you are going to drill a small hole through the concrete to see if this location will work well. Drilling a hole where the concrete will later be cut out minimizes the number of holes you will be drilling through the concrete.

Chapter 6: Slabs and Basements

Planning Step 8:

Confirming you have selected a good suction point.

Let's assume you have picked a convenient and appropriate suction point location. Now let's see if you chose wisely. What you are about to do is simulate a sub-slab system. You will be using a highly technical piece of equipment you may already own, called a sub-slab suction simulator, otherwise known as a big shop vac. You will also need an incense stick or smoke bottle.

This is an important step even though you could go ahead and install the system and hope for the best. All of the tools needed for this suction test will be needed for the installation of the actual system anyway. Besides, you have been looking for a reason to buy a big shop vacuum, right?

Concept of the suction test:

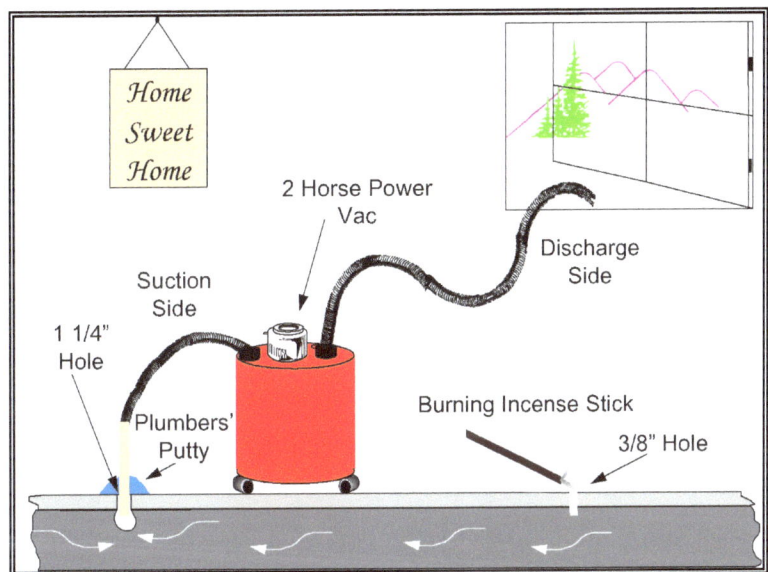

- Drill a 1 ¼ inch diameter hole through the concrete about 8 inches down into the soil at the location of the primary suction hole (see previous planning step). ***Watch out for sub-slab pipes.***

- Drill a few 3/8-inch diameter holes, called test holes, through remote parts of the slab.

- After inserting the wand of the vacuum cleaner suction hose down into the 1 ¼ inch hole and sealing with plumbers' putty, run a length of vacuum hose attached to the discharge out a window.

- Next, you will turn on the vacuum.

- With a smoke or incense stick -- observe if smoke is drawn down the smaller test holes when the vacuum is turned on and off.

If the smoke is pulled down a test hole **only** when the vacuum cleaner is on, you know that the sub-slab suction system is impacting that portion of the slab between the vacuum hole and the 3/8-inch test hole. Repeat this for other test holes at various locations around the slab to be sure the vacuum can impact the entire slab area.

Smoke drawn down test hole-Score!

If there are parts of the slab that you cannot impact, pick a secondary sub-slab hole using all of the criteria listed before. Repeat the process with the vacuum cleaner suction attached to this secondary hole. Perform this process until you have identified the number and location of suction points that will be needed to create a vacuum under the entire slab. A more detailed description is given in the next planning steps.

Protecting Your Home from Radon

Avoid Sub Slab Pipes or Utilities

There can be more things under a slab than just dirt and rock. You may have any of the following:

- Sewer lines
- Water lines
- Ductwork
- In-Floor heating pipes.

Typically, water and sewer lines are a few inches below the bottom of the slab. If you are careful, you can tell when your drill bit breaks through the bottom of the slab when you drill down. When you penetrate the bottom of the slab –STOP. You don't have to go any further for a diagnostic hole.

When you are coring your suction point later, follow the same practice of just cutting out the concrete, then digging the dirt out by hand.

In-Floor Heating

In-floor heating can be very problematic because the piping can sometimes be in the concrete slab or just below it. This piping is often plastic and when you drill down you will have no idea you have drilled through until water starts spraying up. Repairing busted in floor heating pipes can be very expensive.

If you have in-floor heating you may want to hire a mitigator, or at the least have someone with a special instrument that can spot where these pipes are to avoid damaging them.

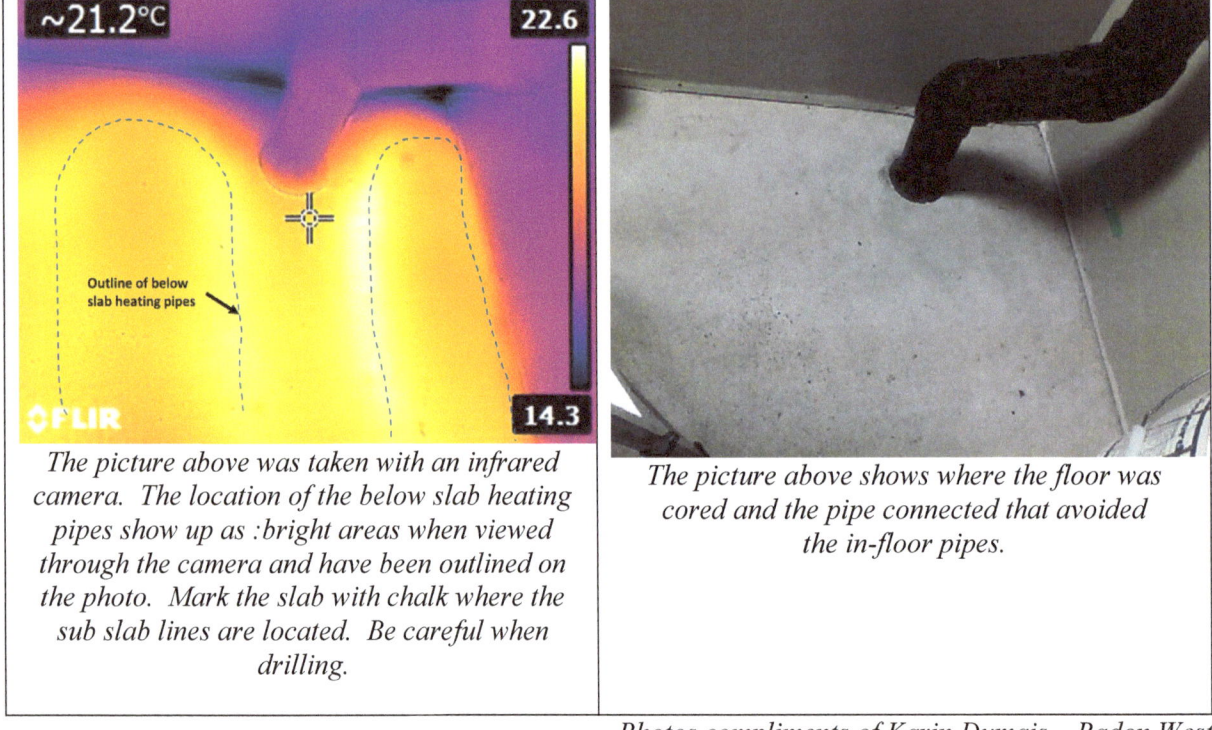

The picture above was taken with an infrared camera. The location of the below slab heating pipes show up as :bright areas when viewed through the camera and have been outlined on the photo. Mark the slab with chalk where the sub slab lines are located. Be careful when drilling.

The picture above shows where the floor was cored and the pipe connected that avoided the in-floor pipes.

Photos compliments of Karin Dumais – Radon West

Chapter 6: Slabs and Basements

Planning Step 9:

Sub-slab depressurization simulation diagnostics.

This step is to determine the number and location of the suction points that will be necessary to create a suction field beneath the concrete slab area. Before beginning this work assemble the following tools and safety equipment. You should also read the general safety practices described in Chapter 10 of this manual before commencing the work.

The following is a checklist of equipment and materials you will need before starting.

Area	Item	√
Safety		
	Safety eye goggles	
	Dust mask	
	Leather gloves	
	First aid kit	
	Assistant	
	Ear protection for you and your assistant	
Material		
	Jar of plumber's putty	
	Duct tape	
	6 in. by 4 in. PVC or ABS schedule 40 reducing bushing Or 5-inch by 4-inch Uniseal bushing	
Tools		
	Shop vacuum (2 horsepower or greater)	
	2-inch diameter vacuum cleaner suction hose Two lengths of hose at least 6 foot long each	
	Length of flexible dryer vent - long enough to attach from vacuum cleaner discharge hose to the nearest operable window and out of the window at least two feet.	
	Vacuum wand -- 1 ½ in. on one end and 2 inches on other end. This is a normal accessory when you buy shop vac hose.	
	Electric hammer drill (1 ½ inch -- not your typical hand drill; these can usually be rented along with bits from most tool rental houses)	
	1 ¼ inch by 12-inch bit for hammer drill	
	3/8 inch by 12-inch bit for hammer drill	
	Heavy duty, grounded extension cord (three prong)	
	Flashlight	
	Smoke stick (see Chapter 8)	

Planning Step 10:

Performing the sub-slab simulation.

The following is a step-by-step procedure for performing the sub-slab simulation as was briefly described in the previous planning step.

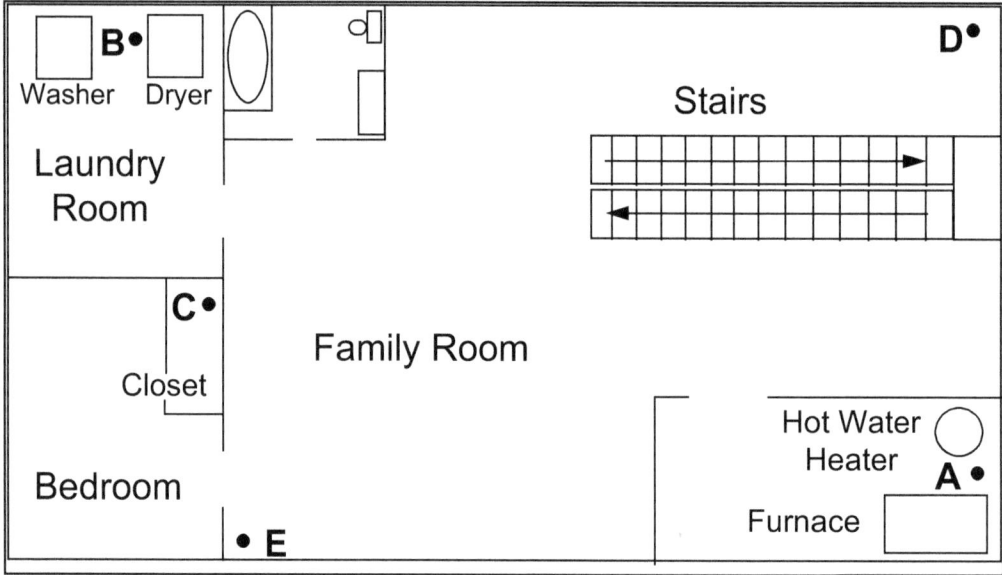

Step 1. Make a sketch of the concrete floor area like the one shown above. Mark your preferred suction point location. In this example, we will choose **Point A** in the furnace room. We did this because it is near an outside wall and would be in an area where the pipe could be concealed. We are hoping this one suction point will be sufficient to impact the soil under the entire slab. This process will prove or disprove this assumption.

Step 2. Using the dimensions provided in Planning Step 7, or according to your own piping installation design (see Chapter 7), set the 6-inch by 4-inch reducer on the concrete floor in the exact location that you plan to install it. Mark a circle on the concrete floor with a marking pen or grease pencil, using the outside circular edge of the 6 by 4 reducer as a guide. Make an "x" mark in the approximate center of the circle.

Step 3. Put the suction hose on your shop vac and plug it in. Tape the suction hose to the floor so it is within a couple of inches of your "x" mark. This is to catch the dust you will be making when you drill through the concrete at the "x" mark. Run the discharge hose out of the window because some fine concrete will get through the filter of the vacuum and make a mess if you don't run it outside.

Step 4. Attach the 1 ¼ inch bit to the hammer drill and set the drill to the rotary hammer setting.

Step 5. Put on your eye, ear and respiratory protection and turn on the vacuum cleaner.

Step 6. Drill a 1 ¼ inch hole <u>straight</u> down through the concrete at the location in the center of the circle that you had marked with an "x." Be careful! These hammer drills can bind up on a piece of reinforcing wire in the concrete. When the drill binds up it can deliver quite a twist. Make sure you are standing in a position so when this happens you will not be caught between the drill and the wall or have the handle whack you in the knee cap. Stand out from the drill with the drill between you and the wall. To reduce the chance of binding up the drill, hold the drill as vertically as you can. Pull the bit out frequently as it is turning in order to clear the hole of concrete dust. *Note:* **Do not push down on the drill**. The weight of the drill alone is enough to drive the bit through the concrete. If you get anxious and try to make things happen faster by pushing it, you will only cause undue stress on your wrists and elbows and increase the chance of the bit binding up.

Chapter 6: Slabs and Basements

Drilling through the concrete should only take 3 to 4 minutes unless you hit something. Generally, the drill bit will cut through reinforcing wire in the concrete. Sometimes it won't. If you have drilled at a location where you cannot get through the concrete, move a couple inches away from your "x" mark and try again.

If you bind the drill up in the hole and cannot pull it back out with the drill, then remove the bit from the drill. Extract the bit from the floor by taking a pipe wrench and secure it to the bit near the floor. Put a block of wood between the wrench and the floor. By twisting the drill bit and using the leverage provided by the wood block you should be able to free it up. **Don't put your wrench on the splined portion of the bit that connects to the drill!**

Take your time. As you get close to the bottom of the slab take it easy. ***Caution:*** Once the drill goes through the bottom of the slab, it could drop very quickly and hit a plumbing line that you didn't know was there. Once you get through the slab, look down into the hole with a flashlight to make sure nothing is in the way. Drill further down, look frequently to make sure you don't hit a pipe. Keep drilling until you have drilled as deeply as you can, at least 6 inches below the slab.

Pay attention to what happens as the bit goes through the concrete.

- Does it drop sharply? This could mean there is a cavity under the slab. This is good.
- Are rocks or pea gravel visible at the bottom of the hole or are drawn up alongside the bit? This indicates loose permeable fill beneath the slab. This is excellent!
- Is the dirt at the bottom of the hole or on the bit a damp plastic like clay material? This means the soil may be impermeable and difficult for air to flow through it. Don't stop, though; go on to the next step as you may get lucky and still be able to create a decent vacuum field beneath the slab.

Step 7. After the hole has been drilled, vacuum up the dust around the hole. *Don't put the hose down into the hole yet.*

Step 8. Change the bit in the hammer drill from the 1 ¼ to the 3/8-inch bit. Go to opposite corners and ends of the slab. Look for inconspicuous places to drill these test holes through the concrete. Corners of closets are good. Corners of rooms are good even if they are carpeted. You can always pull up a corner of the carpet with a pair of square nose pliers, and pound it back into place with a block of wood and a hammer -- <u>*don't drill through carpet!*</u>

Step 9. Drill the pilot holes with the same technique described above for the big hole. Locate them approximately 6 inches out from the wall to avoid drilling into the footing. If the drill does not drop through the bottom of the concrete, drill at an alternate location. Mark the location of the test holes on your drawing. In our example, we have drilled pilot holes at **Points B, C, D** and **E** on the preceding sketch.

Step 10. After cleaning the dust around the small holes, take the shop vacuum back to the location of the big hole. Attach the second length of vacuum hose to the discharge port of the vacuum cleaner and run it out an open window (use dryer vent to add necessary length).

Warning: **If you do not exhaust the vacuum out the window you could be exposed to high levels of radon gas.** If the length of hose is insufficient to reach the window, stick it in one side of a cheap flexible dryer vent hose. Tape this connection together with duct tape so it is tight. Then run the dryer vent hose to and out the window.

Step 11. Attach the 1 ¼ inch wand to the end of the vacuum cleaner suction hose and stick it down into the large hole (hole A). Seal the wand to the hole by pressing plumber's putty all around the side of the wand where it meets the top of the concrete.

Step 12. Get your incense stick (or smoke device) and flashlight and go to one of the test holes. With the vacuum cleaner "off" observe which way the smoke moves when held right next to the hole. It should rise into the room. Now have your assistant turn the vacuum cleaner "on." Is the smoke now being pulled down through the hole? Use a flashlight to be able to see this subtle change in direction. Turn the vacuum cleaner "on" and "off" several times to confirm that you are seeing the effect of the vacuum cleaner rather than the kids opening and closing doors upstairs.

If the smoke is drawn down a hole when the vacuum cleaner is turned on, you can conclude a suction point installed at the location of the vacuum cleaner hole (point A) would positively impact the area beneath the slab between the vacuum hole and the particular small test hole.

Shop Vacuum Connected to Proposed Suction Hole Location

Smoke stick used at pilot hole to see if operating shop vac "pulls" smoke down

Step 13. Repeat this testing procedure at each of the small holes that you drilled. Note the results either on your sketch or on a table such as the one below: (arrows show direction of smoke)

Vacuum Cleaner on Hole ID:____	Test Hole:__ Smoke ↑ or ↓ Vac **Off**	Test Hole:__ Smoke ↑ or ↓ Vac **On**	Test Hole:__ Smoke ↑ or ↓ Vac **Off**	Test Hole:__ Smoke ↑ or ↓ Vac **On**	Test Hole:__ Smoke ↑ or ↓ Vac **Off**	Test Hole:__ Smoke ↑ or ↓ Vac **On**	Test Hole:__ Smoke ↑ or ↓ Vac **Off**	Test Hole:__ Smoke ↑ or ↓ Vac **On**

For example, assume the following data was obtained for the house plan illustrated below:

Vacuum Cleaner on Hole ID:___	Test Hole:__ Smoke ↑ or ↓ Vac **Off**	Test Hole:__ Smoke ↑ or ↓ Vac **On**	Test Hole:__ Smoke ↑ or ↓ Vac **Off**	Test Hole:__ Smoke ↑ or ↓ Vac **On**	Test Hole:__ Smoke ↑ or ↓ Vac **Off**	Test Hole:__ Smoke ↑ or ↓ Vac **On**	Test Hole:__ Smoke ↑ or ↓ Vac **Off**	Test Hole:__ Smoke ↑ or ↓ Vac **On**
	B	B	C	C	D	D	E	E
A	↑	↓	↑	↓	↑	↓	↑	↓

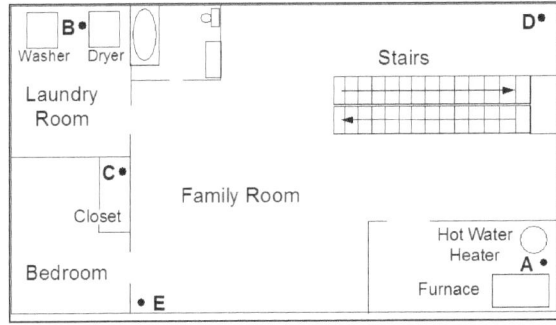

This data indicates the vacuum cleaner connected to suction point A was able to cause the direction of smoke to be reversed at all test hole locations (shown by the arrows pointing down at test holes B, C, D and E). This means a single suction point located at point A would work well, and we can assume one suction point is all that is needed.

On the other hand, what if the data had turned out as follows:

Vacuum Cleaner on Hole:__	Test Hole:__ Smoke ↑ or ↓ Vac **Off**	Test Hole:__ Smoke ↑ or ↓ Vac **On**	Test Hole:__ Smoke ↑ or ↓ Vac **Off**	Test Hole:__ Smoke ↑ or ↓ Vac **On**	Test Hole:__ Smoke ↑ or ↓ Vac **Off**	Test Hole:__ Smoke ↑ or ↓ Vac **On**	Test Hole:__ Smoke ↑ or ↓ Vac **Off**	Test Hole:__ Smoke ↑ or ↓ Vac **On**
	B	B	C	C	D	D	E	E
A	↑	↑	↑	↓	↑	↑	↑	↓

You can see that the vacuum cleaner was able to reverse the direction of the smoke at points C and E, but **not** at B and D. This means a suction point located at A will only affect the soil under half of the slab. What do we do now?

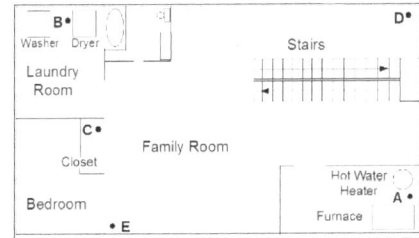

If the primary suction point does not impact the entire slab, you may need to install more than one suction point. To confirm the location of a second suction point, move the vacuum cleaner to that location. Drill a 1 ¼ inch hole and 106stick the suction hose and wand into this hole and repeat your test. *Be sure to follow all of the steps previously described to drill these holes, especially exhausting the shop-vac outside so you do not fill your house with radon while it is running.* One of the test holes that was drilled previously can be re-drilled with the larger bit to become the second vacuum test point.

Let's assume in our example that point B was chosen as the secondary suction hole and the preceding table now looks like this:

Vacuum Cleaner on Hole:__	Test Hole:__ Smoke ↑ or ↓ Vac **Off**	Test Hole:__ Smoke ↑ or ↓ Vac **On**	Test Hole:__ Smoke ↑ or ↓ Vac **Off**	Test Hole:__ Smoke ↑ or ↓ Vac **On**	Test Hole:__ Smoke ↑ or ↓ Vac **Off**	Test Hole:__ Smoke ↑ or ↓ Vac **On**	Test Hole:__ Smoke ↑ or ↓ Vac **Off**	Test Hole:__ Smoke ↑ or ↓ Vac **On**
	B	B	C	C	D	D	E	E
A	↑	↑	↑	↓	↑	↑	↑	↓
	A	A	C	C	D	D	E	E
B	↑	↑	↑	↑	↑	↓	↑	↑

The data now shows that a suction point at location B will positively affect point D but not C, E or A. However, from the previous testing we saw that a suction point located at point A positively influenced points C and E.

Conclusion: A vacuum simultaneously drawn on both points A and B would treat all areas of the slab. This would mean that two suction points would be installed at points A and B. You can install both suction points or just one and plan to add the second one if your post-mitigation test results are not satisfactory. There are times that full coverage is not always necessary. However, the amount of reduction will be better with full sub-slab coverage. It is a good idea to design and install the depressurization piping system with the option of being able to add an additional suction point (see Planning Step 5).

Important: If you find that more than three suction points are required you probably have very impermeable soils, and you should consider calling a professional mitigator.

After you have determined the location of the suction points you can either fill the small holes up with plumber's putty or just duct tape over them. You will want to access them later. Since you have already rented the hammer drill for the day, enlarge the hole in the concrete for the suction point and install the suction pit as described later in this chapter.

Chapter 6: Slabs and Basements

Planning Step 11:

How to handle multiple slabs in a single home.

Some homes have more than one portion built on isolated slabs. A common example of this is a split-level home. The figure above illustrates such a home. You could install separate suction points on each slab and connect them to a common fan or to independent depressurization systems.

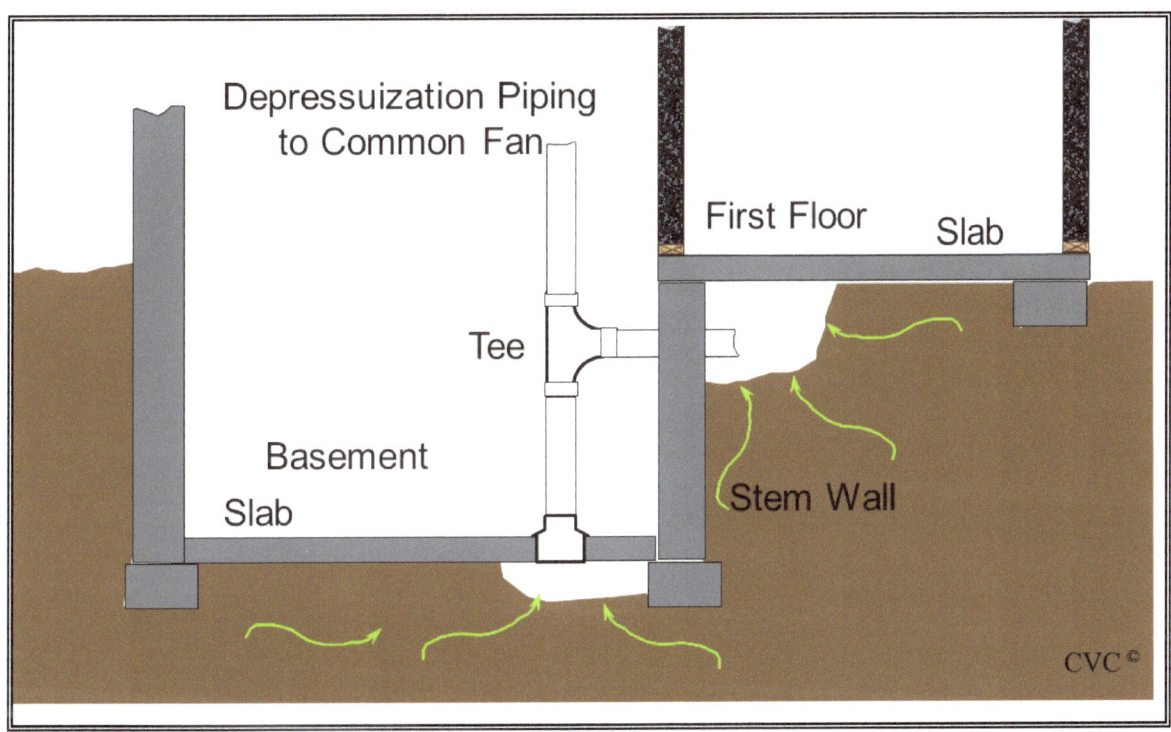

The split-level home shown above has two slab areas that are separated by a stem wall. This style of construction is common with multi-level homes. The furnace or utility room is generally located in the center of the home in the lowest level and adjacent to the stem wall. This makes the utility or furnace room an excellent place for the primary suction point since they are also good places to conceal suction piping. Establish the location of your primary suction so it is next to the stem wall. Plan to install a tee in the depressurization piping system that can be connected to a pipe which will penetrate the stem wall. You should be able to treat both the lowest and the adjacent slab area with two suction points in the utility room.

To test how this will work, repeat the previous diagnostic test with the vacuum cleaner. However, in this case you will drill your vacuum cleaner hole through the stem wall and drill your test holes through the floor above. After following all the precautions and methods detailed in Planning Step 10, you can determine if this stem wall suction point will be able to treat the upper slab area.

Plan the location of this stem wall penetration to be on a vertical line with the depressurization system riser. Instead of inserting a 6 by 4-inch reducer into the wall, use a 4-inch diameter pipe inserted through a hole drilled in the wall. At least two 5-gallon buckets of soil should be removed. Insert the pipe into the hole (minimum of 6 inches past the back side of the concrete). Use expansive foam or non-shrink grout to seal the gap between the wall and the pipe (see Chapter 8 on sealing techniques). If the stem wall is hollow block, be sure to extend the pipe **completely** through the block, and completely foam the void of the hollow block around the penetrating pipe to avoid losing the vacuum at this point.

Locate stem wall suction point near the bottom of the upper slab and dig dirt out up to bottom of the slab. This reduces the potential for dirt caving in on your horizontal suction hole.

Protecting Your Home from Radon

Planning Step 12:

Sub-Footer Depressurization: Total external routing of sub-slab system.

Sometimes it may be desirable to have your depressurization system located outside. This may be the case if your lower-level slab is completely finished and there are no good locations to place your suction point. If your footing is not too deep, or if you have dug down to find a foundation drain and it wasn't there, you can actually excavate a little further and create a suction pit from outside of the foundation as illustrated below. This is referred to as "sub-footer depressurization system".

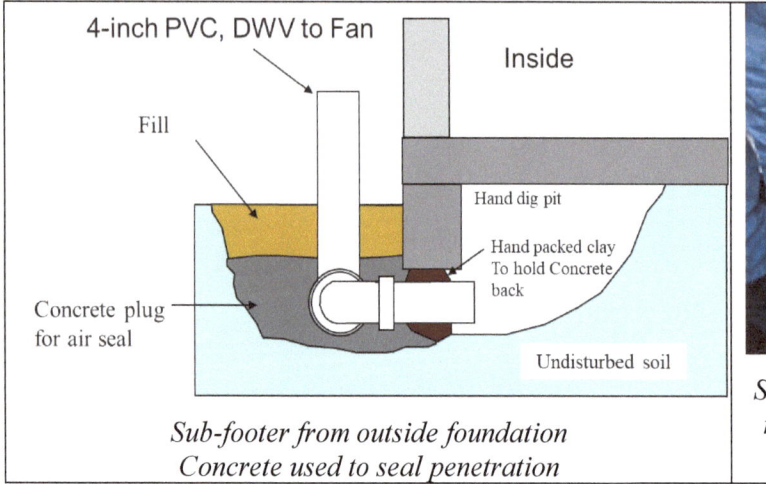

Sub-footer from outside foundation
Concrete used to seal penetration

Sub-Footer System. Two penetrations made on either side of a grade beam

When installing a sub-footer system, you should try to locate it where the depth to the bottom of the footer is not too deep. If you do this, remember to shore up your hole so it won't cave in on you. When you reach the bottom of the footing you will need to excavate at least one five-gallon bucket of dirt from beneath the footing and adjacent slab. Don't remove too much dirt on either side of the hole to where the footing would be undermined. Wear gloves and use hand tools to do this. Dig horizontally under the footing as far in as possible and until the soil becomes looser. Also dig up inside the footing until you can "tickle" the bottom of the slab. This will prevent dirt from falling down and plugging your suction pipe later. To finish the pit, do the following:

- Glue a length of 4-inch PVC or ABS pipe to a 4-inch PVC or ABS elbow. This length of pipe should be long enough to extend a few inches beyond the inside edge of the footing. Glue another length of 4-inch PVC or ABS pipe to the other end of the elbow. This second piece needs to be long enough to extend above grade outside and to connect to your fan.

- Set the pipe system in and <u>solidly</u> pack dirt around the pipe where it passes beneath the footing.

- Support the bottom of the elbow by solidly packing dirt beneath it to provide vertical support.

- Using polyurethane caulk, attach a scrap of plastic sheeting to the outside of the exposed footing just above where your pipe passes beneath the footing. Make a slit in the plastic so it can pass on either side of your pipe and caulk these edges to the pipe as best as you can.

- Add dirt to the hole and pack the plastic as tightly as possible into the hole. This is to reduce air leakage back into the hole.

- Backfill the hole. Pause each time you have added 6 inches of dirt and tamp it well to improve the compaction of dirt you are replacing.

- Attach the balance of the fan and piping system as described in Chapter 7.

Chapter 6: Slabs and Basements

Installing the Sub-Slab Depressurization System

Installation Step 1.   Making the suction hole and installing the riser.

In this section you will cut concrete. A pit will be dug. A fitting will be sealed into the opening. A riser will be attached to the fitting. Later, the depressurization system piping will be attached to this riser. Before proceeding with this work, read Chapter 10 on safety and Chapter 7 on depressurization piping systems. At the conclusion of the installation, the technique described in Chapter 8 on sealing should be followed.

Before starting this work assemble the following materials and equipment:

Area	Item	🕒
Safety		
	Goggles	
	Dust mask	
	Leather gloves	
	First aid kit	
	Assistant	
	Ear protection for you and your assistant	
	Ventilation fan (window fan)	
	Coveralls	
Material		
	Can of expanding urethane foam	
	Duct tape	
	6 in. by 4 in. PVC or ABS schedule 40 reducing bushing (one for each suction point planned)	
	tube of polyurethane caulk	
Tools		
	Shop vacuum (2 horsepower or larger)	
	2-inch vacuum cleaner suction hose at least 6 foot long	
	5-gallon bucket or pail	
	Hand spade or other small hand digging tools	
	Crowbar	
	Heavy wire cutters	
	Electric hammer drill that can function both as a rotary hammer and an electric chisel (1½ inch -- not your typical hand drill, these can typically be rented along with bits from most tool rental houses)	
	3/8 inch by 12-inch bit for hammer drill	
	Heavy duty extension cord (three prong), with ground fault interrupter	
	Caulking gun	
	Rags	
	Chisel bit for hammer drill	

© Copyright 2023 • Center for Environmental Research and Technology, Inc.

Protecting Your Home from Radon

Installation Step 2:

Making the suction hole and piping connection.

Warning: Wear your safety goggles, ear protection and gloves!
Failure to do so can result in permanent injury.

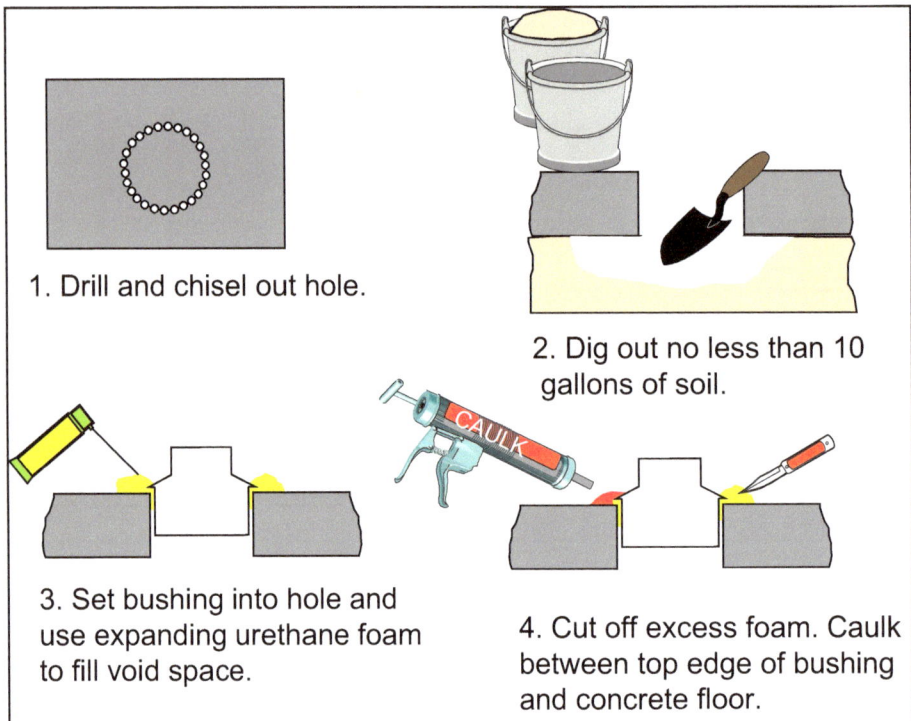

1. Drill and chisel out hole.
2. Dig out no less than 10 gallons of soil.
3. Set bushing into hole and use expanding urethane foam to fill void space.
4. Cut off excess foam. Caulk between top edge of bushing and concrete floor.

1. Draw a circle on the floor with a magic marker or a grease marker around the 6 by 4-inch schedule 40 PVC or ABS bushing that will later be inserted into the hole (see Planning Step 7 for guidance on placement). Using the hammer drill with a 3/8-inch bit, drill several holes along the line of the circle. Check to make sure that when the bushing sets down into the hole the lip on the bushing will cover the jagged parts of the hole. Replace the drill bit with the chisel bit and change the setting on the drill to "chisel." Use the chisel to bust out the center and smooth the edges. Keep chiseling until the bushing sits down into the hole with the flange resting on the top of the concrete slab. *Wear safety goggles!*

2. Set up a window ventilation fan to blow fresh air into the room in which you are working. This will reduce your exposure to high radon levels that can be released when large openings into the soil are made. Plus, it helps evaporate the sweat you will be generating. Wear leather gloves to dig out a pit beneath the opening. Dig out at least 2 five-gallon buckets of dirt. Don't skimp! This is a critical detail. The harder it is to dig, the more important it is to get the full amount of dirt out. If you find reinforcing wire, cut it, or bend it back and forth several times until it breaks. It is better to dig the pit wider than deep.

3. After you have removed the soil, clean up the mess with the shop vac. Insert the bushing into the hole and apply the expanding urethane foam into the voids around the bushing. Don't add so much that it fills the pit! (See Chapter 8 regarding sealants.)

4. After the foam has cured and is rigid, cut the excess away from the top. Apply a ½ inch wide bead of caulk to the edge of the bushing where it meets the top of the concrete. Using a piece of cardboard, smooth the caulk into the joint between the bushing and the floor in a continuous circular motion all the way around the bushing. Let this set for several hours before proceeding.

The following photos illustrate a typical installation sequence using a 6 by 4 PVC bushing which is preferred. However, if you cannot find a 6 by 4 bushing a more common "Uniseal" fitting can be used as is shown on the installation sequence on the next page.

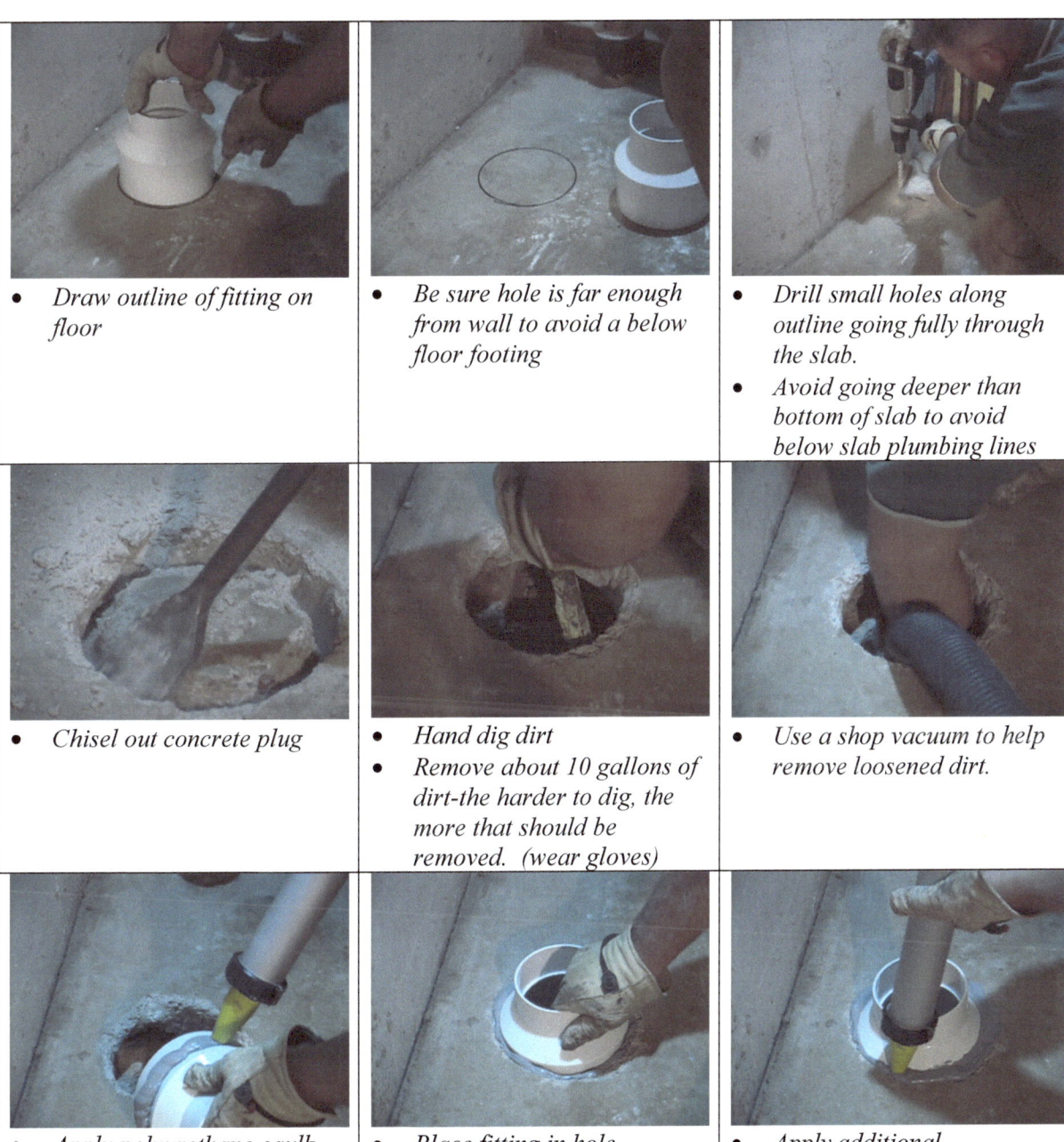

- Draw outline of fitting on floor

- Be sure hole is far enough from wall to avoid a below floor footing

- Drill small holes along outline going fully through the slab.
- Avoid going deeper than bottom of slab to avoid below slab plumbing lines

- Chisel out concrete plug

- Hand dig dirt
- Remove about 10 gallons of dirt-the harder to dig, the more that should be removed. (wear gloves)

- Use a shop vacuum to help remove loosened dirt.

- Apply polyurethane caulk around fitting

- Place fitting in hole

- Apply additional polyurethane caulk between slab and fitting.

Protecting Your Home from Radon

Installation Sequence using a Uniseal Grommet. Note this requires a smooth hole made by a core bit. Be careful! Use this if you can't find the 6 x 4 reducing bushing.

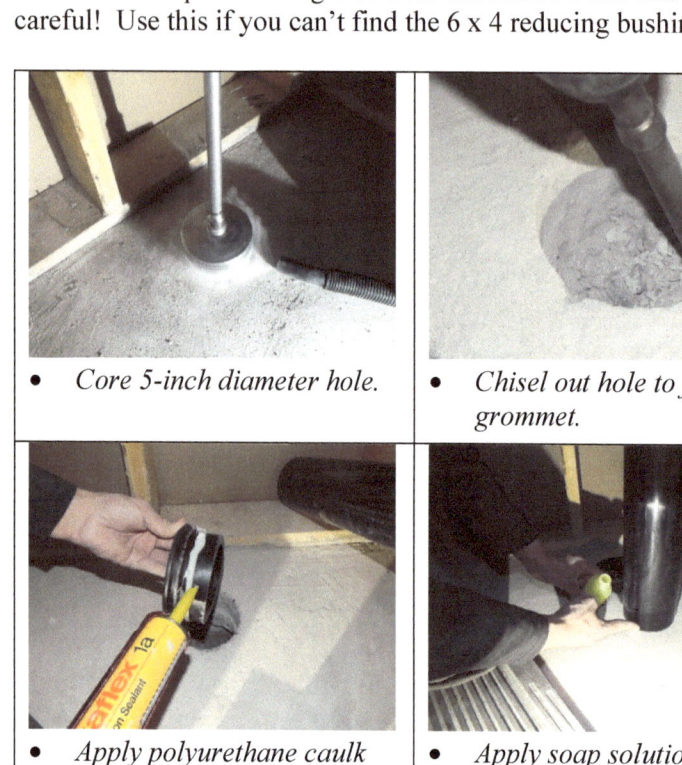

- *Core 5-inch diameter hole.*
- *Chisel out hole to fit Uniseal grommet.*
- *Remove 2 5-gallon pails of dirt and rock.*

- *Apply polyurethane caulk around portion of Uniseal to be inserted into hole.*
- *Apply soap solution to outside of radon vent pipe.*
- *Force pipe into grommet for a tight fit.*

- *Insert grommet into hole.*
- *Pound grommet (wrap plastic around pipe to protect it from hammer).*
- *Apply polyurethane caulk between slab and grommet to seal penetration.*

- *Tool caulk into gap between floor and gromett.*
- *Finished suction point.*
- *Secure pipe above suction point to prevent it from moving up/down or sideways.*

Photos compliments of Radon West

Chapter 6: Slabs and Basements

Installation Step 3:

    Connect the suction point to the depressurization system.

Now you can install the depressurization piping as described in Chapter 7. If you have installed the 6 inch by 4 inch bushing as part of your planning exercise and have not acquired all of the necessary piping yet, tape off the top of the bushing so kids do not "accidentally" throw something into it or mice don't find a new home to live in. When you are ready to run the depressurization piping, remove the tape and glue your 4-inch PVC or ABS pipe into the bushing's throat.

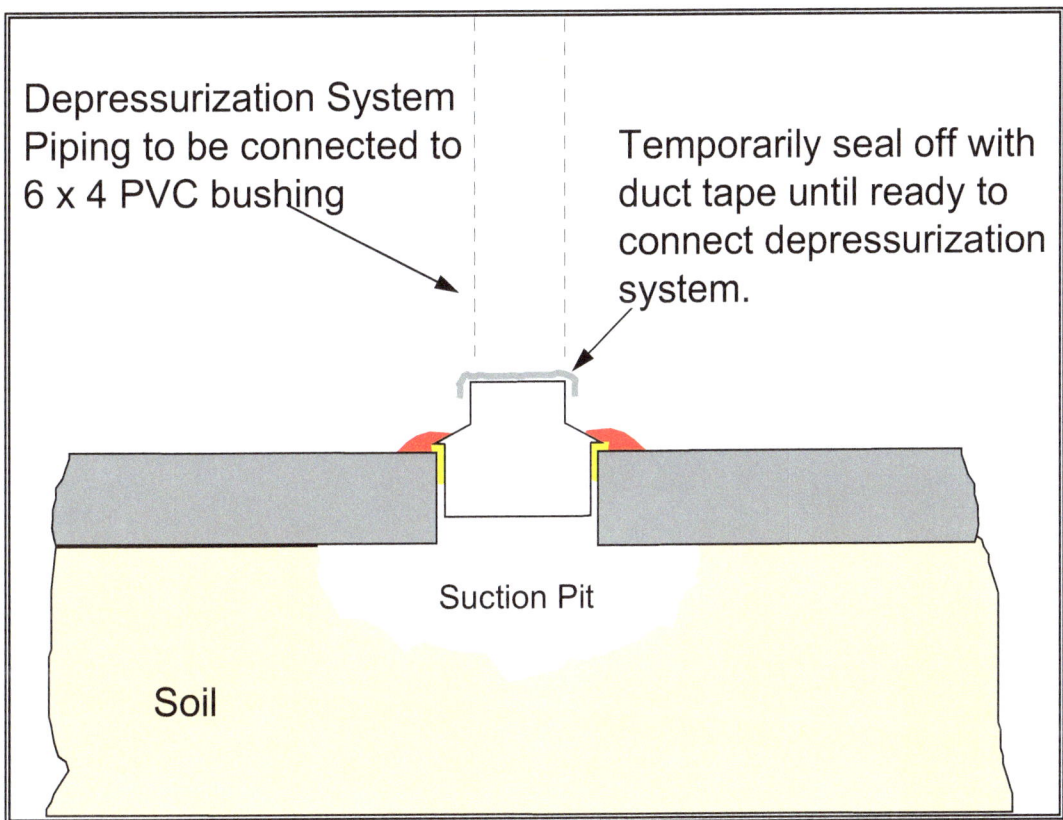

If during the vacuum cleaner suction test, you found that greater than three points were going to be needed and you called a professional mitigator, he will be able to connect to the 6 inch by 4 inch bushing for this system. What the professional mitigator will do is install a higher vacuum fan than is typically required. This will be done because you have unusually tight soils. The system the mitigator installs will probably use different size piping than the standard 4 inch. This isn't a problem since the bushing throat is a standard pipe size and that fittings are available to adapt to other pipe sizes.

Installation Step 4:

    Check for air leaks.

After you have completed the installation of the depressurization piping, turn on the system and look for air leaks through concrete cracks, floor joints and at the suction hole. Do this by using a smoke stick and a flashlight and the techniques described in Chapter 8. If you find leaks, seal them by following the methods in Chapter 8.

Installation Step 5:

> **Backdraft test.**

Have a professional perform a combustion appliance backdraft test to ensure that the drafting ability of your combustion appliances has not been changed by the radon system you have installed. It is rare that these systems will cause backdrafting. This is especially true if you have done a thorough job of locating and sealing air leaks. *However, the consequences of carbon monoxide poisoning are severe*. So, turn off the system until you have the combustion flues tested by a professional. Test this with the radon system both on and off.

Active Radon Vent System

An active sub-slab depressurization system has been installed in this home. It is designed to draw radon from beneath the concrete slab. Suction points are located_____. These are attached to a fan located_____. If the system must be disconnected for any reason, turn off fan. The shut off for the fan is located:_____. The fan is powered from breaker #____ in the electrical breaker panel.

*US EPA recommends bi-annual testing.

Installation Step 6:

> **Label system and re-test home.**

After you have performed the air leak tests and have had the combustion appliance flues tested for backdrafting, it is time for some finishing touches.

Label your piping system at all visible sections of pipe.

Place a system label at each of the suction points. If there is more than one suction pipe, place a label on each section of pipe as it comes out of the floor. Make sure you list all of the suction points on the label. This is important in case someone cuts one of the pipes and does not turn off the fan. This could seriously effect radon reductions, heating costs and, most hazardous of all, an increased potential of backdrafting.

Install a carbon monoxide alarm to alert you if your combustion flues backdraft and increase carbon monoxide levels, as would be the case if your system became damaged.

Finally, re-test the home for radon. Be sure to follow the proper testing procedures described in Chapter 2, conducting first a short-term test as an indication of performance followed up by a long-term test for final verification. It is best to determine how well your system is working by placing the test device in the same location as your original test.

Chapter 7

Depressurization System

Fan and Piping

Deciding How Much You Can or Want to Do

Planning the Piping and Fan

Installation

CHAPTER 7 – DEPRESSURIZATION SYSTEM – FAN AND PIPING

Deciding How Much You Can or Want to Do

This chapter will describe how the piping and fan system is to be installed. In each of the previous radon reduction chapters, individual risers or connection points were detailed. This chapter will describe the piping system that will be attached to these connection points and continued on to a proper discharge location outdoors.

You have a basic decision to make now. Assuming you have either made the attachment to the sump or drain or have laid the plastic sheeting in the crawl space, or you have installed the suction points in the concrete slab, you will have a stub of pipe to which the depressurization system will attach. You can proceed to install the piping system, or you can call a contractor who could install it for you.

In making your decision whether to do this yourself or hire a contractor be aware of the following:

If you do this yourself, you could be:

- Using PVC/ABS glue to attach plastic pipe together.
- Cutting precise lengths of pipe.
- Cutting holes through walls, siding and perhaps your roof.
- Crawling through attic spaces filled with insulation.

If you hire a plumber, be aware of the following:

Most plumbers are not familiar with some of the key elements of installing radon systems, such as preferred pipe materials and the need for condensed water to positively drain back to the suction point. However, if the information in this chapter is shared with the contractor, they should have no problem complying with the specific needs of a radon system.

Alternatively, you could hire a contractor who is certified for radon mitigation and properly licensed as a remodeling contractor in your area.

Getting Power to the Fan

The fan that will create the necessary vacuum is an electrical device. You have three choices:

1. You can hire an electrician to install it, or
2. You can purchase a packaged low-voltage system that is wired just like an alarm systems or stereo speakers and install it yourself; or
3. Use a fan with a 6-foot electrical cord, provided it can extend to an existing receptacle near the fan location.

Unless you opt for the low-voltage systems or the simple appliance cord plug in, it is recommended you do not hard wire 120 volt fans yourself but rather hire an electrician.

Vent Piping Considerations

Depending upon the layout of your home, there are several options as to where you locate the radon fan and how you route the vent piping system. Your actual routing will depend upon the layout of your home as well as your own personal preferences and skills. When deciding the approach, there are four key elements that you need to take into consideration:

1. **Where the system passes through cold spaces such as attics or outdoors, the surface of the pipe is cooled to the point where water will condense and form water droplets inside your vent pipe.** This can be a considerable amount of water even several liters per day. Consequently, absolutely no traps or low spots can exist in the system that would quickly fill the pipe and render the system inoperable. In fact, the pipe should slope back to the suction point to allow the condensate to drain back into the sub grade from which it came. Note, experience has shown this will not cause a ground swelling problem at the suction point and the overall net effect of a radon system is that soil moisture is reduced, which is typically a good thing.

2. **Where the system is exposed to freezing temperatures, the condensed moisture within the pipe can freeze and reduce the efficiency of the system or completely shut it down until it thaws.** This can be reduced by insulating the pipe, but better yet is to minimize the amount of pipe exposed to freezing temperatures.

3. **The soil gas collected and exhausted by your system will have a high concentration of radon, so locate the discharge in a location where it is not likely to re-enter the home through windows and doors, ventilation system intakes or be close to areas where people may gather outdoors such as a deck.**

4. **The system should be designed and installed as a durable, operating system that will now be a part of your homes operating system just like your furnace or water heater.** Consequently, it should be made up of solid PVC or ABS pipe capable of withstanding abuse, well supported, and the joints properly primed and glued such that radon does not leak out of the system into the house or interior air be drawn into the system.

Differences Between Canadian and U.S. Approaches to System Routing

The four elements above must be taken into consideration regardless of where in the world a radon system is being installed. However, there certainly are different climate conditions that would result in more or less condensation or freezing of the water conveyed through these systems. Due to colder overall temperatures in Canada, the potential for icing issues is more likely for Canadian installations than it would be south of the Canadian border. For this reason, research, and experience with radon system installations in Canada allow for different recommendations or standards of installations than what one may find referenced for other countries.

For example, in the United States, concerns regarding the re-entry of exhausted radon-laden gases into the home via windows etc., led U.S. standards to dictate that the discharge point be terminated above the roof line of the home. Although this prescriptive approach may minimize re-entry of gases it can also expose a great deal of the vent piping to freezing temperatures that can impact performance and durability. Consequently, Canadian guidance allows lower discharge locations to minimize freezing. This can also be accomplished if the entire system is routed through the interior of the home and vented through the roof.

Another example is the location of the radon vent fan. In the U.S., there are concerns that the fan housing may leak or that discharge piping can be broken, both of which could vent radon into the living space. Consequently, U.S. standards require the fan and discharge piping to be located outside the living space or in a location so that if there was a leak it would not introduce radon into the home. This aspect of U.S. standards has had the effect of most vent systems being installed outside, which would cause a large portion of the system to be exposed to freezing temperatures in a climate such as Canada's. Consequently, and as

Chapter 7: Piping and Fan System

a means of extending the performance of the systems, radon fans and discharge piping can be routed within the living space of **Canadian** homes. Of course, the potential for leakage can still exist. To minimize this risk, proper vent pipe materials and well-sealed radon fans should be used.

The key differences between the U.S. and Canadian installations are summarized below:

Element	Canada	U.S.
Location of Fan	• Inside or outside of home • Can be in crawlspace below home • Can be in garage if below living space	• Must be outside of living space • Cannot be in crawlspace below home • Cannot be in garage if there is living space above garage
Portion of vent piping above fan	• Can be routed through living space	• Cannot be routed through living space
Discharge point	• Does not need to be above roof • No closer than 30 cm to ground or any other passive openings into home (such as windows) • Do not direct discharge towards soffit vents or other building entry points. If moist air from system strikes soffit vents, you should consider sealing off vents for 1 meter on either side of contact point to reduce entry of moist air into attic which could cause mold problems. Use metal flashing or aluminum tape with adhesive on back side of vent diffusers.	• Must be above eave of roof • No closer than 10 feet from ground and no closer than 10 feet from any opening 2 feet below discharge.

The balance of this chapter will focus on approaches prescribed for use in the United States.

Protecting Your Home from Radon

Planning the Piping and Fan

Planning Step 1:
    Deciding the pipe route

The illustrations below provide different fan locations and vent pipe routings that you may want to consider. All of these will work equally well, and your choice will be a function of cost, degree of difficulty and how it will look when you are done.

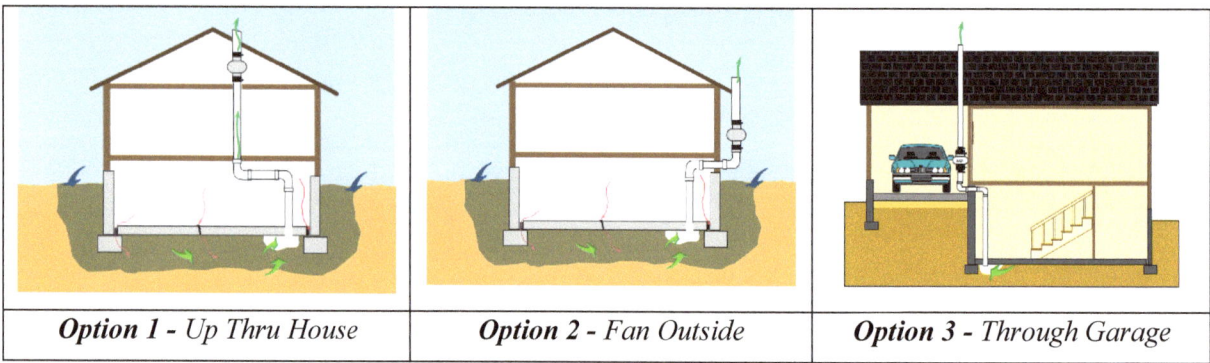

Option 1 - Up Thru House *Option 2 - Fan Outside* *Option 3 - Through Garage*

The fan and all the discharge piping should be in a location where should a leak occur in the piping or fan case that radon-laden air will not enter the occupied space. More on this later, but that is why the illustrations above show the radon fan either in an unconditioned attic, outside or in a garage provided - there is no living space above the garage. For the same reason, we would not see fans in crawlspaces where sub-membrane depressurization has been used.

An important element is the discharge of the system must be at a location that will not allow the exhausted gases to re-enter the building through windows, doors, skylights, or fresh air make-up vents. It is also important it does not discharge into an area where people may spend time, such as a sandbox or a patio. It is equally important the discharge does not enter or affect neighboring properties. Here are some key separations between the discharge point and openings into the home. Note: all these criteria are to be met rather than choosing one or another:

- Minimum of 10 feet above grade

    AND!

- Exhaust point at least 10 feet horizontally away from operable openings

    AND!

- Not less than 4 feet* above operable openings closer than 10 feet away

    AND!

- Not less than 6 inches above edge of roof (eave) or surface of roof when penetrating roof

Note: the 4-foot separation between an operable portion of a window and the discharge is a new requirement since the previous edition of this book where the minimum separation was 2 feet.

Chapter 7: Piping and Fan System

Planning Step 2:

More on selecting a discharge point.

The figure below shows four examples of discharge point locations. According to the guidelines presented on the previous page, the following statements can be made about these examples:

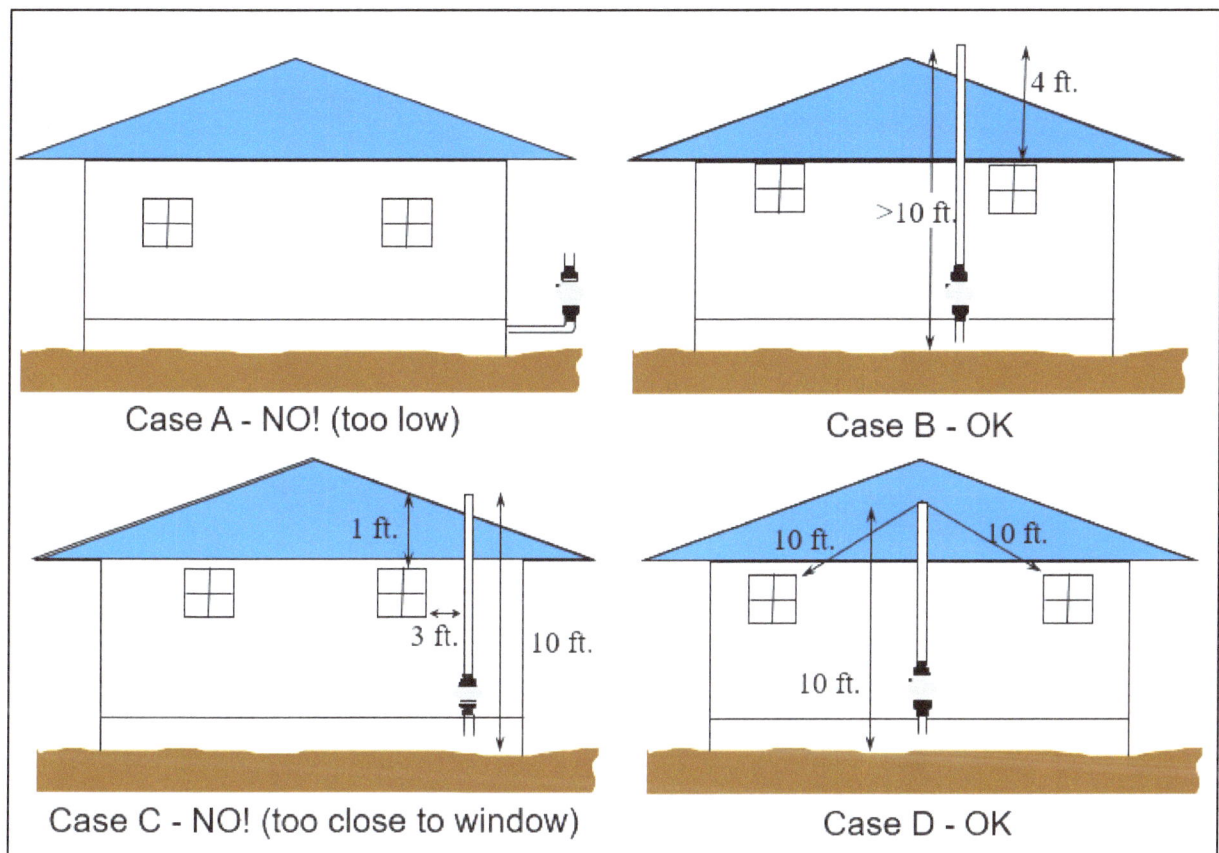

Case A. This is an incorrect location because it is too close to the ground. The potential for the discharge gases entering the home via a window or even through the side of the house is too great. This is a "trick" that some people use to unethically cut costs. This is unacceptable and unwise. You may cause radon to be reintroduced into the home.

Case B. This follows the guidelines. Ten feet above the ground. Even though it is closer than ten feet from the window on the right this is acceptable because the window is more than 4 feet below the discharge of the pipe when a vertical measurement is made from the top of the window when an imaginary horizontal line drawn from the discharge point. *Note: This assumes the discharge is straight up. Do not turn down or use a rain cap. See discussion later on regarding rain caps.*

Case C. This is an incorrect location because it is too close to the window. Although it is 10 feet above grade it is not 10 feet away from a window less than 4 feet below the discharge.

Case D. This is acceptable even though the window is only 1 foot lower than the discharge, because the discharge is ten feet away from the windows, and ten feet above ground level.

> *Running the piping up through the attic reduces these discharge concerns. However, attic routing can involve more work. Don't discharge through a low roof on a multi-level home that has an adjacent wall with windows.*

Protecting Your Home from Radon

The photos below show proper discharge points as well as improper discharges.

Proper Discharge Points:

6-8 inches above eave and has ½ inch bird screen on end

Exterior fan in accessory enclosure and well above edge of roof

Vent through roof with fan in attic space

Improper Discharge Points

Through low roof and discharged near window of upper story.

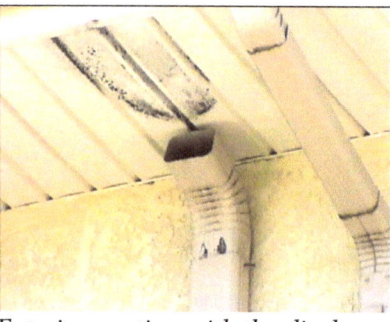
Exterior routing with the discharge impinging on soffit causing mold, mildew, and damage to overhang.

This needs to be routed around the eave and at least 6-inches above the roofline

Discharge too low at grade level

Fan can be outdoors, but discharge needs to be up to above roof,

Not above eave

Discharge near air intake

Fan is inside basement with low, thru wall discharge
(This works for Canada but not U.S.

Planning Step 3:

Planning the end of the discharge.

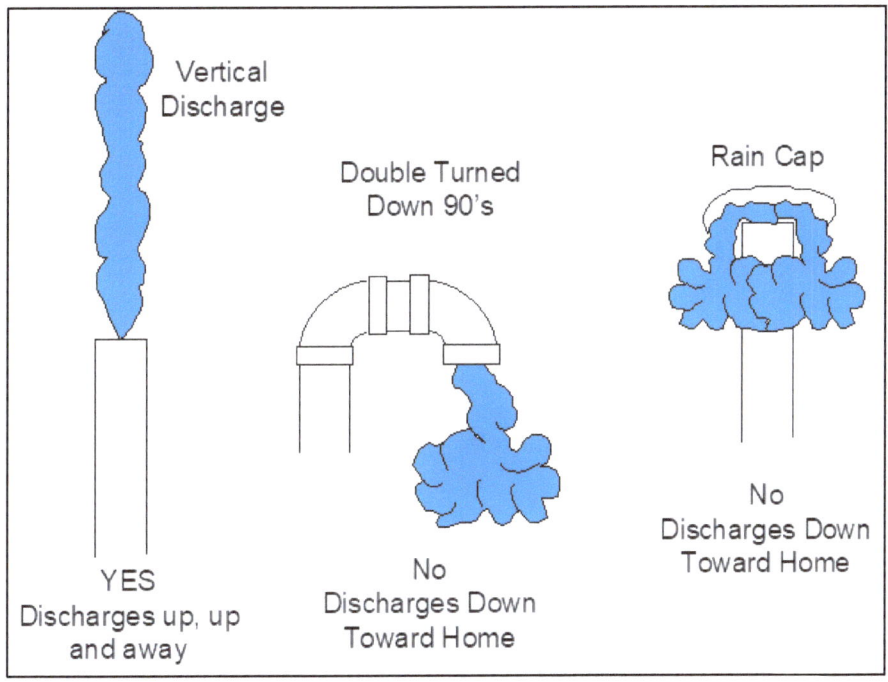

One of the things that people invariably want to do is to put something on the discharge of the piping system to prevent rain from falling in. Rain does not present a concern for two reasons. First, the air coming out the pipe blows the rain away. Secondly, the cross-section area of the pipe is only 12 square inches. Even if the rain fell straight down and the air stream did not eject it, only 1 gallon of water would be collected if your average rainfall is 20 inches per year. So, there really is no need to utilize rain caps and, in fact, they could cause problems with the system.

If you put a rain cap on or install some type of rain diverter on the discharge you will:

- Cause the exhaust gas to be blown down towards the home. This will increase the potential for the exhausted gas to re-enter the home. If this happens you will not be able to recognize it. The above figure illustrates the direction of air flow of three different discharge configurations. (Note that for the purposes of the illustration, an exhaust stream is shown, in reality you cannot see the exhaust.)

- Increase the likelihood of condensate from the system to freeze and form an ice ball on the end of the pipe, thus causing the system to malfunction.

- Decrease the operating vacuum of the fan and effect your system's ability to reduce radon.

Just put a rodent/bird screen in the end, and point it up and away from the home.

½ inch screen on discharge to keep birds out but not too small to cause frost to form

Planning Step 4:

Determining where the fan will be located.

The fan you will be using is installed as part of the piping system itself. Therefore, as you are planning your pipe routing, you need to determine a suitable fan location following the criteria below:

Fan Location Criteria

The fan should not be located inside the home or in areas where fan leakage would allow radon to enter the home.

Good Locations:
- Unoccupied attics
- Outside the house
- In garage that has not living space above garage

Bad Locations:
- In crawlspace beneath house
- In basement
- In attic where there is conditioned and mixes with air in living area.

Orientation:

First and foremost, the fan must be mounted vertically. This allows condensed moisture to flow by gravity back to the soil.

Mounting the fan horizontally will cause water to accumulate in the fan housing. Since the motor is also within the fan housing, water filling the housing will cause the motor to short out. I think we all learned in grade school that water and electricity is a dangerous combination. So, if the fan is vertical, water droplets will be flung to the outside of the casing away from the motor. Fans installed this way can last for years. Fans installed horizontally can last for hours (not good).

Noise:

Radon fans have come a long way. If you use a fan specifically designed for radon, they are pretty quiet. But on a still night when you are trying to fall asleep you can notice an annoying hum. So, select a location away from sleeping areas if possible. Here are a few other considerations:

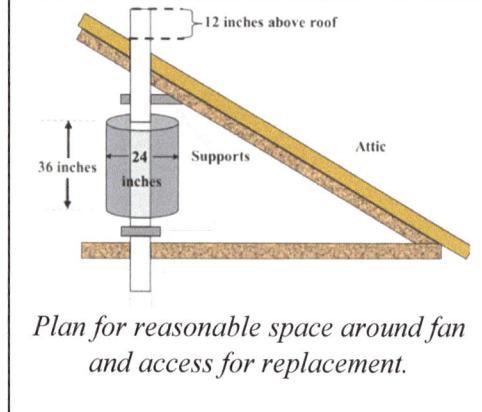

Plan for reasonable space around fan and access for replacement.

1. If you put the fan in the attic, locate it so it is easy to get to. Select a location with a minimum of 36 inches between the top of ceiling joist and the underside of the roof decking. *The fan must be installed vertically.*

2. If you put the fan outside, make sure it is rated for outdoor installations and protected from freezing.

3. Special precautions will need to be taken if you put the fan in an attached garage and penetrate the fire resistive wall between the garage and house (see fire barrier discussion in Planning Step 11.)

Chapter 7: Piping and Fan System

Planning Step 5:

Type and size of pipe to be used.

The air stream that will be running through the pipe will be very humid and at times will have water condensation. Therefore, the piping material should be resistant to water damage. Plastic pipe is very suitable for this purpose. There are two materials of plastic pipe construction that can be found in local plumbing or building supply houses. They are PVC and ABS solvent welded piping. *Note:* **You should choose one or the other, based on cost and availability. Don't mix piping types - do not glue pieces of PVC to pieces of ABS.** When you purchase the pipe be sure to also purchase the appropriate cleaner and cement for that type of pipe.

Piping	
Type of pipe:	PVC or ABS
Thickness of pipe:	Schedule 40
Pipe standard:	DWV
Size of pipe:	4-inch diameter (100 mm)

The durability of the pipe is also important. You may have kids trying to climb these pipes. The strength of the pipe is a function of its schedule number. The schedule number refers to the thickness of the wall of the pipe. Schedule 40 is the minimum pipe wall thickness that should be considered.

There are different service ratings given to pipes. These ratings are a function of the interior pressure that you expect to see within the pipe. Since the system you are installing does not need to withstand high pressures, a non-pressure rated pipe is adequate. The rating that is the most cost effective yet durable is Drain and Waste Vent or DWV. This is the same kind of pipe your plumbing vent stack is most likely made of. It is also sometimes referred to as foam core. Some code designations that may help you identify necessary pipe are:

Pipe Material	ASTM Numbers	NSF Designation
PVC	D-2665 or F891-91	NSF-DWV
ABS	F-628 or D-2661	NSF-DWV

Four-inch (100 mm) diameter pipe is the size that seems to work the most universally. If you install smaller diameter pipe, you are running the risk of not having sufficient capacity for the radon to be removed from the soil. Pipes smaller than 4-inch (100 mm) may also create a whistling noise in the pipe. This can be very objectionable if you like a quiet home. If the air volume to be removed by your system turns out to be rather small and a smaller pipe could have been used, you have only lost the small incremental cost between 4-inch (100mm) and 3-inch (75mm) pipe. On the other hand, if you had undersized the pipe, you would have no recourse other than to rip it out and start again or buy a more expensive and noisier fan to overcome the restriction presented by the smaller pipe.

Planning Step 6:

Allowing for condensation within the piping.

Active soil depressurization systems draw other soil gases besides radon from beneath the home, one of which is water vapor. The air in the soil beneath a home can be high in humidity. The potential for water vapor condensation exists when this humid air passes through a section of the piping system in a cold part of the home or is routed outside the home. **Figure A** in the illustration below depicts the formation of water droplets on the inside of the pipe. The majority of the condensation occurs inside the portion of the piping that is on the discharge side of the fan.

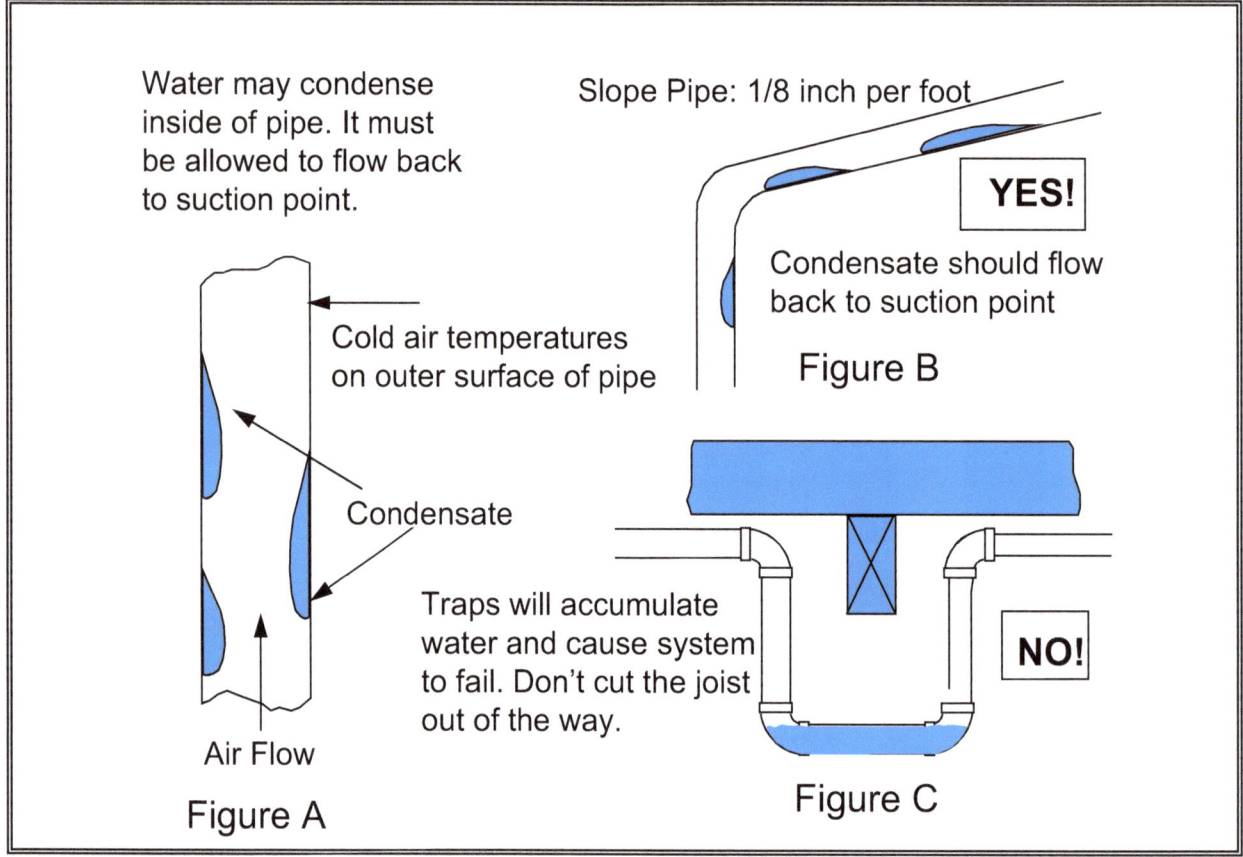

The following factors increase the amount of condensation that occurs:

- As moisture content of the soil increases. Some parts of the country are more humid than others. The authors have seen as much as two liters of water per day produced from these systems.

- With outside temperature variations. As the temperature drops outside, the temperature of the pipe wall also drops, thus increasing the amount of condensation.

- When the length of cold pipe varies. The more pipe that runs through a cold attic or up the outside, the larger the condensation surface area. This also increases the contact time the air has inside the cold pipe to condense.

Note: The piping system must be installed so when the moisture condenses, the water can drain back to the suction point. Do not install low spots in the piping where the water can accumulate. Figure C above depicts a common mistake that people make. Plan your piping so it slopes back to the suction point. Plan a slope of 1 inch per 8 feet of pipe or 1/8 inch per foot (see Figure B). It is just like running a sewage line.

Chapter 7: Piping and Fan System

Planning Step 7:

Insulating pipes to reduce condensation and noise.

One of the ways to reduce the amount of condensation that occurs inside the pipe is to prevent the wall of the pipe from getting too cold. This is especially important in very cold climates where the surface of the pipe gets so cold that the condensed water will actually freeze inside the pipe. This ice can build up and restrict, or completely choke off the desired airflow.

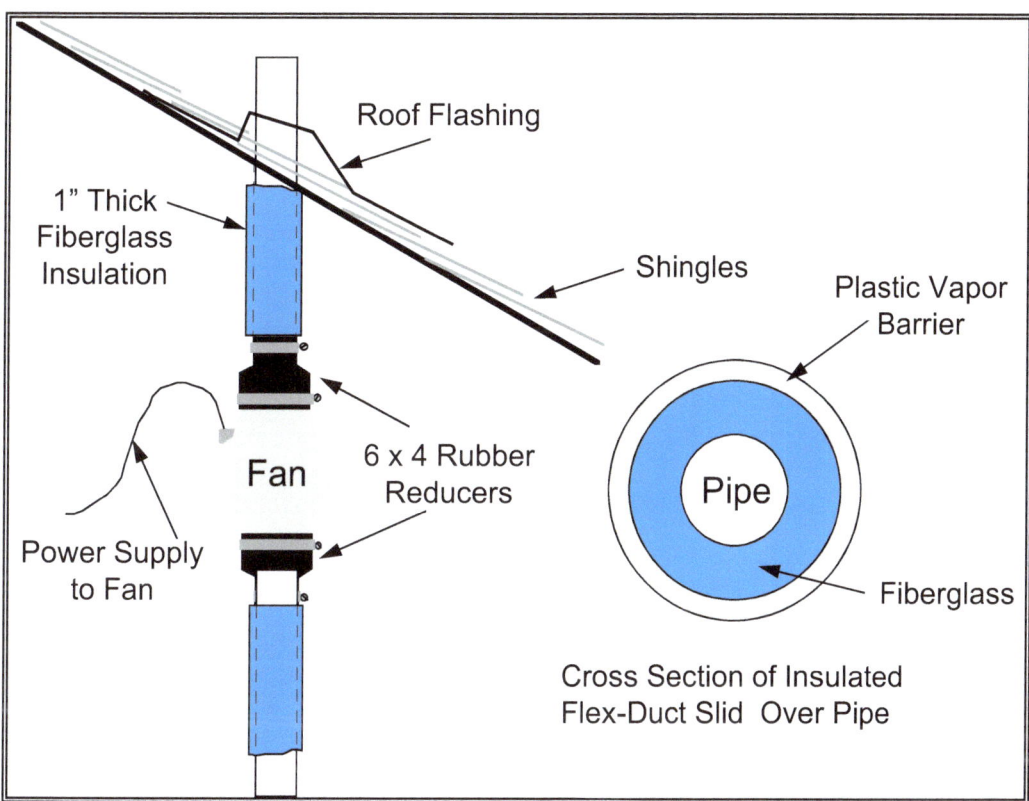

Insulate the outside of the pipe where it goes through cold areas. The figure above illustrates how this was done on the piping inside of a cold attic space. The easiest material to use is an insulated flex duct. Heating and ventilating contractors typically use this. This material has a 1-inch layer of fiberglass wrapped around a flexible plastic tube. There is also a plastic jacket around the outside of the fiberglass that can serve as a vapor barrier. It also makes the installation a lot neater. This material can be purchased in 25-foot lengths. For ease of installation, the insulated ductwork can be cut to length and slid over the piping *before the joints or fittings are glued together.*

Also use insulated ductwork as a jacket around the piping inside the home to reduce the noise caused by air flowing through the piping. If you buy a 25-foot length of the ductwork and only use a few feet in the attic for insulation, use the rest on the piping to dampen noise where it runs through the house. It makes for a quieter installation.

Another reason for insulating the ductwork inside the house would be if you live in a warm, humid climate. The air temperature in the pipe could be cooler than the temperature in the home. When this occurs condensation could form on the exterior surface of the piping. The insulation will reduce this "rain making" effect inside your home. Carefully seal the jacket of the insulation to the surface of the pipe and tape any punctures in the jacket to ensure a good moisture barrier, which could soak and ruin the insulation.

Protecting Your Home from Radon

Planning Step 8:

Dealing with ice and condensation on exterior fan locations.

Systems installed on the exterior of buildings are subject to freezing temperatures. When this occurs, the high moisture content of the exhausted gases will condense, and ice can form. Since the air in the pipe is warm, the ice will eventually thaw, causing ice chunks to fall down into the fan, damaging it.

Hose-style systems that route condensed water from the discharge of the fan to its suction piping can be problematic due to the potential for water freezing in the by-pass hose. Devices that protect ice from falling into fan or drain condensate onto the ground have proven effective in cold climates. There are two ways in which ice can be precluded from entering the fan housing:

Criss-Cross

Install two lengths of stainless all thread (3/8 inch) in the pipe immediately above fan.

- Drill pipe from outside with holes at 12, 3, 6, and 9 o'clock positions.
- Insert all thread in and secure with washers and nuts.
- Caulk penetrations.
- This cross pattern will stop large chunks from falling into the impeller without significantly impairing airflow.

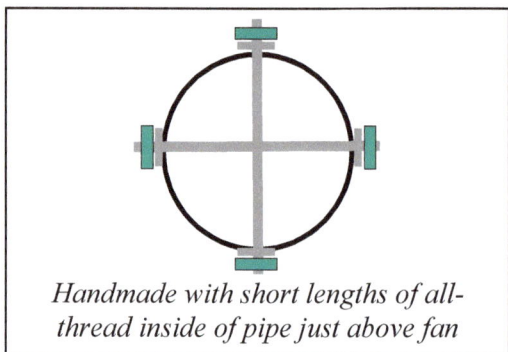

Handmade with short lengths of all-thread inside of pipe just above fan

Hydro-Sep Water Diverter

- A Hydro-Sep water diverter can also protect the fan from ice because it has a nozzle within it that will stop large ice chunks from falling into the fan housing.
- It also allows water to drain out on the area around fan.
- Do not use a Hydro-Sep on a fan located in attic or garage. Only use this type of device when fan is outdoors and where dripping water will not cause damage.

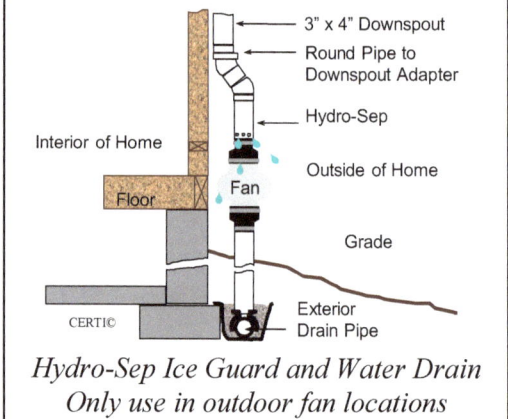

Hydro-Sep Ice Guard and Water Drain Only use in outdoor fan locations

Chapter 7: Piping and Fan System

Planning Step 9:

    Using downspout on exterior pipe sections.

Downspouts can be used for the exterior portion of the vent system if you want to vent above the eave of the roof. This is because the downspout looks more natural on the side of your house than a 4-inch pipe. It can be plastic or metal, which can be painted to match the color of your other downspouts.

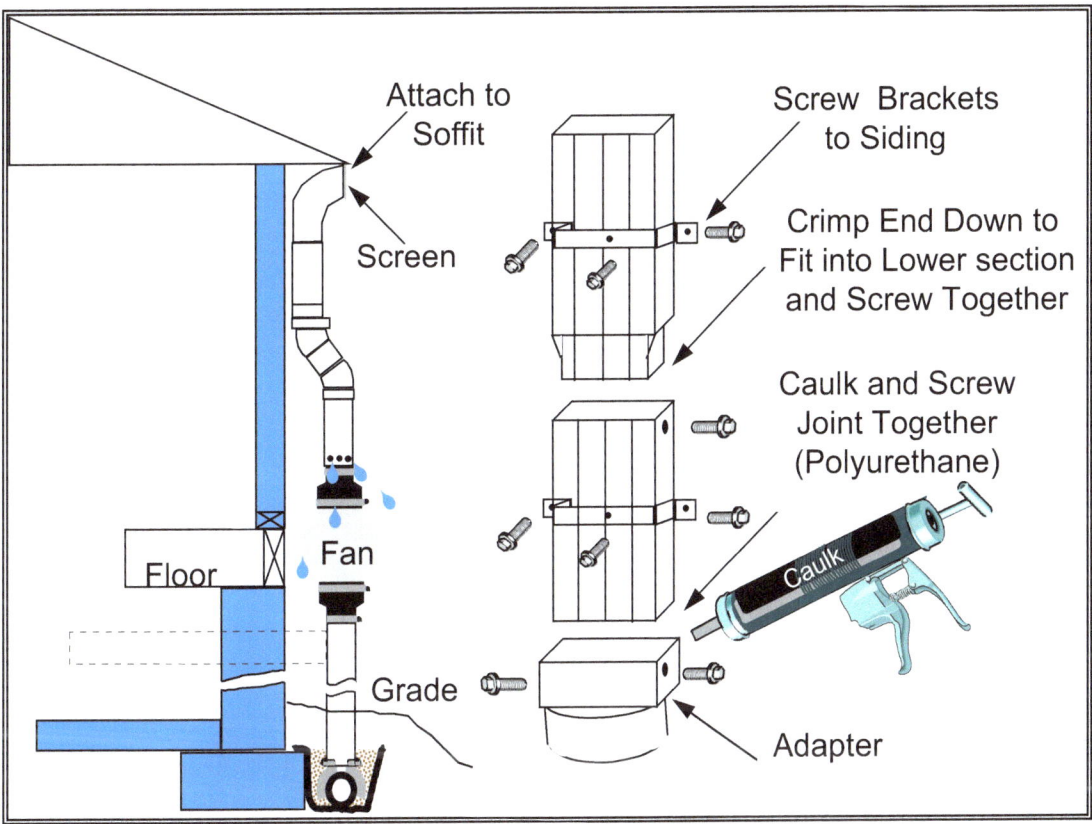

If you plan to do this, you need to keep the following things in mind:

1. A downspout should **only** be on the discharge side of the fan.
2. It should never be run inside of the house.
3. If you use metal downspout the potential for ice buildup in cold climates is greater than if you use PVC or ABS. *Hint:* **See previous step on the use of water separators.**
4. The downspout joints should be caulked and screwed together to minimize leakage.
5. Try to locate it on the sunny side of the house.

In the illustration above, that round PVC piping is used from the discharge side of the fan through two 45-degree elbows. Use PVC pipe for this due to the physical stress that can be placed on the system at this point. After you have reached the side of the house, install a round pipe to rectangular downspout adapter. Cosmetic enclosures are also available for the fan that allow for an offset to occur inside of the housing.

Be sure to use 3 by 4-inch downspout. This is a larger size than what is typically seen on homes. Use of a smaller downspout can severely restrict the air flow and decrease efficiency of the system.

Planning Step 10:

Do You Need a Fan Enclosure?

Sometimes a person may want to have an enclosure around the fan. The reasons for this would be to conceal it, or perhaps to protect it from children, or from the elements. If you use a fan that is rated for outdoor use, you do not need an enclosure. If you live in a very cold climate, you could insulate the fan and place it inside an enclosure or alternatively route the piping up through the house rather than outside.

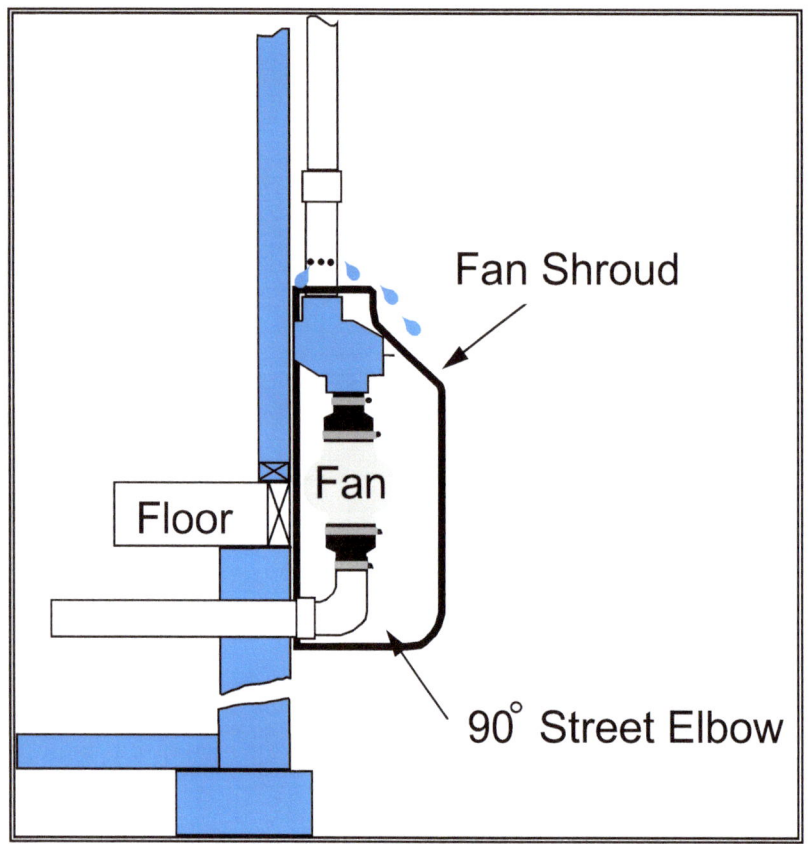

If you use a fan enclosure, realize there are two basic types from which to choose:

- One that attaches to the wall and is very durable. This type of enclosure is used most often on school or commercial installations where protection from abuse is a priority. This is the one illustrated.

- The other enclosure commercially available is a set of plastic clamshells that fit over the fan with pre-molded holes for the suction and discharge piping. These do not provide much structural support if your reason for using the fan enclosure is abuse prevention.

Regardless of the type you use, be sure to install the water separation device on the discharge piping outside the enclosure to prevent water from accumulating inside the enclosure.

External Radon Fan in Shroud

Chapter 7: Piping and Fan System

Planning Step 11:

Penetrating garage walls, fire walls and fire ceilings.

As you plan your routing, be aware you cannot cut a hole through just any wall to run the piping through. Some walls and even ceilings are constructed in a manner to retard the spread of fire from one area of the house to the next. A common example of this would be if you plan to run your piping into an attached garage where the fan can be located. The wall separating the garage from the house is a fire resistive wall. This is in accordance with building codes.

If the fire resistive wall does not extend up to the roof, the ceiling of an attached garage is a fire rated ceiling. Partition walls between units and condominiums, townhouses and duplexes should also be fire rated walls. If the fire walls between separate housing units do not extend to the roof, the ceiling of an individual unit is a fire ceiling also. Fire rated ceilings require fire stops just as much as fire walls do when running PVC pipe through them.

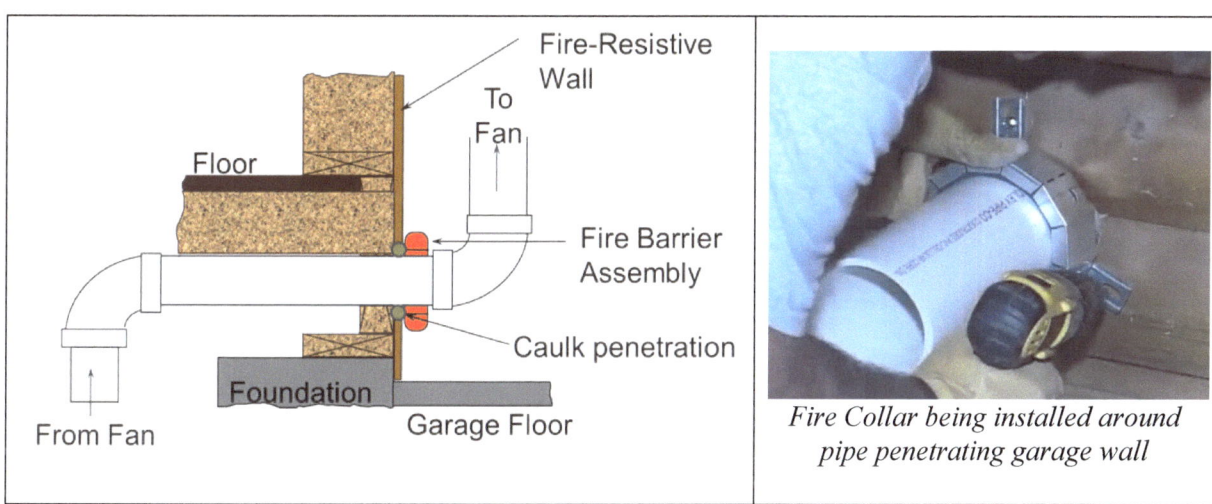

Fire Collar being installed around pipe penetrating garage wall

You may penetrate fire resistive walls, provided you install a "fire stop." A fire stop is a device that will maintain the fire resistance rating of the wall the pipe is penetrating. The device that is the most commonly used for radon piping is the intumescent style fire barrier. The diagram and photo above show how a penetration is made into a garage. The fire barrier itself is a series of strips of material that are wrapped around the exterior of the pipe. A sheet metal collar is then placed over the top of the strips and screwed into the wall. **Only one of these assemblies is needed on one side of the wall per penetration of a fire wall.** Figure B illustrates the pipe with the collar attached.

Note: The barrier and collar must be installed on the side of the wall that presents the greatest fire hazard and must be mounted directly on the wall.

In the case of a garage wall penetration, the assembly would be on the garage side of the wall as shown in Figure A above. These devices are readily available. To order from building supply stores or radon specialty stores supply store, you must specify the pipe size you are fitting over and the fire rating desired (typically 1 hour).

It is recommended that even if your garage wall or ceiling is not fire rated, you use a fire collar in addition to caulking around the outside edge of the penetration.

Planning Step 12:
Planning your pipe supports.

As the pipe will be routed through the home, it will have to be well supported. Even though it will only be full of air and not contain much weight - kids love to climb on them or people are known to hang deer from them (all true stories). Therefore, pipes need to be well supported so they do not crack or break. A broken pipe could cause serious depressurization within the home. This could also cause the combustion appliances to backdraft. Poisonous carbon monoxide gas can accumulate when backdrafting occurs. The figure below shows three methods of pipe support.

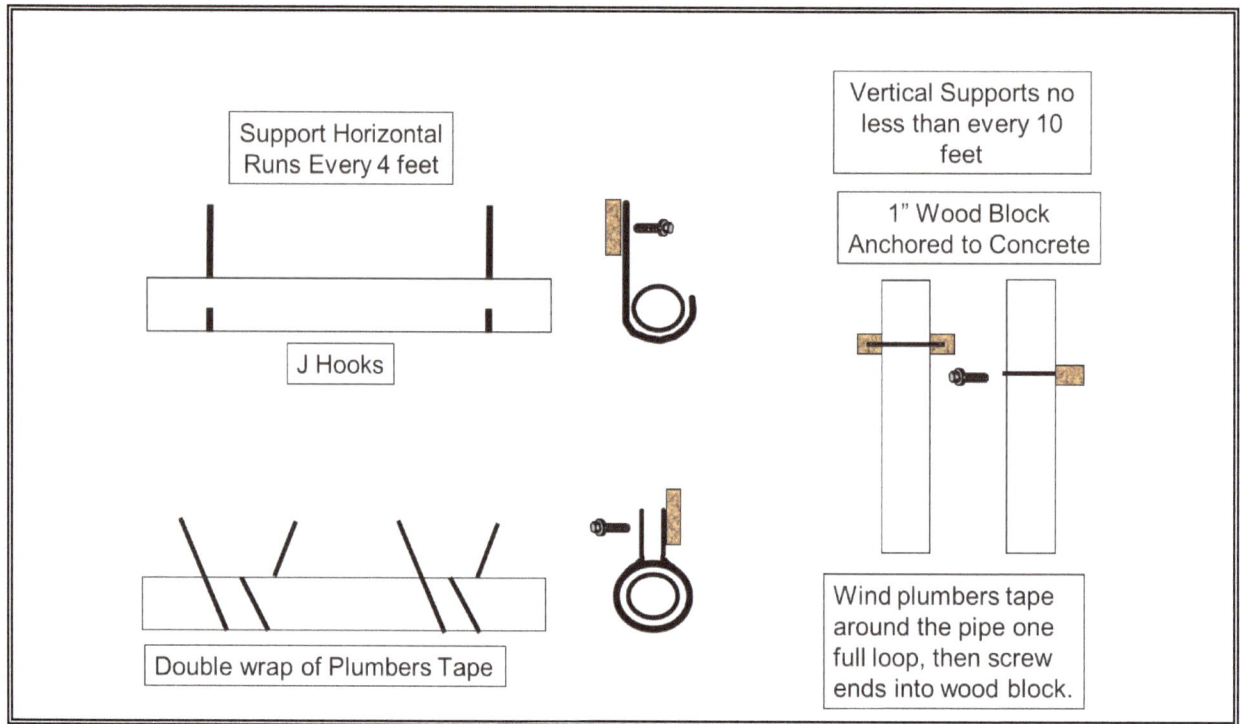

Horizontal pipe is often supported with either J-Hooks or Plumber's tape. Regardless of the method used, the pipe should be supported every 4 feet. Don't forget to slope the pipe.

J-Hooks: J-hooks are plastic hooks that can be nailed or screwed into a wall or floor joist. The pipe snaps into the open end of the hook. There are several holes on the straight section of the hook with numbers on them to help you mount the hooks at different elevations. This is helpful in making sure you have the proper slope to the pipe (1 inch per 10 feet).

Plumber's tape: Plumber's tape is a 3/4-inch-wide metal or plastic tape that has had holes pre-punched into it. It can be purchased in rolls. Just uncoil as much as is needed and cut it with tin snips. Make sure you cut enough off so you can wrap it completely around the pipe once and screw the two ends to the wall or floor joist. Actually, the plastic plumber's tape is a lot easier to work with and has adequate strength.

Plumber's tape screwed into floor joist for pipe support

For providing lateral support for vertical pipes, attach a 1-inch by 1-inch by 8-inch block of wood to the wall. Use wood screws if you are attaching to a wood wall and anchors if you are attaching to masonry or drywall. Wrap plumber's tape completely around the pipe, fasten one end to the wood block, take up the slack with the free end and screw it to the block as well. Vertical supports should not be more than every 10 feet. Additionally, install one at every floor level.

Chapter 7: Piping and Fan System

Planning Step 13:

Planning exterior wall penetrations.

You may prefer to run the piping through an outside wall and avoid the difficulties of running pipe through the interior of the house. If you are depressurizing a basement sump or installing a sub-slab suction system in a basement, or you are depressurizing a plastic barrier on a crawl space floor - exterior piping might be used if your climate is more temperate. The figure below shows how this is done.

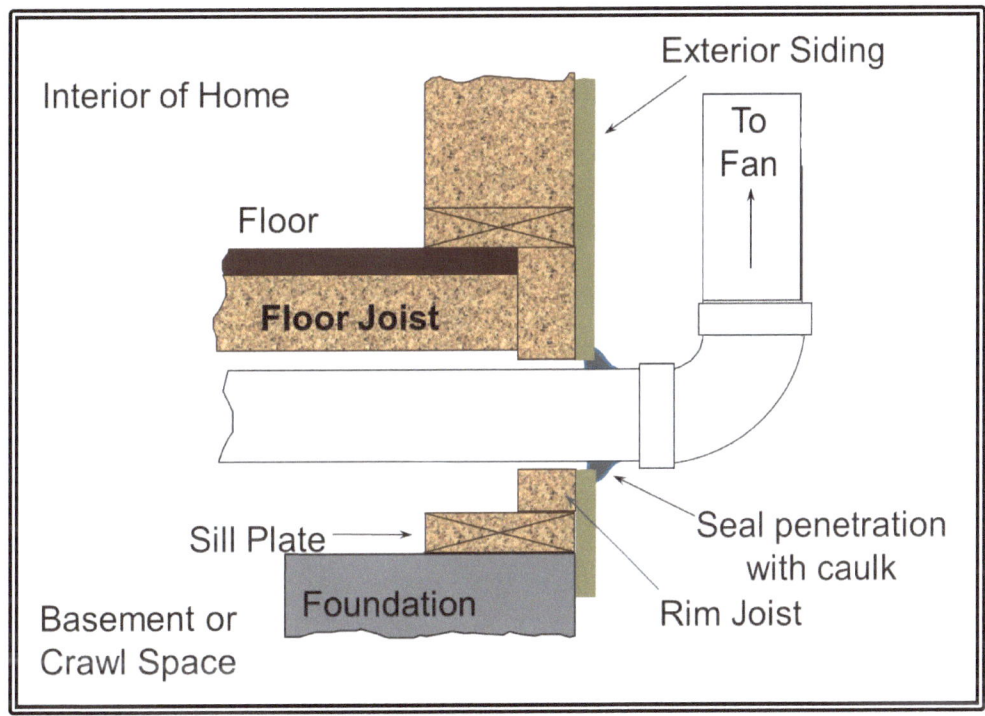

Use a 5-inch hole saw or a reciprocating saw (sawzall) to make the hole. Drill a pilot hole with a small but long drill bit to make sure of the location. Seal around the pipe with outdoor rated caulk like latex or butyl caulk.

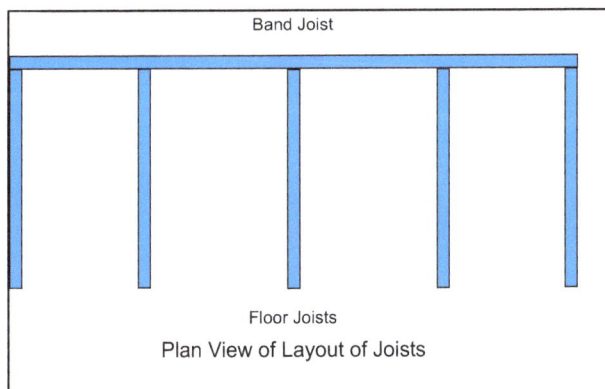

The penetration should be through the rim joist. It should run through the board that sets on the edge on the foundation wall.

- **Do not cut floor joists or run through the wall at a location below grade.**
- **Do not cut holes through structural members or through the foundation wall below grade.**
- **Do not cut a hole through a basement wall below grade unless you want water in your basement (another true story).**

Planning Step 14:

Fan mounting.

The fan that creates the needed vacuum can be installed in many locations. The figure below illustrates a fan mounting for an attic.

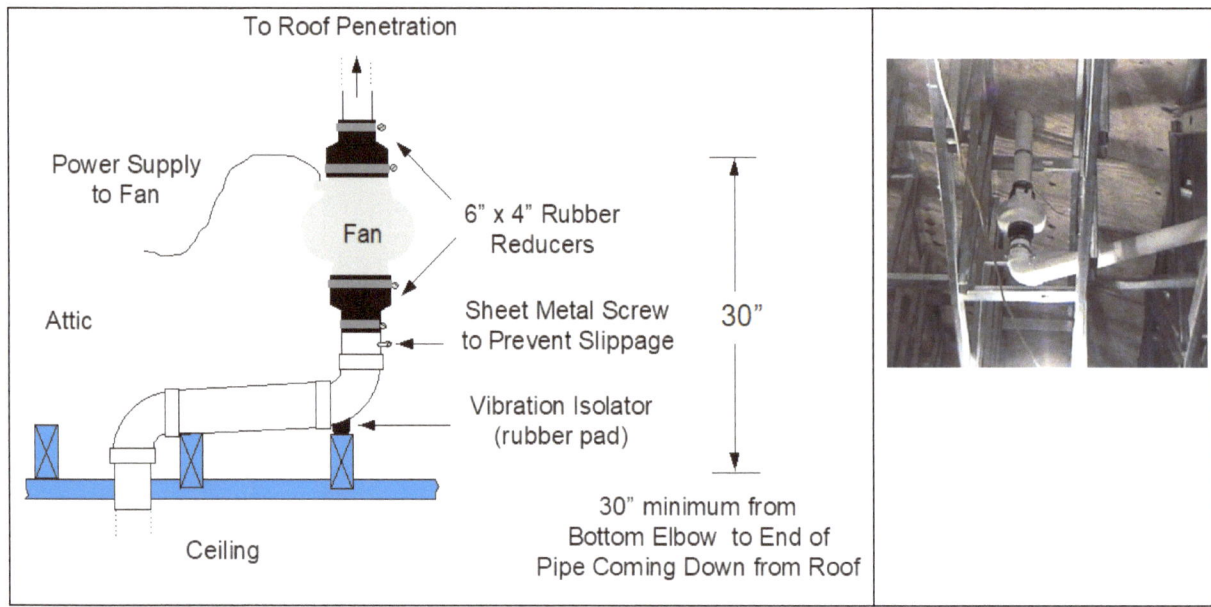

Regardless of the location for the fan, it must be installed in the following manner:

- It must be mounted vertically to allow condensed water to drain down through the fan housing.

- There must be a way to remove the fan from the piping system. The best way to do this is to use 6 inch by 4-inch rubber reducers with hose clamps. These can be loosened so the fan can slide out of the piping system (see the screw shown in the drawing just below the bottom reducer). This screw is a # 8 self-tapping stainless-steel screw that is run into the pipe just below the bottom rubber reducer. This prevents the fan from accidentally sliding down onto the pipe. In hot attics, or for other reasons, the rubber reducer could loosen up. If this were to occur and allow the fan to slide down, the lower pipe would stick into the fan blades. This will stop the fan dead, and likely ruin it. So be sure to install the screw in the pipe below the reducer.

Fan mounted outdoors with flexible connectors above and below fan

Note the way the horizontal piping has been run from the ceiling penetration to the fan. The ceiling joists are supporting the pipe. A piece of rubber has been placed between the joist and the pipe to isolate any vibration from the joist and provide the proper slope to the fan.

The rubber connectors also help isolate fan noise from the piping system and the rest of the home.

Important: *Do not mount the fan at any orientation other than vertical, and do not glue the fan directly to the piping. Use rubber couplings.*

Planning Step 15:
Fan selection.

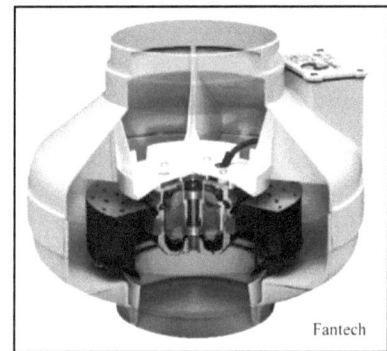

In-line duct fans have proven to be the most universally applicable fan for the types of radon reduction systems described in this book. People have tried duct booster fans, wafer fans, and various other types of fans. These have not shown the satisfactory results for radon reduction and durability as the in-line fans have. In-line fans are located directly in the air flow of the pipe and are supported by the pipe. Their inlet and discharge opening sizes are typically 6 inches in diameter, but they can also be 4 inch. You will need to obtain an appropriately sized flexible coupling to connect the fan to the pipe. Do not glue the fan to the pipe! The flexible couplers reduce noise as well as make it easier to replace the fan when needed.

Radon vent fans come in many sizes and capacities, but they have one thing in common -- they are manufactured specifically for use in radon systems. The use of other HVAC types of fans and blowers (e.g., squirrel cage fans) are unable to deal with the moisture conditions presented with radon systems. In particular, radon fans have the following attributes:

- Inline installation
- Internal motors and impellers
- Casing design that when mounted vertically allow condensed water in the discharge piping to flow around the inside of the casing to the suction side of the fan where it can drain by gravity to the suction point
- Rated for outdoor installation
- Sealed bearings requiring no maintenance
- Rated for continuous service
- Sealed and gasketed electrical connection box
- Thermal overload protection (self-resetting)

There are several manufacturers of the fan units to choose from and often will supply the fan with the appropriate flexible connectors. The following is some technical data regarding some of the fans.

Manufacturer	Model #	Comments	Max. Watts	Max. flow CFM	Max.Vac in. W.C*.
Fantech	HP - 190	For interior/exterior use	84	157	2.0
Fantech	RN-2	For interior/exterior use	90	270	1.5
Festa	Maverick	For interior/exterior use	85	237	2.3
PDS	KTA-150	Low-voltage, Class 2 wiring, built in indicator Fan is interior or exterior. Power supply is interior only	90	270	1.5
Radonaway	RP145	For interior/exterior use	75	155	2.0

* in W.C. = inches of Water Column (fans ability to create vacuum, described as how far its vacuum could pull water up a pipe).

The table above shows a maximum power usage of 90 watts. Most systems usually draw approximately 60 watts or less. There are smaller sizes as well as higher vacuum fans available. However, for the systems described in this manual, any of these fans should be adequate. If the sub-slab simulation test described in Chapter 6 should indicate very tight soils, then the homeowner should follow the recommendation to call a radon professional to size an alternate fan in this unusual instance. One can also seek advice from the radon supply houses when selecting a fan.

Protecting Your Home from Radon

Planning Step 16:

Electrical requirements for the fans.

Radon fans now come in two electrical configurations 120-volt, direct wired or low-voltage with a power supply arrangement. In either approach the power consumption is low enough that neither one would require a separate circuit from your electrical panel (draw one amp or less) unless the circuit you are connecting to is already overloaded (80% or more loaded). Regardless of the approach there are some common elements of either system.

Common to All Radon Fans:

- Fan to be mounted vertically, so condensed water can drain down.
- An electrical disconnect should be within eyesight of the fan for safe removal of the fan for servicing.
- Proper wiring or conduit appropriate for the location of the fan and its wiring.
- Do not connect to a switched circuit.
- Label the circuit to which the fan is powered in the electrical panel.

Circuit Powering Fan Labeled in Power Panel

120-Volt Direct Wired:

These are the systems most commonly installed by professionals utilizing a licensed electrician to wire them.

- Identify a nearby branch circuit
- Connect into an existing junction box or receptacle
- Route wire to fan location
    - Within conduit if outdoors
    - Or as romex cable
- The power can be run with 14-3 wire (ROMEX), unless it is on a 20-amp circuit which requires 12-3 wire.
- Install an inline electrical disconnect within eyesight of fan

120-volt fan direct wired on exterior.
- *Wiring in weatherproof conduit*
- *Disconnect switch adjacent to fan*

120-Volt Plug in Fans

If there is a receptacle within a few feet of your fan location, such as an attic receptacle planned during new construction, an electrical plug not exceeding 6 feet can be attached to the fan and plugged in.

- Corded fans **should not** be used outdoors (locations)
- Maximum cord length: 6 feet
- A disconnect is not needed since the cord can be unplugged form the receptacle for service.

Chapter 7: Piping and Fan System

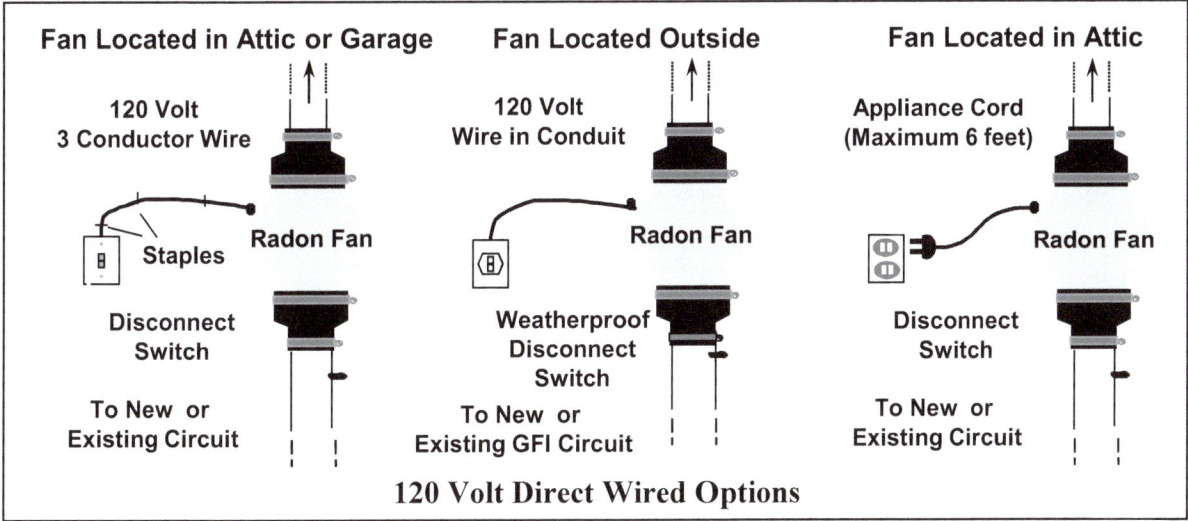

Low-voltage Fans

An alternative fan system that has the same volumetric and suction capacity as the most commonly used 120-volt fans is a unit that can be plugged in to an available receptacle within the home. The voltage is reduced to 24 volts so it can be run in an inexpensive cable to the fan up to 75 feet away. The cable that is typically used with this system is 16-gauge two-conductor cable. The use of the special cable allows for the wiring to be run to the fan without conduit to an exterior fan location. The power supply is modified within the fan, so it operates within the normal airflow and vacuum capacity of the fan.

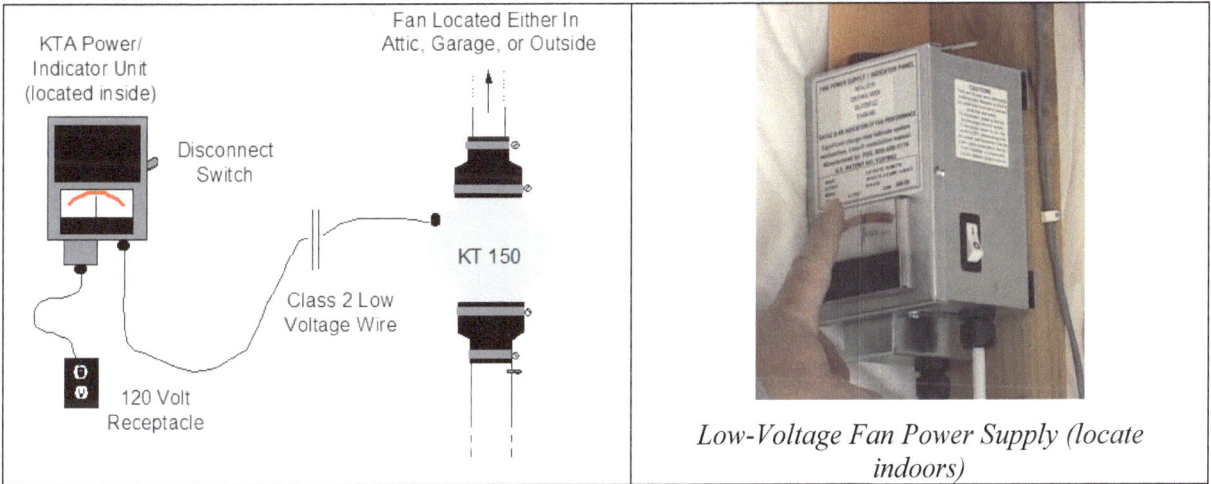

Low-Voltage Fan Power Supply (locate indoors)

The obvious advantage is it can be plugged in, and the power cable strung like one might run a TV cable or a sprinkler wire. Although you still need to follow certain precautions:

- The cable should be supported with cable staples.
- The power supply box **must be located** indoors and at a location where it can be observed since the power supply box has the system performance indicator incorporated into it.

Another advantage to this low-voltage fan system is the indicator system is electronic, and a pressure indication system is not needed. This can overcome the humidity and freezing problems often seen with pressure tubing (see Planning Step 17).

Note that other manufacturers have develop low-voltage fans that work well. Verify any low-voltage fan system meets Class II wiring requirements of the National Electric Code and are approved by UL or CSA.

Planning Step 17:

Types of system indicators.

As part of the installation of a depressurization system, an indicator must be installed which will tell the homeowner if something has changed the performance of the system. This is in addition to re-testing the home for radon after the installation and repeating this test every year. You could purchase a continuous radon monitor. However, it is also recommended an air pressure or air flow meter be installed to alert you if either the vacuum characteristics or the air flow characteristics of the system have changed. A fan stall, a blockage in the pipe, or a breach in the system could cause this to happen. There are two basic types of indicators as follows:

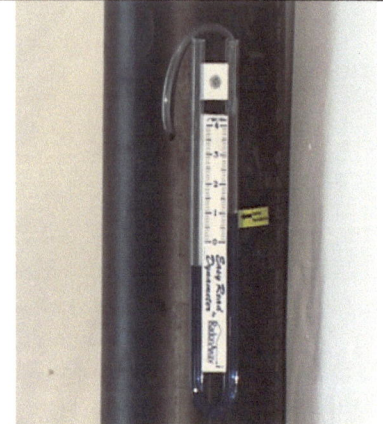

Pressure Based
U-Tube Manometer
Senses changes in system vacuum
Mounts on radon vent pipe

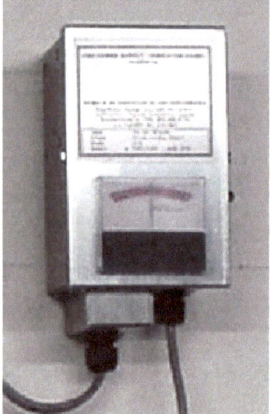

Air Flow Based
KTA-Low-Voltage System
Provides power to fan.
Needle on meter shows changes in air flow

Pressure Based. The above figure illustrates two common types of system performance indicators.

The first is a U-Tube Manometer and is typically mounted directly on the suction piping of the system. When a 1/4-inch tube is run from the "low" side of the manometer to the suction side of the piping system and the "high" side port is left open, the liquid level will change as the vacuum of the system changes. This allows you to identify fluctuations in the radon capture efficiency of the system. Pressure based indicators have the potential to falsely indicate problems because of condensation or freezing within the ¼ inch pressure sensing tubing if the tubing is exposed to cold temperatures.

Chapter 7: Piping and Fan System

As of 2022, an additional monitor requirement was incorporated in the ANSI/AARST standards requiring remote monitoring either by producing an audible alarm, or a flashing light or notification via a telemetric means. An example of both a U-Tube indicator and a pressure monitor with audible signal is shown in the picture to the right.

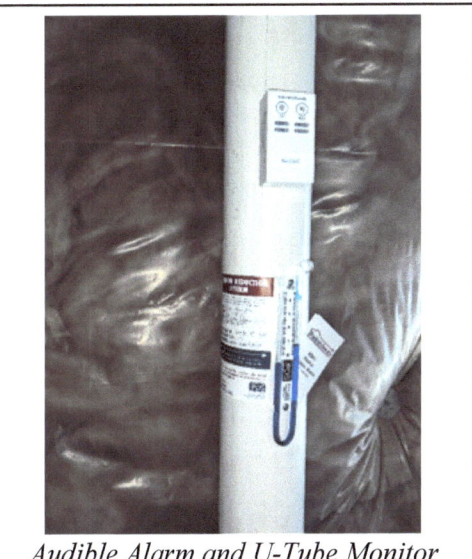
Audible Alarm and U-Tube Monitor

Air Flow Based. Another device is a packaged system that provides both power (low-voltage) and a means for monitoring system air flow. It does this electronically by monitoring the current draw of the fan. Slight changes in air flow due to small leaks, or piping blockages that can develop in the system, are indicated. These electronic monitors are sensitive to problems and also do not require pressure sensing tubing, thus eliminating false signals with condensation, and freezing.

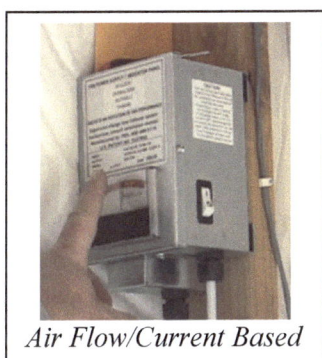
Air Flow/Current Based

Radon Monitors.

Relatively inexpensive radon monitors can be very useful in detecting system failure problems. Although they may not meet all of the criteria for being designated for use by some certification boards for determining the need for mitigation or the success of mitigation, they can certainly indicate to the homeowner if there are changes in radon levels within your home. If one uses these and there is a significant change in radon levels from when the system was installed, the homeowner should check the system for problems and, when corrected, verify low radon levels with devices as described in Chapter 2.

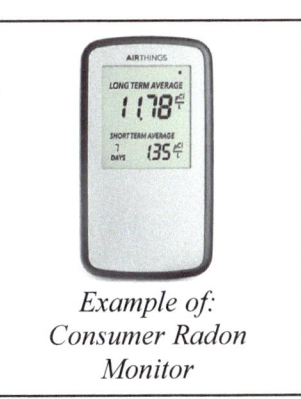
Example of: Consumer Radon Monitor

Protecting Your Home from Radon

Planning Step 18:

How to penetrate the roof if you plan an internal pipe routing.

If you choose to route your piping through the interior of the home and through the roof, you will need to cut a hole in the roof for the pipe and to repair the hole, so the roof does not leak. For those roofs that have asphalt shingles or shakes, the process is relatively straightforward. If it is a flat roof, or a clay tile roof, or if the shingles contain asbestos, the repair is more involved and should be done by a roofing professional. The figure below illustrates how a shingle roof penetration can be made with a roof jack.

1. From inside the attic, drill a pilot hole to mark the center of where you intend the pipe to go through the roof. Push a stick up through the roof, so you can find the pilot hole from the roof. With a circular saw or a sawzall, cut a hole that is 6 ½ inches by 6 ½ inches, or a circular hole that is 6 ½ inches in diameter. ***Warning: Wear safety glasses, gloves, and use a fully grounded extension cord. Failure to do so can result in permanent injury. Before cutting the hole, be in a secure position on the roof, or rope yourself off. The chance of hitting a roofing nail is pretty high, and the saw will kick***. Also, the fine rocks in the shingles will spray when cut and will probably dull your blade. Use an old blade.

2. Install the pipe and secure it both laterally and vertically as described previously in this chapter. With a flat bar or putty knife, loosen the shingle uphill from the pipe. Slide the roof jack down over the pipe with the seal side up. Run two concentric beads of caulk around the underside of the jack where it will set on the roof.

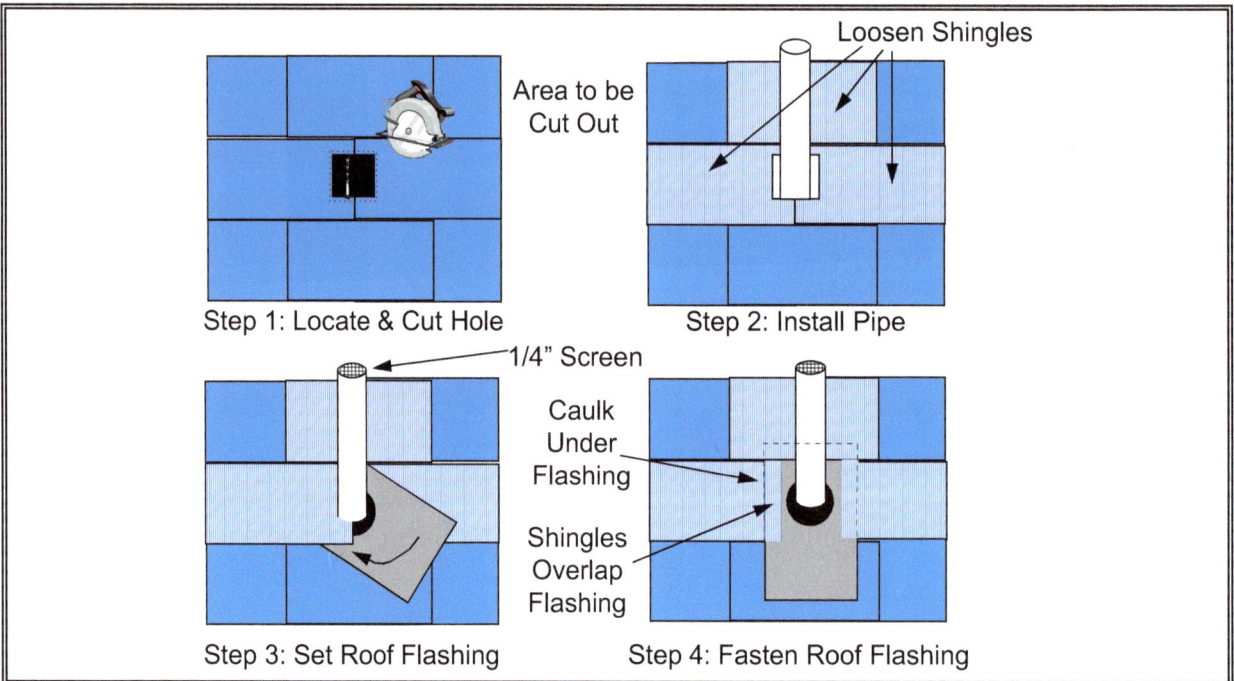

Installing Roof Flashing

3. Tuck one of the upper corners of the roof jack and rotate it under the shingles that were loosened above.

4. Drive a roofing nail into each of the four corners and caulk with roofing caulk.

Be careful getting up on roof make sure it is not slippery with moisture and consider fall protection equipment and definitely secure ladder at top and bottom.

Chapter 7: Piping and Fan System

Installation

If you plan to install the piping system yourself, be sure you are familiar with the items in the safety chapter and that you follow the instructions for the glues and caulks you will be using. Don't get pipe glue in your eyes. Think about how you are going to provide electricity to the fan. If you are using a plug-in approach or the low-voltage system, this is a snap. However, if you are going to mount the fan in the attic or outdoors you should hire an electrician or obtain a permit /inspection from the local building department.

Installation Step 1:

Assemble the materials for installing the depressurization system.

The following is a table that lists many of the items that you may need for the installation of the system.

Safety		QTY	⏱
	Goggles, safety glasses, i.e. eye protection		
	Ventilation fan		
	Gloves		
	First aid kit		
Materials			
	PVC Pipe-Schedule 40 DWV or ABS Schedule 40 DWV Feet:		
	4-inch 90-degree elbows-PVC or ABS		
	4-inch 45-degree elbows-PVC or ABS		
	4-inch tees PVC or ABS		
	4-inch 22.5-degree fittings		
	Pipe solvent and cement - compatible for pipe material used		
	4-inch by 4-inch rubber couplings		
	4-inch PVC or ABS couplings		
	Fan enclosure if desired for aesthetics		
	Roof jack		
	Tube of roofing caulk		
	Plumber's tape		
	# 8 self-tapping screws (at least 50)		
	1 square foot of ¼-inch hardware cloth		
	Rubber vibration isolation strips		
	Flexible duct insulation		
	Duct tape		
	Flexible connectors between the vent pipe and the fans inlet and outlet	2	
	3-inch by 4-inch downspout		
	Type A downspout elbows (turn out)		
	Type B downspout elbows (turn right or left)		
	Downspout to pipe adapter		
	Downspout straps		
	Continued on Next Page		

Protecting Your Home from Radon

			QTY	🕒
FAN	**120 Volt Fan Option**			
		Fan		
		Electrician		
		Pressure and electronic indicator		
		¼-inch tubing		
		Cable staples		
Fan	**Plug in Option**			
		Fan		
		Appliance cord no longer than 6 feet		
FAN	**Low-voltage Fan Option**			
		Integral power supply / indicator with matching fan		
		Two conductor sprinkler cables		
		Cable staples		
Equipment				
	Extension ladder for roof			
	Step ladder (6 foot)			
	Cordless drill with ¼-inch nut driver			
	Flashlight			
	Extension cord			
	Hole saw (5-inch) and drill (right angle with clutch is safest)			
	Circular saw or reciprocating saw			
	Rags			
	Hack saw or PVC saw (PVC saw works best)			
	Measuring tape			
	Marker			
	Plumb bob or weight on a string			
	Level			
	Hammer			

Considerations:

- <u>Before</u> you start this work - think carefully about how you will run the piping system. Try to run the pipe through closets and unoccupied spaces as much as possible.

- Make sure you pick a good weather day to do this work if you are planning to get up on the roof and cut a hole.

- You will need a helper for this work. Someone to hold onto the other end of the pipe is very helpful.

- Don't attempt electrical wiring of the 120-volt systems unless you are trained and licensed to do so or are using a 6-foot appliance cord or a low-voltage approach.

- Wear your safety glasses. Plastic pipe glue is a solvent that glues the pipe together by dissolving the plastic. It will also dissolve your cornea if it gets into your eye.

- ***ABSOLUTELY NO CONTACT LENSES*** while doing this work.

Cutting and Fitting Pipe Together

Measure twice and cut once. One method that professional mitigators use is to "dry fit" the pipe. They cut the pipe and push the fittings on without glue. This can help with the layout of the piping. If you do this, be careful that you allow for at least an extra half inch on each side of a fitting. This is because you cannot push the fitting on a dry pipe as far as you will be able to after you apply the glue.

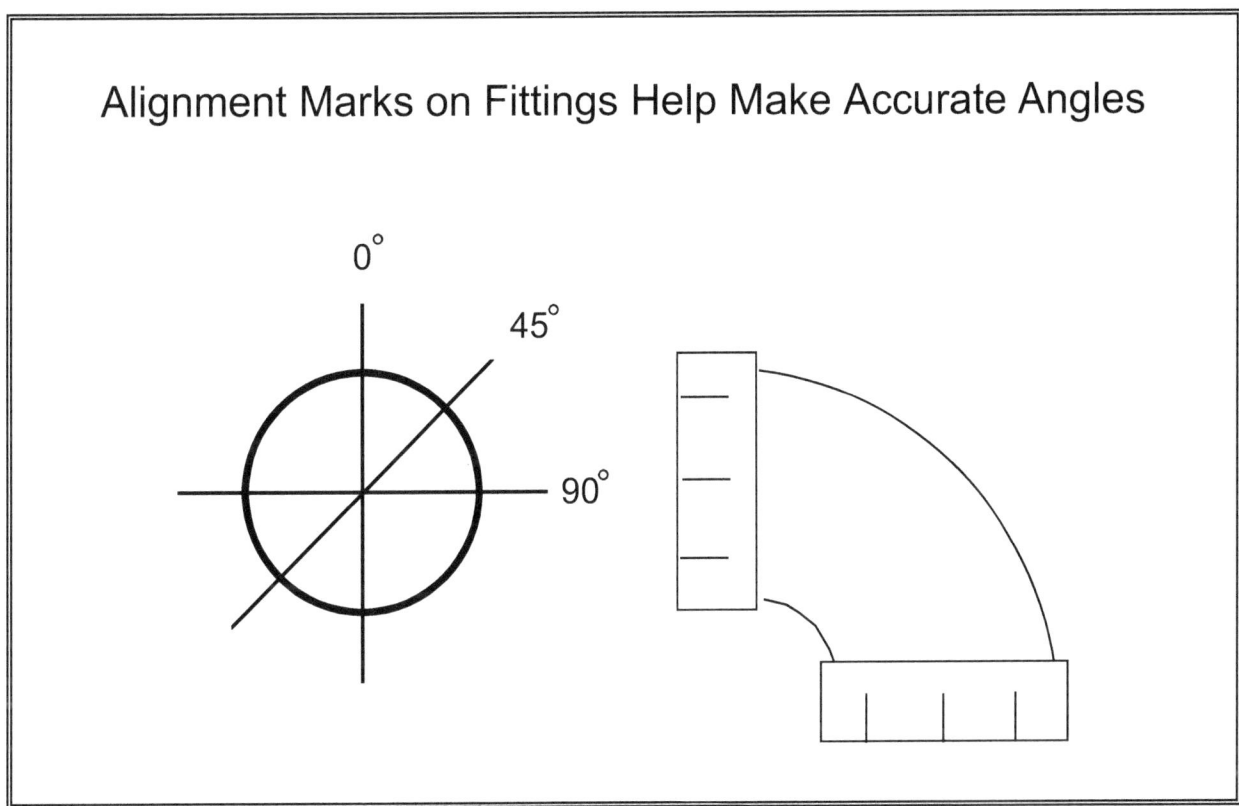

The above illustration depicts how some fittings have marks on their sides to show increments of 22.5 degrees. When these marks are lined up on opposing fittings a perfect 45- or 90-degree angle can be made.

After you dry fit a connection, mark the fitting and the pipe with a marking pen and cut it with a hand saw. These marks will allow you to break the fitting, apply the glue and reconnect the fitting exactly as you had planned. There are special PVC saws that work best for cutting the pipe, but a hack saw will also work for this. After you have made a cut, remove the debris from inside the pipe with a utility knife or a file before applying the glue.

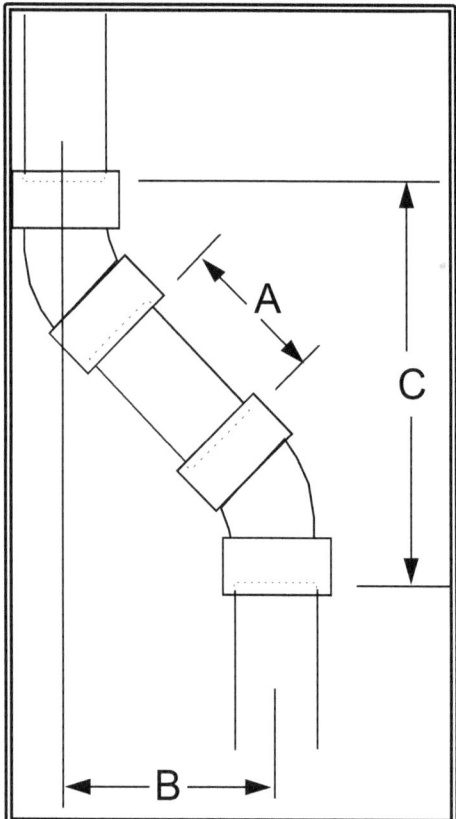

The figure to the left, and the table below may be of assistance in calculating vertical and horizontal offsets with 45-degree elbows.

Dry fitting pipe is a good method as well.

A	B	C
Pipe Length between two 45-degree fittings	**Lateral Offset** between centerlines of vertical pipes	**Vertical** distance between pipes – assuming 1 ¾ insertion for each pipe
inches	inches	inches
0	6.00	10.00
1	6.53	10.85
2	7.05	11.70
3	7.58	12.55
4	8.10	13.40
5	8.63	14.25
6	9.15	15.11
7	9.68	15.96
8	10.20	16.81
9	10.73	17.66
10	11.25	18.51
11	11.78	19.36
12	12.30	20.21

Gluing Pipe

Once you have cut the pipe, you are ready to begin putting it together. The fittings are designed to slip over the pipe to form the connection within the socket of the fitting. The bond is achieved by melting both the pipe and the fitting with a solvent chemical. **WEAR YOUR GOGGLES SO AS NOT TO GET THIS SOLVENT IN YOUR EYES!**

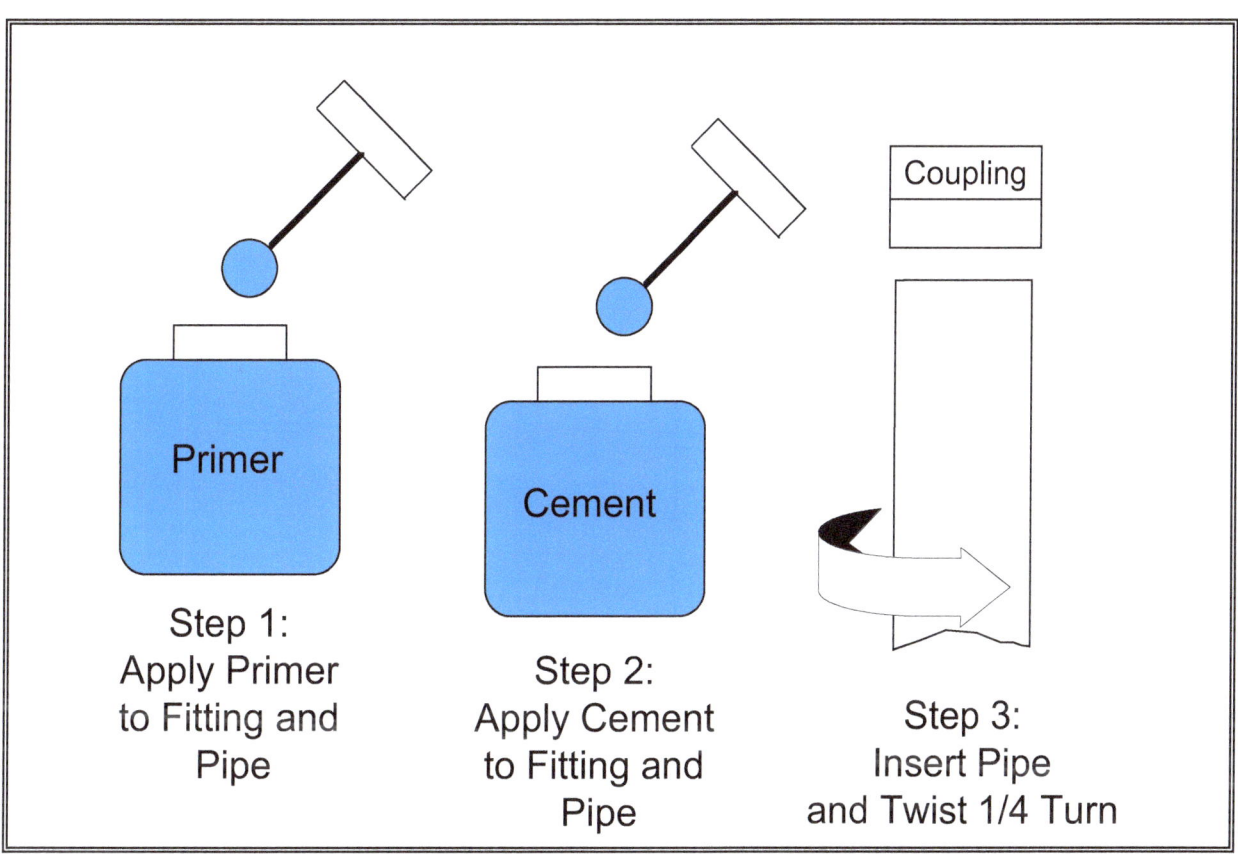

Follow the specific instructions from the supplier of the glue. Once you apply the glue you should be prepared to immediately make the connection. Some general procedures are as follows:

Step 1. After removing debris on the pipe or the fitting, swab a solvent pipe cleaner (primer) on the inside of the fitting and on the outer edge of the pipe where it will be inserted into the fitting.

Step 2. Apply the cement all around the outside edge of the pipe and inside the socket of the fitting that the pipe will slide into.

Step 3. Push the pipe into the fitting as far as you can (1 3/4 inches) and give it a 1/4 turn so the glue smears inside the fitting. The connection will set in just a few minutes, so you can continue on with the next fitting.

Prime and glue fittings

Sequence of Installation

The sequence of installing the pipe is dependent upon the layout of your home. It is generally easier to start at the suction point or riser for the system and work up. Sometimes it is convenient to make the cut through the roof or exterior wall and feed pipe down. Regardless of the approach you use, the following general sequence will apply:

Step 1. Install the main depressurization system, whether it be the plastic sheeting in the crawl space, or the suction holes in the slab or the connection to the sump or drain tile.

Step 2. Install the piping system including the fan and insulation where it passes through cold areas but do not install the rodent screen on the discharge of the pipe until later.

Step 3. Turn on the fan and let the system run for at least five minutes to allow it to blow out any debris that may be in the pipe (e.g., plastic burrs and insulation).

Step 4. Install the rodent screen, a ½-inch or larger hardware screen inserted into end of pipe and screwed into place.

Step 5. Check system for leaks and seal them (see Chapter 8).

Step 6. Install pressure or air flow indicator and active monitor per manufacturer's instructions.

Step 7. Label the pipe on all visible portions. Labels can be purchased, or you can make one of your own. An example label is shown below:

RADON VENT PIPE
DO NOT CUT OR DAMAGE

A fan is attached to this pipe and is located _____.

If this pipe must be removed for maintenance purposes, turn off the fan. Disconnect for the fan is located _____ _____, and is connected to circuit #_____ in the electrical breaker panel. After repairs have beeen made turn fan back on.

*U.S. EPA recommends bi-annual testing.

Step 8. Shut off the system until you have your combustion appliances (hot water heater, furnace) checked for backdrafting with and without the system on. If it backdrafts, get the flue repaired. If it doesn't, install a carbon monoxide monitor, turn the system on and let it run continuously.

Step 9. Re-test radon levels in home (See Chapter 2).

Chapter 8

Sealing to Improve System Performance

What is the Value of Caulking and Sealing?

Planning

Caulking and Sealing

CHAPTER 8 – SEALING TO IMPROVE SYSTEM PERFORMANCE

What is the value of caulking and sealing?

When it was first determined that radon could easily enter into a home via floor cracks, around plumbing penetrations, through block walls, etc., it was theorized you could seal all of these openings to prevent radon from seeping in. It was a good theory, but did not work in practice. Caulking and sealing cannot be relied on as a stand-alone mitigation technique.

The reason you cannot fully seal out radon is because it takes only a very small opening to account for a large amount of radon to enter a home. Many openings are not readily accessible and therefore cannot be adequately sealed. Examples are beneath showers, tubs, toilets, floor-to-wall joints behind finished walls, etc. Granted you can get at some of the openings; however, think of radon like a balloon. If you squeeze it in one place it will bulge in another spot. If you seal at one location, more radon can be forced through the openings you cannot access and seal.

There is still value in caulking and sealing. The more a concrete slab can be sealed for example, the less interior air will be drawn down through the concrete slab by the depressurization system. The reduction of this lost air has many benefits:

- It reduces the potential for backdrafting combustion appliances.
- It improves the vacuum created by the depressurization system.
- It reduces the loss of household air which would otherwise increase the heating or air conditioning load on the home.
- It reduces the electrical cost of running the fan.

All of the reasons listed above make caulking and sealing very desirable and, in the case of the backdrafting concern, mandatory. Seal at the most accessible openings and those which will have the greatest benefit.

Determining which openings and cracks should be sealed is actually very easy. You simply install the depressurization system and turn it on. Using a smoke stick and a flashlight you can see where air is being drawn into the system through openings. Once you have located these points seal them and re-check with the smoke stick.

Although some of the caulking needs will be determined after the radon system is installed, there are some areas that you can visually determine to help plan your material needs. These are:

- The edges and seams of a sub-membrane depressurization system (see Chapter 4).
- The suction points of a sub-slab depressurization system (see Chapter 6).
- The lid of a sump or where the depressurization piping system attaches to a drain (see Chapter 5).
- The floor-to-wall joints that are exposed.
- The concrete slab cracks greater than 1/16 of an inch where it is determined that air from the home is being drawn down through the crack.

Planning

This chapter is devoted to methods of sealing openings in the slab that hurt the operation of an active soil depressurization system. Special sealing activities associated with the specific radon system installed are covered in the chapters describing those systems.

Note: Because caulking materials contain solvents that can generate harmful vapors, proper ventilation must be used during this operation. If you are especially sensitive to chemical fumes, you should seek the assistance of a professional. Read Chapter 10 and the Material Safety Data Sheets for the product you plan to use.

Planning Step 1

Determine what areas will probably need to be sealed.

The areas of greatest need for sealing are ranked as follows, in order of their importance:

1. Floor-to-wall joints in areas nearest the suction point location.
2. Floor cracks greater than 1/16 inches within a 6-foot radius of the suction point.
3. Floor-to-wall joint areas on the far end of slab.
4. Floor cracks greater than 1/16 inches further than 6 feet from suction points.
5. Concrete slab control joint cracks and where separate pours of a concrete slab adjoin each other.
6. Hollow block walls near floor suction points.
7. Floor drains themselves as well as cracks around edges of floor drains.

You should assume that when dealing with an unfinished slab area, items 1 through 5 will be necessary.

Open areas beneath bathtubs and showers are major leakage areas. These often do not need to be addressed if you have planned your system so the suction points are as far as possible from them. If they cause a concern, **silicone** caulk can be used to seal the bases to the floor to minimize the loss and still allow access to the fixtures. However, there may still be significant openings to the soil behind the tub within the wall the tub was constructed against. This is why it is good practice to locate your suction points away from tub block outs, but if you have to address this, you may need to open up an access panel (or create one) to apply expanding foam into the cavities.

When dealing with a finished area where access is limited by firred out walls and carpeting, item 1 is usually not practical. After the system is installed, the reduction of radon achieved and whether or not the drafting of the flues in the home has been affected will determine the need for additional sealing.

Protecting Your Home from Radon

Planning Step 2

Determining what kind of floor-to-wall joint you have.

There are basically three ways that the builder of your home may have formed the joint between the concrete slab and the foundation wall.

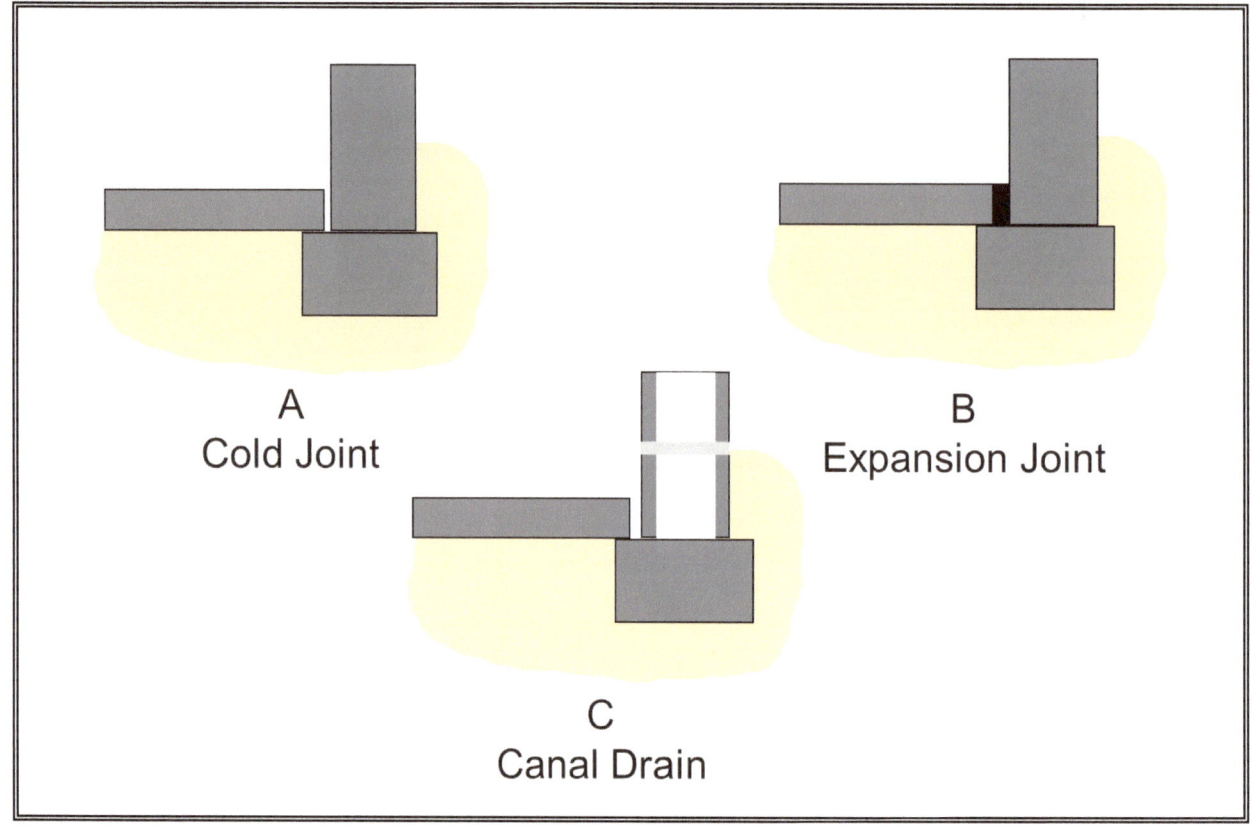

You will need to inspect your floor to determine how your home was built. The above illustration shows the three basic methods:

A. Cold Joint. This is where the concrete slab was poured right up to the wall. As the concrete cured it contracted and pulled slightly away from the wall. Although this may look like a small crack, it can be a major entry route and cause a significant air leak for a suction point located nearby. Sometimes this joint may have been grooved with a corner edging tool that will provide a ¾-inch deep trough at the joint. To seal this area, the joint should be wire brushed and vacuumed and a bead of caulk applied which spans between the floor and the wall. If the joint does not have a groove, plan that a 11-ounce tube of polyurethane caulk will cover 12 linear feet. If there is a groove, plan a tube of caulk to cover 8 feet of perimeter length.

B. Expansion Joint. This is where a ½-inch asphalt-impregnated board is placed against the foundation wall and the concrete is poured up to it. This prevents attachment of the concrete to the wall so the slab can "float." This is often found in areas where expansive soils cause a heaving concern. Plan an 11-ounce tube to cover 8 feet of perimeter length

C. Canal Drains. This is where a 2 by 4-inch board was laid up against the foundation wall and the concrete was poured up to it. After the concrete has set, the board was removed to form a 2-inch channel along the perimeter of the slab. It is designed to either catch water that drains off the face of the wall so it can either drain to the aggregate beneath the slab, or slope towards a sump. If you have one of these, pay particular attention to how this is sealed so as not to restrict the basement's ability to get rid of drainage water.

Chapter 8: Sealing to Improve System Performance

Types of Sealants and Materials to be Used

The types of sealants that you will use will depend upon what you are sealing. Regardless of the type, you must read the material safety data sheets and the manufacturers' instructions.

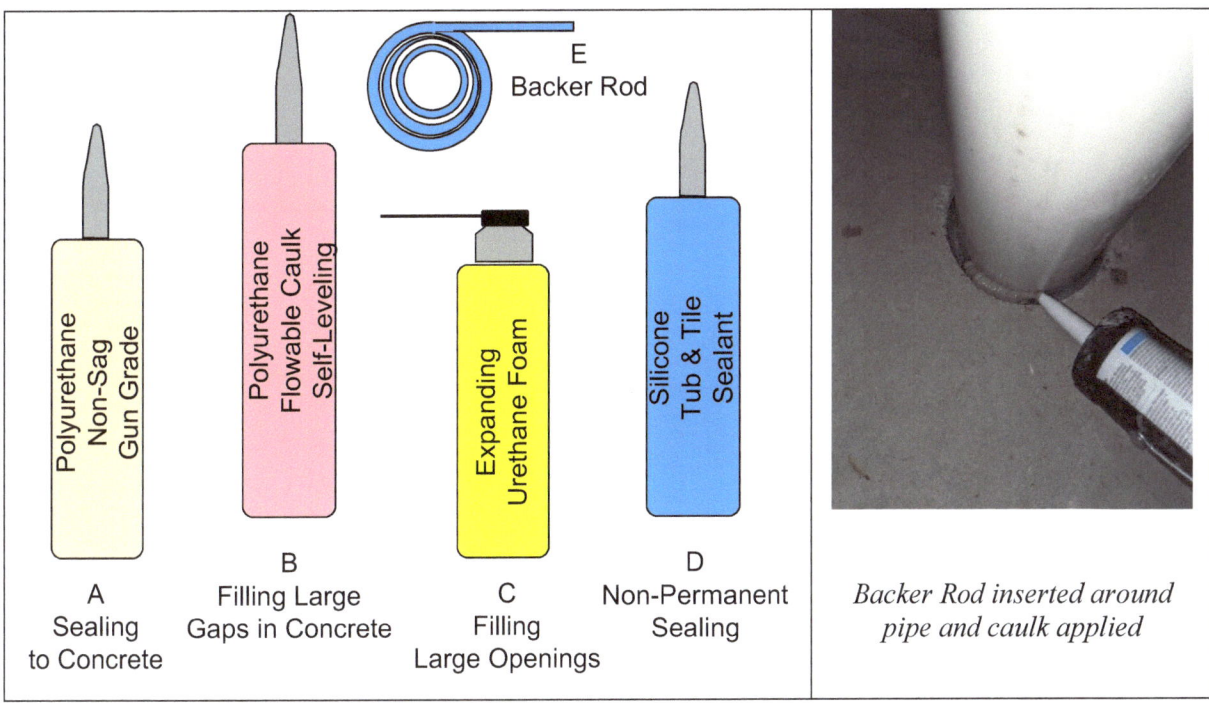

Backer Rod inserted around pipe and caulk applied

Polyurethane caulks are most frequently used. They are used for sealing wherever you want to make a permanent seal. Don't get these tubes wet or they will blow out when used. Keep them in a warm interior location prior to use (cold caulk is hard to use). It comes in two basic forms: non-sag and flowable. Increasingly, low-solvent containing caulks can be obtained which would make the work more pleasant especially in a closed in space like a basement or crawlspace.

A. **Non-sag or gun-grade polyurethane**. This comes in 11-ounce tubes and can be applied with a common caulking gun. Examples for use would be concrete floor cracks, floor-to-wall joints and attaching plastic sheets in sub-membrane systems. This is the most widely used caulk for radon work.

B. **Flowable or self-leveling polyurethane caulk.** This is also used for permanent adhesion to concrete. It is used for sealing large areas such as a canal drain or a concrete control joint. This material flows like ketchup, so the void space must be first filled with a backer rod (E) or gun grade caulk to prevent it from being lost down through the concrete. It requires a large caulking gun.

C. **Canned urethane foams**. This can be purchased and used to fill large void spaces as may be found with a plumbing penetration through a basement wall. Once the material expands, it sets up and can be trimmed with a bread knife.

D. **Silicone caulk.** This is infrequently used but is the caulk of choice for sump covers, toilet bases, etc., where a permanent bond is not desirable. Not used on concrete!

E. **Backer rod.** This is a foam rope-like material for filling large holes or gaps (½ inch or wider) prior to caulking.

Protecting Your Home from Radon

Caulking Floor-to-wall Joints -- Cold Joint and Expansion Joint Types

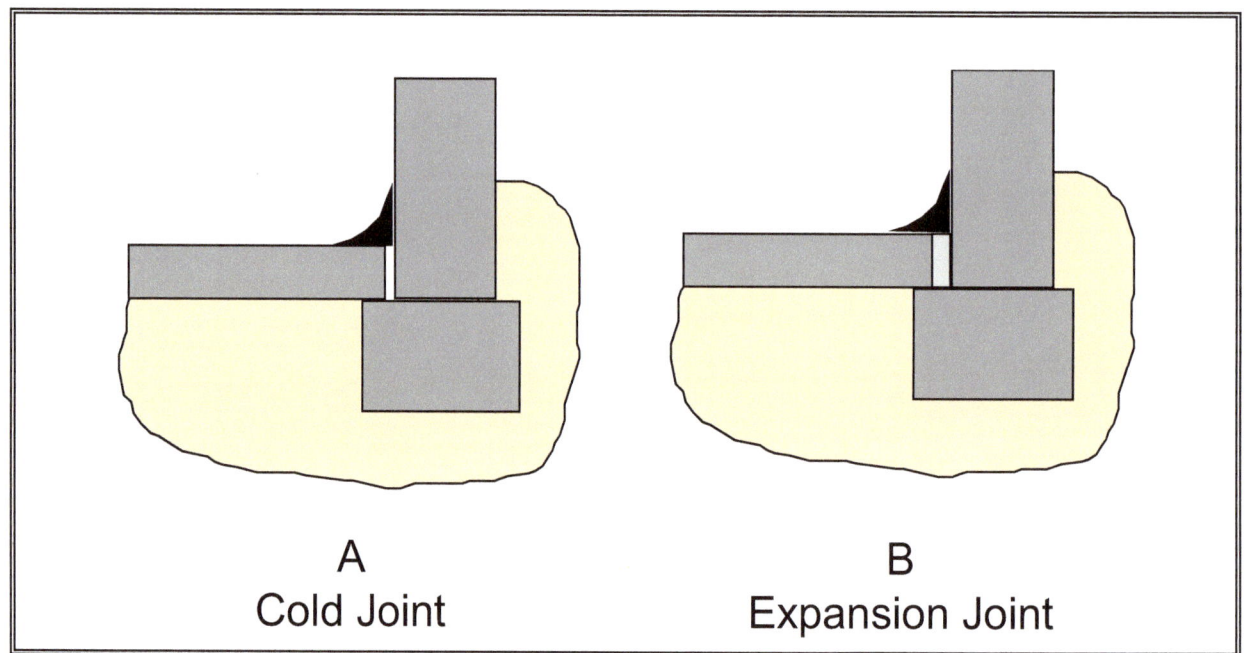

A
Cold Joint

B
Expansion Joint

Cold Joints.

Wire brush the joint to remove loose dirt and concrete spatter. Be sure to brush down into the crack and at least an inch out onto the floor and 1 inch up the wall. *VENTILATE THE WORK AREA* (see later in this chapter and Safety Chapter 10). Use a caulking gun to apply a thick bead of caulk along the joint. *Note:* **You should be applying enough caulk, so an 11-ounce tube goes no further than 12 feet.** Take a spent tube of caulk and run the butt end of it along the joint so the caulk is smoothed onto the floor and up the wall about 1/2 inch. BE CAREFUL - THIS IS STICKY, STRINGY STUFF AND WILL GET EVERYWHERE IF YOU ARE NOT CAREFUL.

Expansion Joints.

If the joint sticks up above the concrete more than 1/8 inch, cut it off with a utility knife or a hammer and chisel. DO NOT TRY TO POUND IT DOWN (it will pop back up and break the seal). Don't use a grinding wheel either unless you enjoy big messes. Use a utility knife. Brush the top of the expansion joint and at least an inch out onto the floor and 1 inch up the wall. *VENTILATE THE WORK AREA* (see later in this chapter and Safety Chapter 10). Use a caulking gun to apply a thick bead of caulk along the top of the joint. *Note:* **You should be applying enough caulk, so an 11-ounce tube goes no further than eight feet.** Take a spent tube of caulk and run the butt end of it along the joint so the caulk is smoothed onto the floor and up the wall about ½ inch. BE CAREFUL THIS IS STICKY, STRINGY STUFF AND WILL GET EVERYWHERE IF YOU ARE NOT CAREFUL.

After applying this material be careful not to step in it or allow children or pets into the area for at least 24 hours. It will take several days for it to fully cure, but it should be tack free after 24 hours.

The important thing to remember with either type of joint to be sealed is that you should apply the caulk in a smooth consistent bead - and do not skimp. It is not a problem if you apply too much since the excess will be removed when you "tool it" with the back of the caulk tube.

Caulking Floor-to-Wall Joints -- Canal Drains

The sealing of a perimeter canal drain is not a trivial affair. The key thing to remember is that this channel was placed there to collect water and that you should not impact this feature. To do this, it is important there is a channel between the top of the slab and the caulking. There should be a relief area beneath the caulking to allow for the water in the hollow block wall to drain to the sub-slab aggregate. Therefore, the caulk will be suspended between the top of the slab and the footing. This is accomplished by the use of a backer rod. A backer rod is a flexible close cell styrene material that can be purchased from most building supply stores. It comes in several widths and lengths.

The canal drain should be cleaned out with a vacuum cleaner. The backer rod should be squeezed down into the canal. Buy the backer rod in a diameter that is slightly larger than the width of the canal. This causes the rod to fit snuggly into the canal. Do not push it all of the way down. Use gun grade polyurethane caulk to seal where ends of backer rod meet at corners.

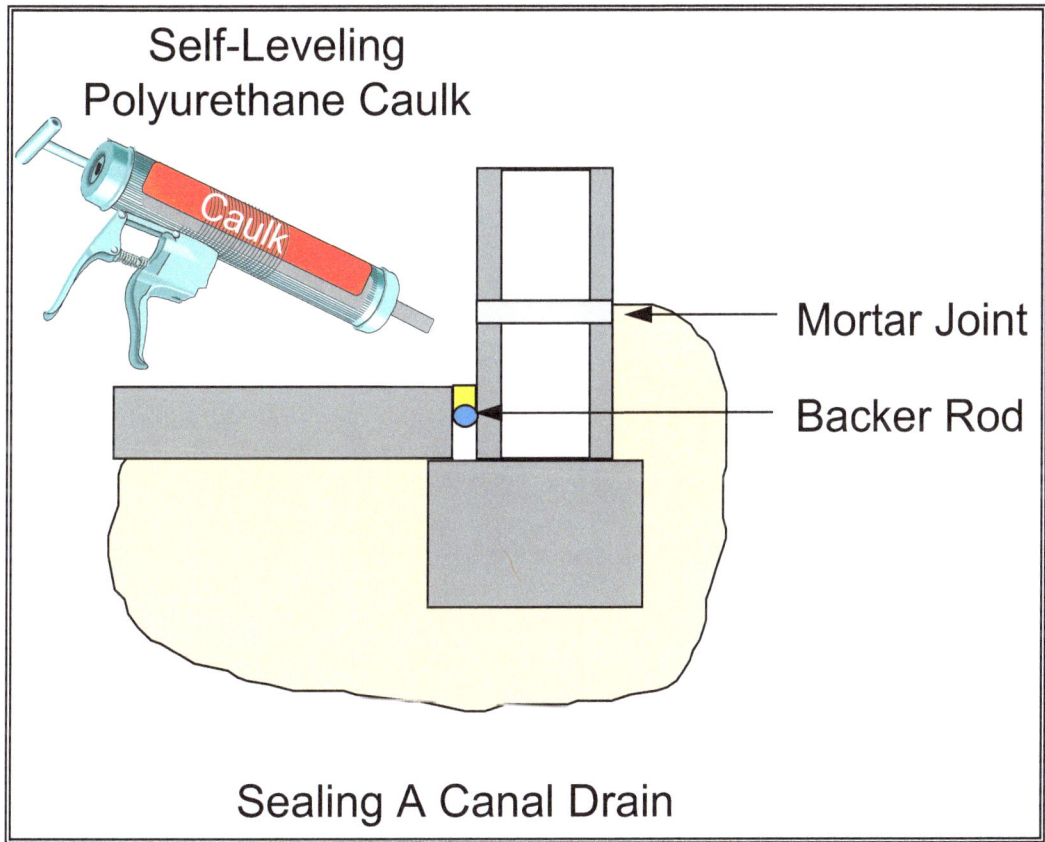

VENTILATE THE AREA. Apply flowable polyurethane caulk to the area above the backer rod. The flowable caulk is a liquid. It will flow to the edges of the canal on top of the backer rod. Make sure you do not fill up the entire channel between the backer rod and the top of the concrete. Leave at least a ½-inch channel for water to collect. Make sure this channel is directed towards a floor drain or sump in the basement.

Sealing canal drains is tricky and may warrant the hiring of a contractor who is familiar with this operation.

Protecting Your Home from Radon

Finding leaks.

After the system has been turned on, a suction will be created in the soil under and around the home. This vacuum catches radon and other soil gases that would have entered the home if a mitigation system had not been installed. The better the vacuum is, the better the radon reduction will be. Finding and sealing leaks through a slab can produce a better vacuum. You should check slab cracks, plumbing penetrations, etc., to see if air is being drawn down beneath the slab. The use of smoke saves a lot of time and expense in determining what should be caulked. Simply, if the system does not pull air down -- don't caulk it. Of course, you have to do this after the system is installed. Plan on purchasing a few extra tubes of caulk beyond what you need for the floor-to-wall joints, so you will have enough for this touch up sealing.

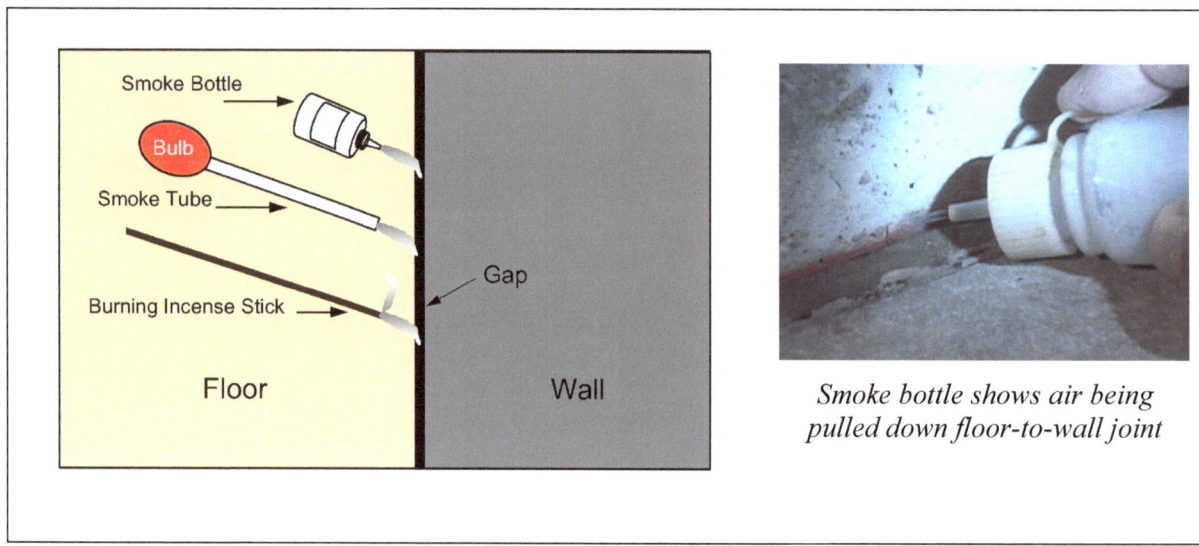

Smoke bottle shows air being pulled down floor-to-wall joint

Sometimes you can hear air being drawn down through a leak. However, it is best to use some type of smoke generator to detect air being drawn down through the leak. The graphic above shows three different types of smoke generators that can be used for this purpose. A flashlight should be used to help see the direction that the smoke moves. If it goes down through an opening, use some caulk to reseal the opening until smoke is no longer seen to flow down. Typically, polyurethane caulk is used to seal openings such as concrete cracks and floor-to-wall joint areas. However, where a seal may need to be broken in the future, the sump lid for example, silicone is to be used. Silicone will allow for future access to a plumbing system like a sump lid, whereas polyurethane will not.

Burning Incense Stick: An incense stick or a "punk" can be purchased and when lit it burns slowly and produces a light smoke. This can be held close to a suspected leak area to see if the smoke is drawn down. If so, seal it with caulk. Because the smoke is warm, it will want to rise on its own; therefore, it is as not as sensitive for finding leaks as the other devices. To compensate for this, put the burning end as close to the opening as possible and shine a flashlight on the smoke and look for small wisps of smoke being drawn down.

Smoke Bottles: These are devices that can be ordered from radon catalog supply houses or sometimes from a heating and ventilating equipment supplier. They are filled with a fine powder that when the plastic bottle is squeezed from a bottle and will float in the direction of air flow. These devices are typically more sensitive than the incense stick and more likely to find leaks. Use a flashlight with these devices as well.

Floor Cracks, Cold Joints and Control Joints

Floor cracks generally do not cause a significant concern unless they are close to the suction point or are very wide (greater than 1/16 of an inch). Even cracks that are greater than 1/16 of an inch may be acceptable if the crack forms a "V" in the concrete. A "V" crack is wide on the top of the concrete and narrow on the bottom so there is not a large pathway for air leakage. An exception to this would be where no reinforcing wire was used in the concrete (areas where there are no provisions for frost or seismic tremors in the local building codes). In these areas, when the concrete cracks, it makes a wide crack all the way through the concrete and present a large air leakage area, which will need to be sealed. You may not be able to tell how bad a crack is until the system is turned on and a smoke stick is used to check it (see previous page.)

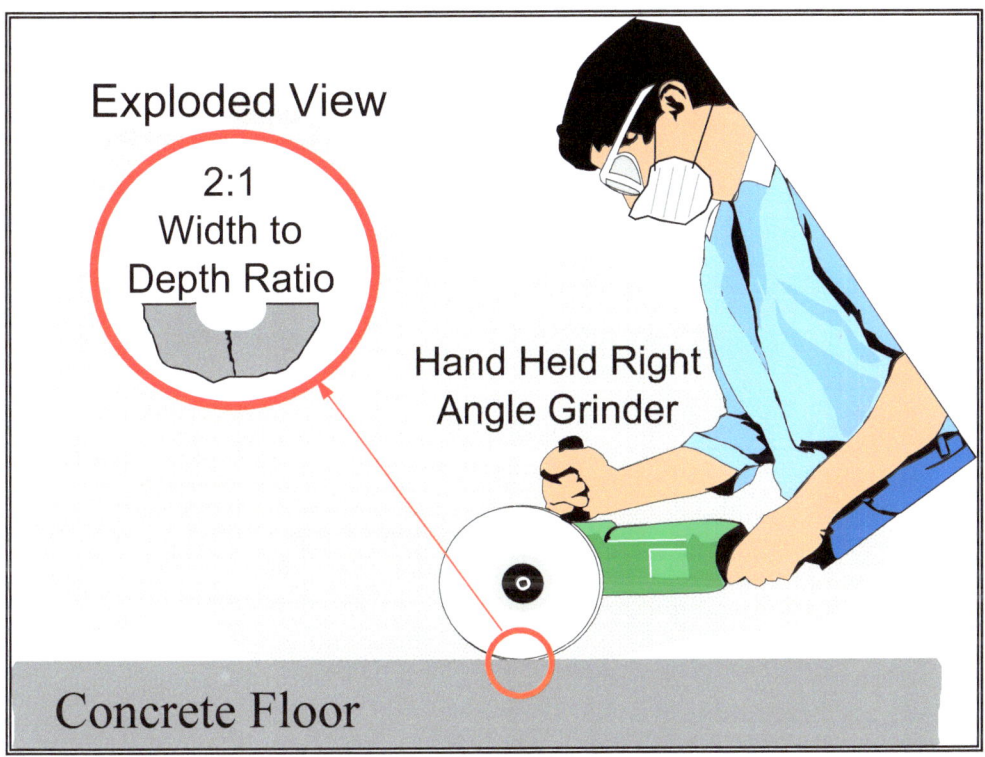

If you do decide to seal the crack, merely forcing caulk into the crack is a waste of time as it will not last very long. You need to grind out the crack with a hand grinder. BE AWARE THIS WILL CREATE A LOT OF DUST. You should have a shop vacuum wand near the grinding wheel to catch as much as you can. You should cover furniture with drop cloths to protect it. You will have to wear gloves, goggles, a respirator, and hearing protection. Grind out the crack to provide a clean surface for the caulk to adhere to and to give it the proper adhesion profile as shown in the exploded view above.

After the crack has been ground out, ventilate the area and apply a non-flowing polyurethane caulk into the crack and smooth it out flush with the top of the concrete using a scrap of cardboard or putty knife. Wipe the excess up off the floor with rags. Don't allow children or pets into the area for at least 24 hours to prevent this from being tracked around the house.

This same approach would be applied to cold joints where separate slabs are poured together. Also, if you have control joints in the concrete (straight ½-inch grooves in the slab) the method for sealing them is identical except that you **do not need to grind** the joint. Just vacuum out the control joint and apply the caulk.

Protecting Your Home from Radon

Hollow Block Walls

Hollow block walls, if open on top, can be significant air leakage points. After turning the soil depressurization system on, use a smoke stick at the top of the wall to see if air is being drawn down. If this occurs, you may have to seal the void space on the top row of blocks. This is especially true if so much inside air is drawn out that the combustion appliances backdraft or the suction pressure beneath the slab is too weak to adequately reduce the radon level. Sealing these areas can be difficult. The illustration below shows four different methods depending upon whether the sill plate (the board that sets on top of the block that the floor joists rest upon) covers the entire block or not, and whether you can access the block tops.

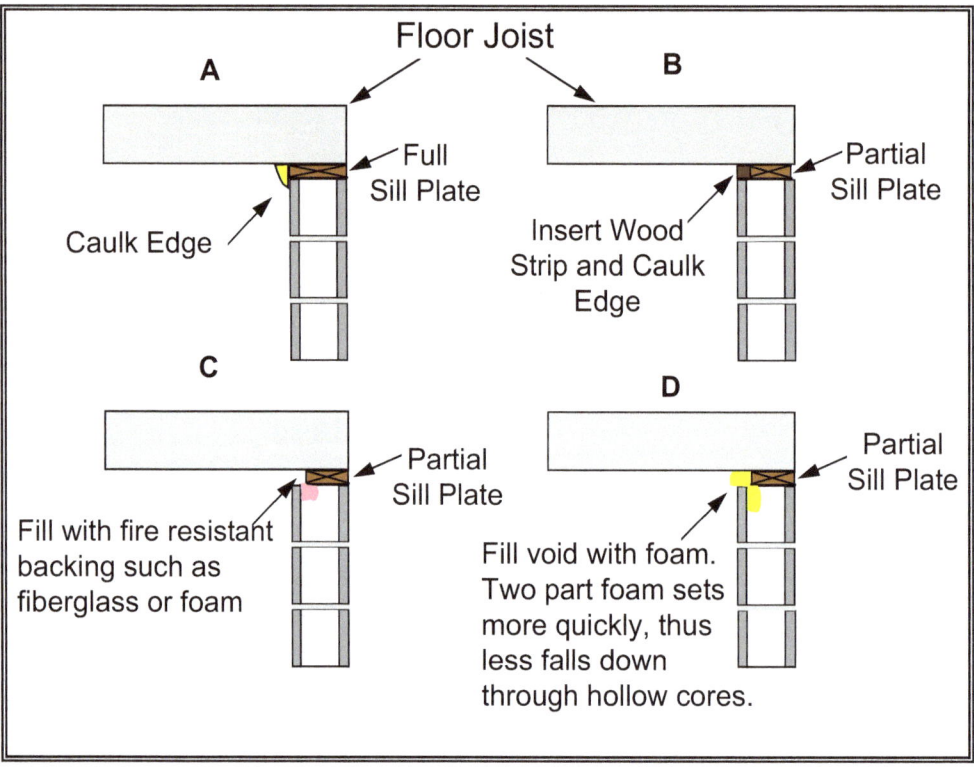

Illustration A: If the sill plate spans the width of the block, wire brush the point where the sill plate and the block meet. Then run a thin bead of polyurethane caulk along the edge. Use your smoke stick to find leaks, seal, and re-check when done.

Illustration B: If the sill plate only spans a part of the width of the block, cut a board of appropriate width and height and place over the gap not covered by the sill plate. Caulk the edge as in A above.

Illustration C: As an alternative to B, you can stuff the top of the block with fiberglass insulation to act as a backing and use expanding urethane foam to seal off the open area.

Illustration D: As an alternative to B and C, where the walls have been finished and you cannot easily get to block tops, purchase a fast-setting two-part urethane foam and shoot it into the block tops either from inside the home or through the exterior side of the block after 3/8-inch holes are drilled into each hollow course from the outside. If you drill holes into the block from the outside, make sure you drill them above grade and seal them with polyurethane caulk when you are done.

USE VENTILATION WHEN USING THESE SEALANTS, SEE CHAPTER 10.

Chapter 8: Sealing to Improve System Performance

Large Wall Openings, Plumbing Penetrations and Wall Cracks

Other places that you should check with your smoke stick to find air leaks are wall and floor penetrations for utility piping.

If the gap is small around the pipe, wire brush it and caulk around the penetration with polyurethane caulk. Make sure you ventilate the area and follow the safety precautions discussed in Chapter 10.

If the gap is large, greater than ½ inch, you will have to stuff it first with backer rod and caulk it with polyurethane. Alternatively, you can apply expanding urethane foam into the opening. Remember this material expands to three times the volume applied. It will grow into the void that you want to seal off. Much of it will expand into the room. After it sets up you can cut the excess off with a bread knife.

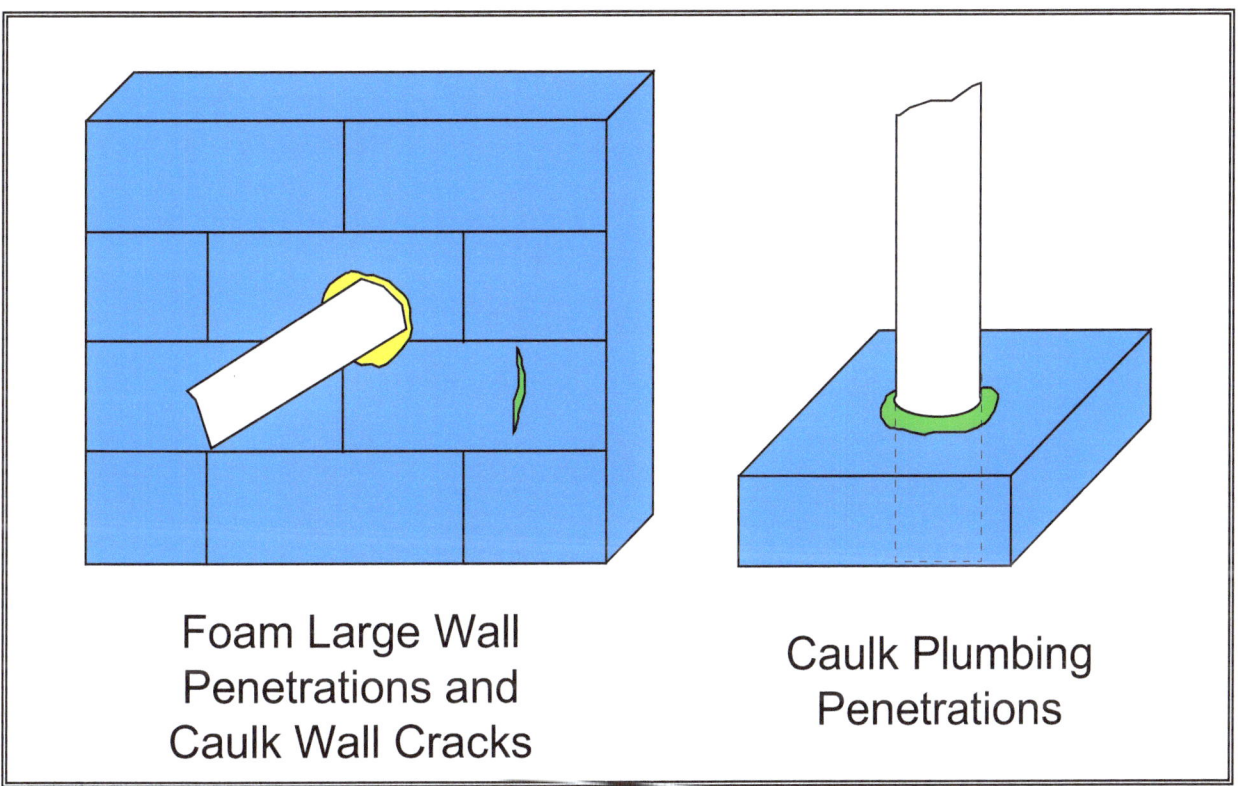

You may want to check wall cracks to see if they are drawing air into them as well. If so, caulk them as you would a floor crack (grind it first).

Floor and wall coatings offer little value for reducing air leakage. The most economical approach is to find the holes and caulk them, rather than covering an entire wall or floor with a material that will crack as the wall moves.

Polyurethane caulk being applied around plumbing penetration

Floor Drains

At times, air leakage can occur around and down floor drains. Use a smoke stick to determine this. Some floor drains have slip joints beneath the drain in the soil. Once a vacuum is applied to the soil, air from inside of the house could be lost. This would especially be true if a suction point was located near a sub-slab plumbing pipe.

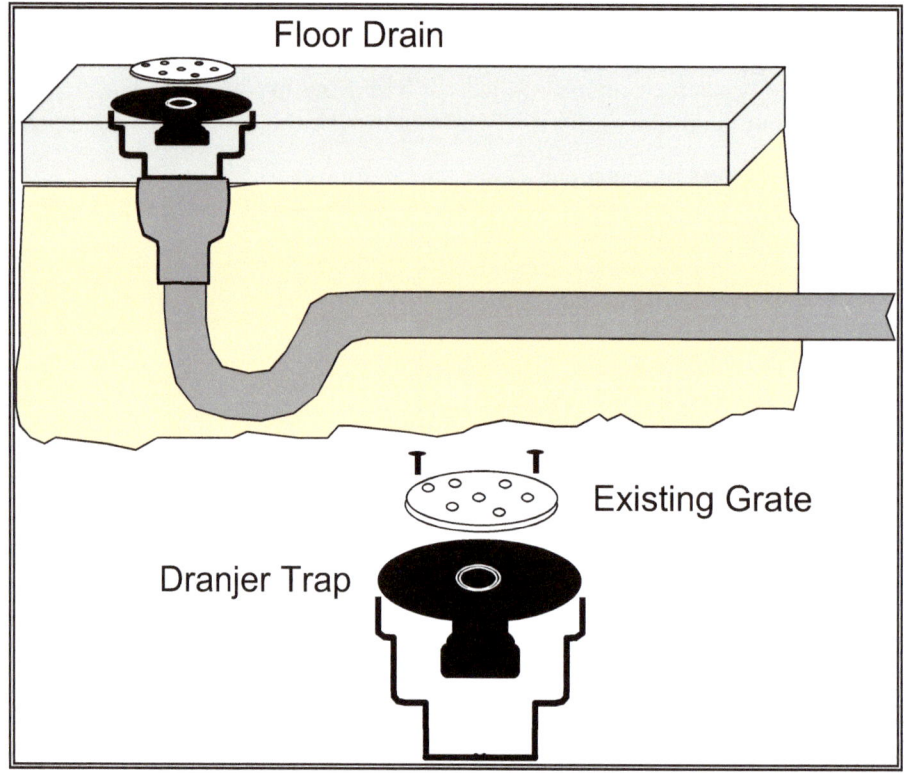

Floor drains can be sealed with a proprietary device called a Dranjer. It consists of a rubber sheet with a drain in the center. Connected to the pipe is a small cup trap. Water can still drain from the floor through the cup trap, but the trap forms a water seal to prevent air passage. It is installed by removing the grate over the floor drain and setting the trap into it. The excess rubber is trimmed off and the grate screwed back down onto the rubber seal.

Note: DO NOT SIMPLY BLOCK OFF THE FLOOR DRAIN WITHOUT A MEANS SUCH AS THIS TO ALLOW WATER TO FLOW INTO IT.

Another use for these water traps, and others like them, are for sump lids. If your interior water drainage system was designed to allow water to weep down walls and across the floor to a sump, and you have sealed the sump with a lid, a trapped floor drain should be installed on the lid to allow for water to get into the sump. This would be the case if you have had to seal off a canal drain as was described earlier in this chapter.

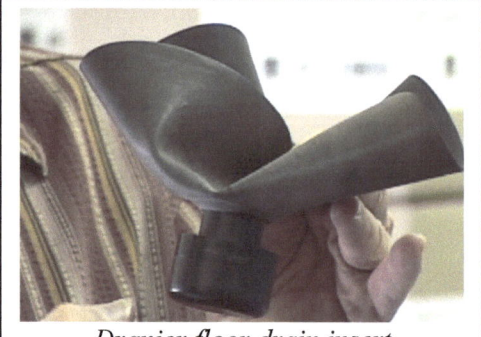

Dranjer floor drain insert

Caulking and Sealing

The following is a list that you can use for determining the materials that you may need for sealing air leakage points. Note that this material would be in addition to the materials that you may need for the actual active soil depressurization system itself.

Area	Item	Feet	Ft/tube	√
Safety	Goggles/safety glasses			
	Dust mask			
	Nitrile disposable gloves			
	First aid kit			
	Ventilation fan			
	Flashlight			
	Coveralls or old clothing			
Material	**Gun grade polyurethane caulk**			
	Perimeter expansion joint		8	
	Cold joints (perimeter or where slabs adjoin)		12	
	Control joints		10	
	Floor cracks		12	
	Wall cracks		12	
	Flowable caulk			
	Perimeter canal drain 2 inch by ½ inch volume		10	
	Backer rod			
	Perimeter canal drain			
	Other large openings (oversize so it squishes in)			
	Silicone caulk			
	For sealing around bathtubs, etc.		12	
	Expanding foam			
	Holes in walls, etc. (one can will expand to 350 cubic inches)			
	Drain trap			
Tools	Smoke stick			
	Hand grinder with composite or diamond wheel suitable for concrete			
	Caulking gun			
	Wire brush			
	Shop vacuum			
	Drop clothes			
	Broom & dustpan			
	Trash container			
	Rags			
	Utility knife			

Protecting Your Home from Radon

Caulking Photographs

The following photographs illustrate the steps for caulking. A video of this can be seen on the CERTI's YouTube site at: Center for Environmental Research and Technology - YouTube

- *Vacuum up loose dirt*
- *Apply thick bead of caulk (Expansion Joint)*
- *Tool caulk up wall and onto floor, covering joint*
- *Tool caulk into cold joints*
- *Apply caulk to cracked control joins*
- *Tool caulk into control joints flush or just below top of slab*

Summary

Relative to the installation of the caulking and sealant material, the only advice that can be provided is:

- Not all openings need to be sealed. Seal the ones that show smoke being drawn down.
- Ventilate the area very well when applying the caulking.
- Use polyurethane caulking unless you are sealing something that you may have to remove in the future such as a toilet base. In that case, use silicone caulk.
- Carefully follow the manufacturer's instructions and obtain **and read** the Material Safety Data Sheets before proceeding (see Chapter 10).
- Keep kids and animals away from caulking until it cures so they do not track it around the house.

Chapter 9

Combining Radon Mitigation Systems Together and Alternate Mitigation Techniques

Phasing Installations

Tying Multiple Systems Together

Other Mitigation Techniques

CHAPTER 9 – COMBINING RADON MITIGATION SYSTEMS TOGETHER AND ALTERNATE MITIGATION TECHNIQUES

If your home is built completely over a crawl space, or completely over a basement, or completely as a slab-on-grade home, the techniques that have been described in Chapters 4 through 8 can be applied as described. However, there are times that a house has both a crawl space and a basement, or both a crawl space and a slab. How do you approach these more complex foundation designs?

The good news is the specific systems previously described can be installed and connected to a **common depressurization system and fan**. This will save considerable cost compared to a separate piping and fan system for each separate foundation area. However, to tie these different mitigation systems together, you will need to plan your piping accordingly.

Phasing Installations

The question that often arises in dealing with homes, which may need a multiple approach, is: Do I need to install all of these systems in order to reduce my radon level? The answer is often no, but the answer is sometimes yes. There are no good methods for predicting this. However, there is an approach used by professional mitigators to minimize the amount of unnecessary work done called **"phasing."**

Phasing is where the individual system that has the greatest potential for reducing radon is installed first. The system is then fine-tuned with as much sealing as is reasonable (see Chapter 8). Next, a short-term test device is placed in the home utilizing the methods described in Chapter 2 to determine how well the first system has worked. If the test shows an acceptable level, you are done. If the result is not acceptable, proceed to the next method or hire a radon contractor until you are satisfied with the post mitigation results.

The key to phasing is to plan your depressurization piping in a manner that will allow you to easily extend it to the next system that may be installed. The other key to phasing systems is to determine which single technique will provide the biggest reduction. The following table of relative ranking should provide some guidance as to what to do first.

> **Relative Ranking of Effectiveness of Reduction Techniques in Homes with Complex Foundation Designs**
>
> 1. Crawl Space Depressurization
> 2. Sump Depressurization
> 3. Foundation Drains
> 4. Sub-Slab Suction Points

The relative ranking of these reduction techniques are guidelines and not hard and fast rules. A crawl space that is attached to a basement generally represents a large entry point for radon and is an area that always has to be treated to adequately reduce radon. In some cases, a vacuum drawn under a plastic sheet in a crawl space that has been sealed well will draw radon from beneath an adjacent slab, even when the slab is at a lower elevation than the crawl space.

An interior sump or a foundation drain approach will provide a better distribution of the applied vacuum under a slab than one or two suction points in a slab. On the other hand, digging an eight-foot hole down the side of a basement foundation may be more than one wants to take on and a sub-slab approach would be more practical.

If there is no crawl space or sump system a sub-slab depressurization system is an obvious choice. The fact that it is listed last should not diminish your confidence in this measure. It is very effective but may require more than one suction point to accomplish the full reduction.

Tying Multiple Systems Together:

To make two techniques work in concert with each other, you need to plan your piping system to be able to depressurize both systems. If you are phasing the systems by installing one, then testing to see if the other system will be needed, you will need to plan the piping system for the first system to allow for easy connection to a second system. If you are phasing the systems, you should install a tee and a cap to allow for the potential connection of the second system.

There are some tricks that will make the connection of multiple foundations a little easier. These techniques are based on experience and the concept that radon can be withdrawn from beneath a foundation horizontally just as easily as it can be drawn vertically. The following examples may provide some help in designing your own combination system.

Combining Sump and Sub-Membrane Depressurization Systems

Typically, when a home has both a sump and a crawl space, the sump is next to the wall separating the two areas. This will make tying a crawl space system to a sump system rather easy. If the sump is on the far end of the basement, you can still tie them together as is shown in the illustration below it is just that the horizontal piping will be longer.

Both systems are to be installed with their own separate risers from the plastic sheeting and from the sump lid. The two risers should be connected by way of the simplest and most direct pathway. Any horizontal run should be sloped to either or both risers (i.e., towards the sump or towards the crawl space).

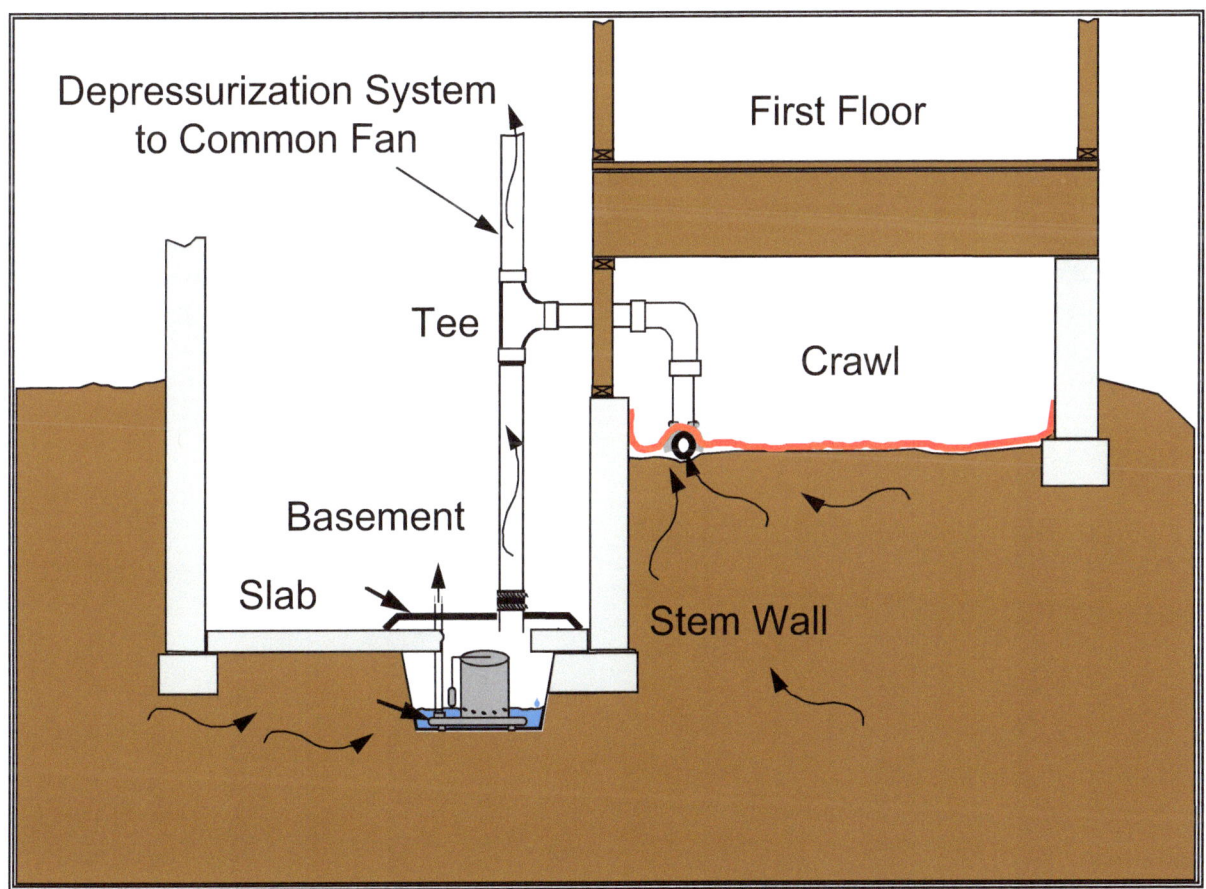

Protecting Your Home from Radon

Combining Drain Tile and Sub-Membrane Depressurization Systems

If you have a home built partially on a crawl space with the remainder on a slab, and there is an exterior foundation drain (as is shown in the figure below), you may be able to treat both areas by combining a sub-membrane system in the crawl space with the exterior drain system. The illustration below shows how this can be done by connecting the sub-membrane system and the drain-tile depressurization system to the same pipe that is then routed to a common depressurization fan. This approach can provide excellent coverage of both the slab and the crawl space areas.

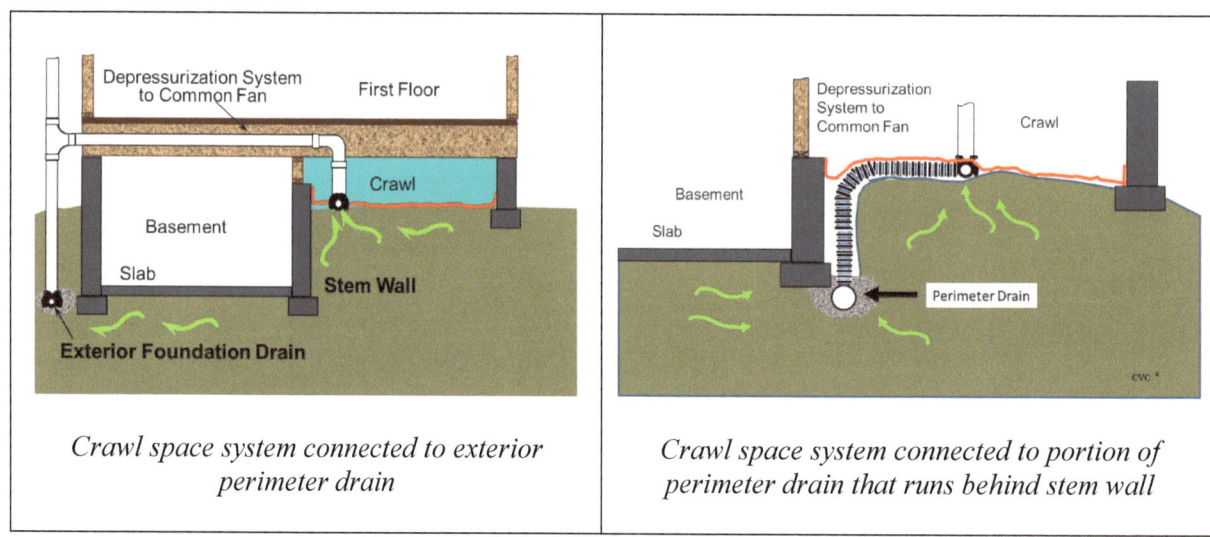

Crawl space system connected to exterior perimeter drain

Crawl space system connected to portion of perimeter drain that runs behind stem wall

Another variation of this method would be to tie into the exterior drain system from within the crawl space rather than from outside of the house. This would be possible when the loop of perforated drainpipe was installed along the lower foundation, which, in many cases, would be along the footing that separates the slab area from the crawl space area. This means you could dig down along the wall separating the basement from the crawl space (from inside of the crawl space) and find the foundation drain. After you find it, you can connect the drain to your crawl space system and again route it to a common depressurization system. Although tying into the foundation drain requires some digging from within the crawl space it has the obvious advantage of reducing the amount of piping that is through the basement.

Chapter 9: Combining Approaches

Combining Sub-Membrane and Sub-Slab Depressurization Systems: Method A

If there is both a crawl space and a basement or a crawl space and a slab-on-grade area that does not have a sump or a foundation drain system, consider installing a sub-membrane depressurization system in the crawl space first. Often the vacuum applied to the plastic sheeting on the crawl space will extend well under the adjacent slab. This extension of the vacuum could eliminate the need for adding a suction point in the slab area. Install the sub-membrane system first then re-test before you install the sub-slab suction point. This is where a phasing process for installing multiple systems is helpful.

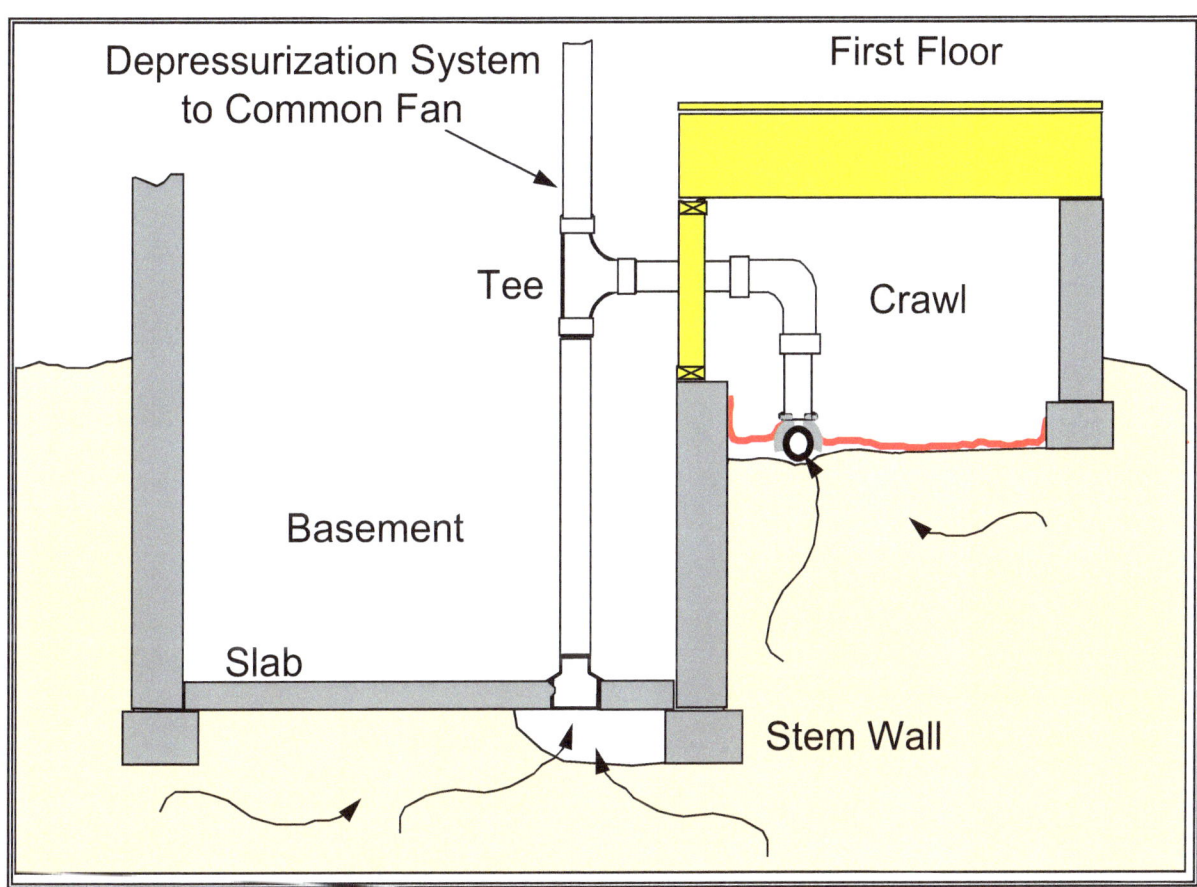

If the sub-membrane system alone does not adequately reduce radon levels, you should go ahead and install a sub-slab suction point which can be tied to your sub-membrane piping system as is shown above or in the variation shown on the next page. The method above involves the use of an actual suction hole placed in the basement slab. Note that depending on the permeability of the soil beneath your slab you may need to install more than one suction point. See Chapter 6 on how to determine this.

Protecting Your Home from Radon

Combining Sub-Membrane and Sub-Slab Depressurization Systems: Method B

Frequently, the area adjacent to the crawl space is finished and would not look good with a suction point in it (other than as a conversation piece). If this is the case, the suction point for the slab area might be installed in the same manner as the sub-footer suction point discussed in Chapter 6. This keeps all the piping in the crawl space and out of the finished area. As illustrated below, the piping to the sub-slab area is the same perforated, corrugated polyethylene pipe that is installed under the plastic membrane. In this instance the piping is extended into an excavation under the adjacent slab.

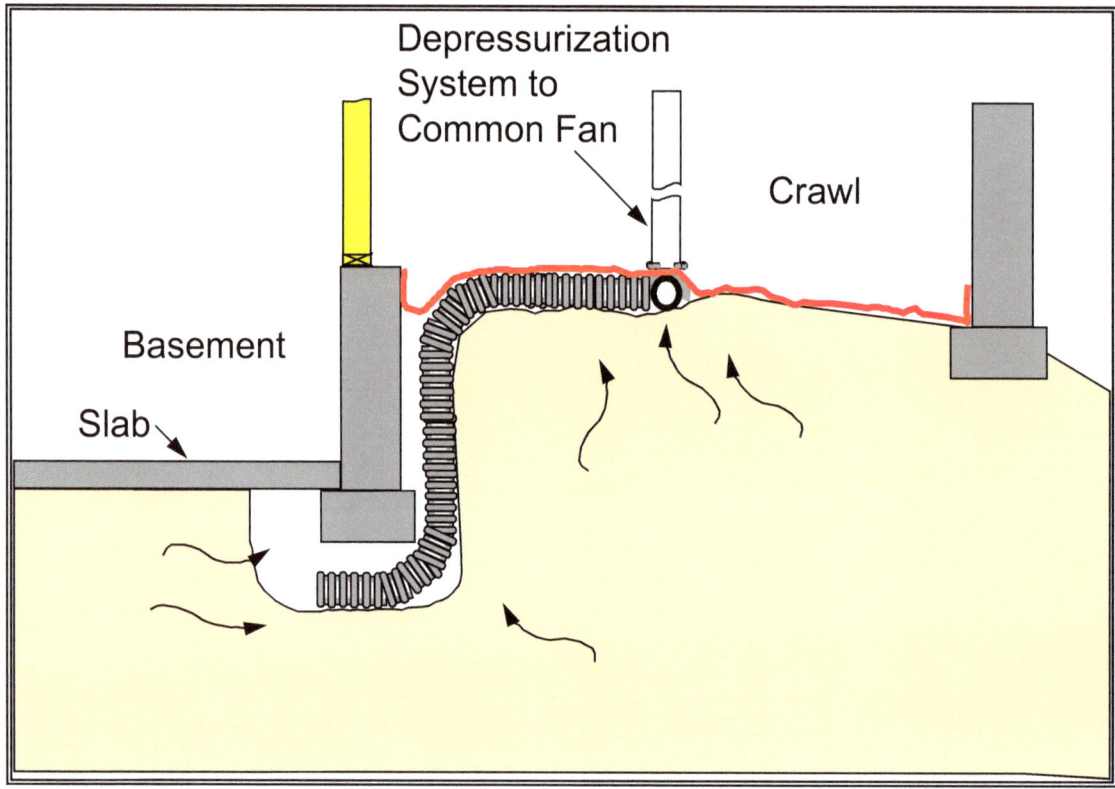

We know that the idea of digging a hole from inside the crawl space sounds a little fatiguing but realize the dirt inside the crawl space along side of the foundation wall separating the crawl space from the adjacent basement is typically fairly loose. This is because this dirt is generally not compacted during the construction process. Provided you have enough room to work in the crawl space, you can dig down along the side of the wall and beneath the footing. Hollow out a pit beneath the footing that extends beyond the inside edge of the footing. This will significantly improve the system's ability to impact the slab area.

Extend the 3-inch flexible perforated pipe that you installed beneath the plastic sheeting for your crawl space system into the pit you dug out from beneath the adjacent slab. You can replace the dirt you removed during the excavation, but it is not necessary, since the plastic sheeting within the crawl space will provide the necessary air seal. If you do replace the dirt, make sure you do not fill the pit beneath the slab and reduce the sub-footer suction pits efficiency.

Note, that you could install the crawl space system first, and then test the home to determine if the crawl space system was able to adequately reduce the radon in the home. If not, you could always go back into the crawl space, cut the plastic, dig the pit, extend your pipe beneath the slab, and reseal your plastic with plastic scraps and caulk.

Other Mitigation Techniques

There are mitigation techniques that can be used other than those detailed in this book. They are techniques that are generally used in the rare case when the basic Crawl, Drainage, or Sub-Slab Systems do not fully reduce the radon. They are also used if there are other problems with the house such as other indoor pollutants or water drainage problems. These approaches have been left out of this book, either because their installation is more complex than that which can be handled by the typical homeowner, or they could present health risks or high operating costs if <u>not properly</u> installed. This is where a professional mitigator is most valuable. Those who have been trained and are nationally certified are instructed in the peculiar aspects of these other systems. See Chapter 12 regarding tips on selecting contractors.

If the homeowner wishes to obtain information on this, the Colorado Technical Guidance "Measuring and Mitigating Radon in Colorado" may be helpful (https://cdphe.colorado.gov/radon-and-real-estate)

The following is a list of some of the techniques that require specialized skills:

Method	Advantages	Disadvantages
Heat Recovery Ventilation	• Can dilute other indoor air contaminants. • Applicable when levels of radon are 8 pCi/L or less.	• Can add additional cost to heating and cooling bills. • Air flows into and out of home should be equal or balance with dampers.
Block Wall Depressurization	• Can reduce radon infiltration by creating a vacuum on the block walls.	• High potential for backdrafting of combustion appliances if the openings in the block tops and sides are not well sealed.
Baseboard Depressurization	• Can reduce radon by creating a vacuum within a channel built over the floor-wall joint. • Can be used for basement de-watering as well.	• Difficult to install properly. If not done right both back drafting and drainage system problems can occur.
House Pressurization	• Can reduce radon by blowing air into home.	• Can result in high heating and cooling bills and introduce allergens into home. • Can introduce moisture into home or force moist air into exterior walls where it can condense and create big problems. • ***<u>Because of the two reasons above be very careful with this approach if it is suggested to you.</u>***
Basement Pressurization	• Can reduce radon by blowing air from upstairs into basement.	• Can backdraft fireplaces and combustion appliances as well as increase utility costs. • Can force humid air through rim joists and cause freezing in walls. • ***<u>Because of the two reasons above be very careful with this approach if it is suggested to you.</u>***

Method	Advantages	Disadvantages
Soil Pressurization	• Can reduce radon by blowing air from outside to beneath a slab in order to force the radon away from the house.	• Can sometimes increase the radon entry into the building. • Its effectiveness can vary with frost or rain content of soil around the house. • The soil depressurization techniques described in this manual are generally more reliable than soil pressurization.
Crawl Space Depressurization	• Reduces radon in home by using a fan to suck air out of the crawl space without the use of a plastic membrane. • Used most often with inaccessible crawlspaces.	• Can cause significant house air to be drawn down into crawl space. • The potential for backdrafting is high with these systems and can increase utility bills.

After the active soil depressurization techniques described in this book (which comprise more than 90% of the mitigation approaches used today), the heat recovery ventilator is the most popular. Its application is best suited in conjunction with addressing other indoor air quality concerns or when the active soil depressurization systems have reduced the radon to very near 4 pCi/L and just a little dilution air (from a heat recovery ventilator) is needed to bring the radon down to below 4 pCi/L.

In any event, do not attempt the techniques described in the previous table unless you have consulted with a professional radon mitigator and have taken into consideration other impacts systems like this can have on the comfort and energy efficiency of your home.

Chapter 10

General Safety Precautions and Backdrafting Concerns

Basic Personal Protective Gear

Work Area Ventilation

Other Hazards

Backdrafting

CHAPTER 10 – GENERAL SAFETY PRECAUTIONS & BACKDRAFTING CONCERNS

Performing the repairs described in this manual will expose a person to many risks. Using power drills, hammer drills, digging holes, working in confined spaces, and working with solvent-containing caulks and glues present many injury opportunities. The risks are greatly minimized if you use caution and do not attempt anything you are not comfortable with or experienced in doing. This chapter is designed to point out some of the potential hazards and to offer advice as to how to avoid them. Most accidents occur because of poor planning and haste. Think first, assemble your materials, and take your time. Remember that although radon levels are certainly a concern, they present a long-term exposure risk and do not require that you take immediate and precipitous action. In other words, you can take a little time to plan out your strategy. Don't ignore radon but you don't need to move out of your home until the radon is reduced. A few general pieces of advice are:

1. Plan and design your system at least two weeks prior to performing the work. It will take a couple weeks to obtain the special materials needed.

2. Assemble everything before starting - especially your safety equipment.

3. If you need to complete the actual installation sooner than a few weeks, such as in a real estate transaction, then you are probably better off calling a professional. Professional mitigators have all the right equipment and can generally complete most repairs in one day. To quote one of the contributors of this manual, "The only difference between an amateur and a professional is the price of his tools and the time it takes to do the job." *Allow yourself sufficient time.*

4. Arrange to have a helper work with you. It is a lot easier to have someone hold the other end of the pipe as you run it, but **more** importantly if one worker gets hurt, the other can call for help.

5. Don't do anything you are **not** trained to do! Don't run your own 120-volt system unless you are a trained electrician. There are alternatives such as hiring an electrician or using packaged low-voltage systems.

6. Read all the instructions and Material Safety Data Sheets (called MSDS) provided by the suppliers of the caulks and glues. Ask for the specific MSDS sheets at the information center of the hardware store you are buying materials from. Note that manufacturers are required to provide these sheets which are most easily obtained from the Internet.

7. **Remember no one ever plans to have an accident**.

The majority of the potential accidents that can occur are minor (if you are careful). The potential for cuts and bruises is high, especially if you find yourself crawling through a crawl space filled with nails, busted glass and an occasional critter. These can be avoided with protective clothing such as gloves, safety goggles and coveralls. If you don't have these, **get them** before starting work. They'll come in handy for other home improvement projects as well.

The primary areas that need specific protection are your skin, eyes, hands, ears, and lungs. The following illustration depicts the basic and most fashionable attire for the do-it-yourself mitigator.

Chapter 10: Safety Precautions

Basic Personal Protective Gear

The illustration below shows the minimum requirement of personal safety gear for different jobs that you may be doing. Note, in all of the operations cited above, the following items are always used:

	Gluing Pipe with Ventilation	Crawl Space	Hammer Drill	Vacuum Cleaner	Caulking or Gluing Pipe - Closed Space
Eyes, Nose, Ears	goggles	goggles + mask	goggles	goggles	goggles + mask
Coveralls	✓	✓	✓	✓	✓
Gloves	✓	✓	✓	✓	✓
First Aid Kit	✓	✓	✓	✓	✓
Knee Pads		✓			

1. **Safety Goggles.** These protect your eyes from glue that can drip into them when applying it to a fitting overhead. They also protect your eyes from those wires and nails that are always hanging down in dimly lit crawl spaces and not easily seen. Goggles also protect you from the flying bits of concrete when operating hand and concrete hammer drills. They are also useful when caulking in closed spaces and when you wipe the side of your face with a sleeve that has caulk gobbed on it. **Wear safety goggles all of the time while working.**

    NEVER wear contacts while doing this type of work. Chemical fumes from the caulks and glues irritate your eyes. However, the biggest concern is when chemicals are splashed into an eye. If this happens, some of the material can get behind the contact lenses and prevent the eye from being quickly and thoroughly washed out. Safety goggles can be purchased that will fit over your glasses. **Don't wear contact lenses.**

2. **Coveralls.** Durable outerwear offers excellent protection from the debris found in crawl spaces, the grunge found in sumps and the insulation in the attic. Although an old pair of pants and a work shirt will help, coveralls offer more protection since they are one piece. The problem with a shirt and a pair of pants is that the shirt comes out and then your mid-section is exposed. Pants will scoop up dirt as you crawl through the crawl area.

3. **Gloves.** A well-fitting pair of leather gloves or garden gloves is a necessity for protecting your hands from sharp objects. Sharp objects are found everywhere in this work, whether it be in crawl spaces, pulling dirt from a suction pit through a basement slab, or when your drill slips off the screw, you're driving in. Gloves won't protect you from cutting a finger if you tangle with a saw and, of course, gloves offer no protection if you do not have them on. Buy a pair of gloves that are not too big and clumsy. If they are too big, you will not be able to pick up anything and they will soon be off and in a corner. A tight-fitting pair of leather gloves works best ("ropin" gloves).

   Gloves can cause problems while caulking if you get caulk on the glove. With a glove, you cannot feel the caulk; therefore, you are not apt to clean it off before you smear it on something you touch. The best advice is to wear good leather gloves, take your time caulking, and do not get it all over yourself. Be prepared to throw the gloves away if you're not careful with the caulk and glue.

4. **First Aid Kit.** A first aid kit that has disinfectant, small and large butterfly bandages, and knuckle bandages are mandatory. Make sure there is running water available to flush an eye if something spills into it.

5. **Tight Spaces:** If you are entering a confined area such as a crawl space realize this can be the home of spiders and snakes. Don't go in if you feel these critters are in there. Call a professional pest exterminator or call your local extension office to find out how you can drive them out. Remember once you are face-to-face with a rattlesnake or a skunk, there is not a lot of freedom of movement to make a hasty retreat. The best thing to do is to shine a lot of light into the crawl space before entering and to make a lot of noise as you go in to scare them away.

6. **Knee Pads.** These are handy for crawl space work since you will be supporting half of your weight by your knees. There are few things as painful as a nail through the knee. Not only do you hurt your knee, but you also whack your head when you react to the pain.

7. **Head Protection.** Wear something on your head. A hard hat is best, but when you are bent over into a sump or are in a crawl space, they are hard to keep on. If you are not accustomed to wearing a hard hat realize it can limit your range of vision. A bike helmet works well and is easier to keep on your head since it has a chinstrap. At least, wear a snug fitting heavy baseball hat to soften a blow when you bump into a floor joist.

8. **Ear Protection.** Hammer drills, electric drills and shop vacuums create more noise than you think, especially if they are all going at once. Get some of the soft insertable, and disposable, foam earplugs. You can also purchase "ear-muff" style ear protectors. However, the foam earplugs provide good protection and are more comfortable to wear.

9. **Lighting and electrical cords.** When working in dark spaces like a crawlspace have good work lights to help you do the work but also avoid sharp objects and "critters." Also, use extension cords or trouble lights whose cords are in good condition and not frayed and don't run them through puddles of water.

Remember: **Prevention is cheap and a whole lot less painful than a gash in your knee or a bump on the head.**

Hantavirus Concerns

An extremely virulent virus has occasionally been found in homes which affects the respiratory tract. Mice and other rodents carry this virus. The virus itself is found within mouse droppings, saliva, and urine in areas inhabited by mice, such as crawl spaces and attics where you may be installing portions of your radon system . ***If you encounter evidence of mice, like mouse droppings, nests, or a dead mouse you should remove yourself from this area immediately.*** Dust in these areas can have the virus attached to it. The virus can enter your respiratory tract, your mouth, and even the tear ducts of your eyes by way of this dust. Consequently, when you exit the area (immediately) you should remove your clothing for washing. You should shower as soon as possible, cleaning your entire body.

Spraying the area containing the mouse droppings with a mild disinfectant solution of bleach or Lysol can neutralize the virus. However, you should not do this until you contact your local health department for current procedures. It typically involves putting on protective clothing and respiratory protection and spraying the entire area with the bleach solution. This would be a good job for a professional.

Do not treat this lightly. Hantavirus has been detected throughout North America and when contracted, the resulting disease has been fatal in close to 50% of the cases. If you will be working in an area where Hantavirus is a potential concern, contact your local health agency for information on its symptoms, treatment, and prevention.

Protecting Your Home from Radon

Respiratory Protection

The picture below shows two alien looking creatures wearing different types of half face respirators. These are designed to offer different levels of protection from breathing airborne particulate and chemical vapors. The next section, on ventilation, will describe a more practical way of protecting yourself from most respiratory hazards. However, you may find yourself in an area where you do not know the hazards when you enter it. Increased ventilation may deal with one problem but stir up dirt and dust at the same time. Respirators are worthwhile protection for the investigation side of your project as well as the actual installation.

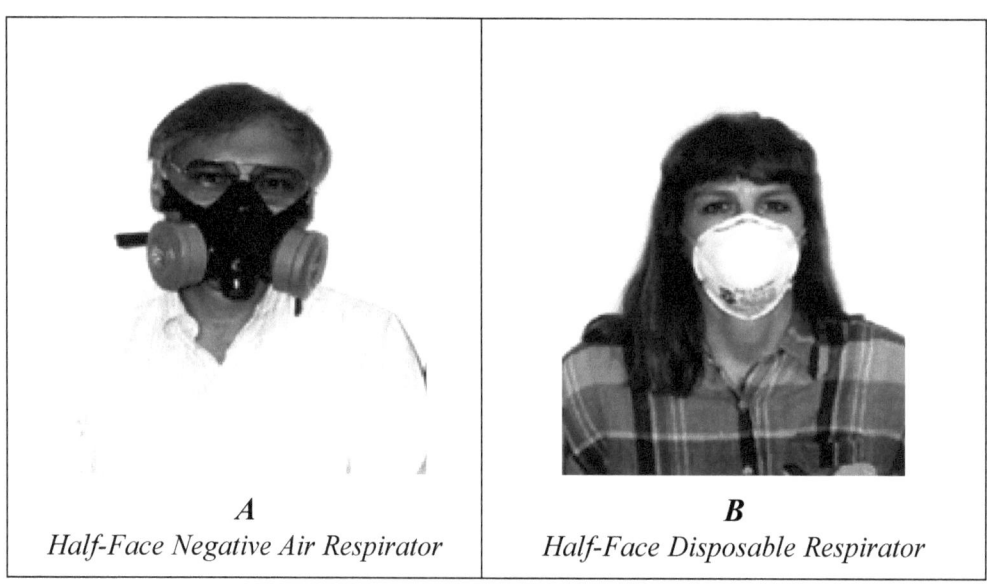

A
Half-Face Negative Air Respirator

B
Half-Face Disposable Respirator

Illustration A: Half-face negative air respirator: This is a respirator that can be used with many different types of filters against different types of contaminants. They are called negative air respirators because you have to suck air in through the filters as you breathe.

NOT EVERYONE HAS THE LUNG CAPACITY TO WEAR THESE ON A PROLONGED BASIS WHILE ENGAGED IN PHYSICAL ACTIVITY. You should **NOT** wear one of these unless your doctor has approved it. They should fit snugly. You should not rely on them to work in an area with asbestos or hantavirus unless you had a physical and have been trained how to use them properly. ***IF YOU FIND ASBESTOS - LEAVE IT TO A PROFESSIONAL.*** Once asbestos gets in your lungs, it stays there and continues to damage the lungs.

Illustration B: **Half-face negative air disposable respirator.** These are often found in hardware stores. They operate the same as respirator A above, except they are not as difficult to breathe through. They do not provide the same level of protection as respirator A. They are suitable if you just need something to keep the dust out. Never depend upon these for full protection against hazardous materials such as asbestos.

When purchasing these devices, look for cartridges for respirator A, or the actual mask in the case of respirator B, that will provide protection against dusts and organic chemical fumes according to the table below.

Protection from:	Respirator A Cartridges NIOSH /MSHA ID #s	Protection From:	Respirator B Masks NIOSH ID #
Radon decay products, asbestos	TC-21C-231 TC - 21C-346	Nuisance level dusts	TC-21C-132
Organic vapors	TC-23C-107 TC-23C-661	Nuisance level organic vapors	TC-21C-234

Chapter 10: Safety Precautions

Ventilate the Work Area to Reduce the Buildup of Chemical Vapors

It is best not to let the vapors from the caulking or glues to build up. This is often easier and more practical than wearing a respirator at all times. The best way to prevent vapor build up is to ventilate the work area. The following illustration shows one method for doing this:

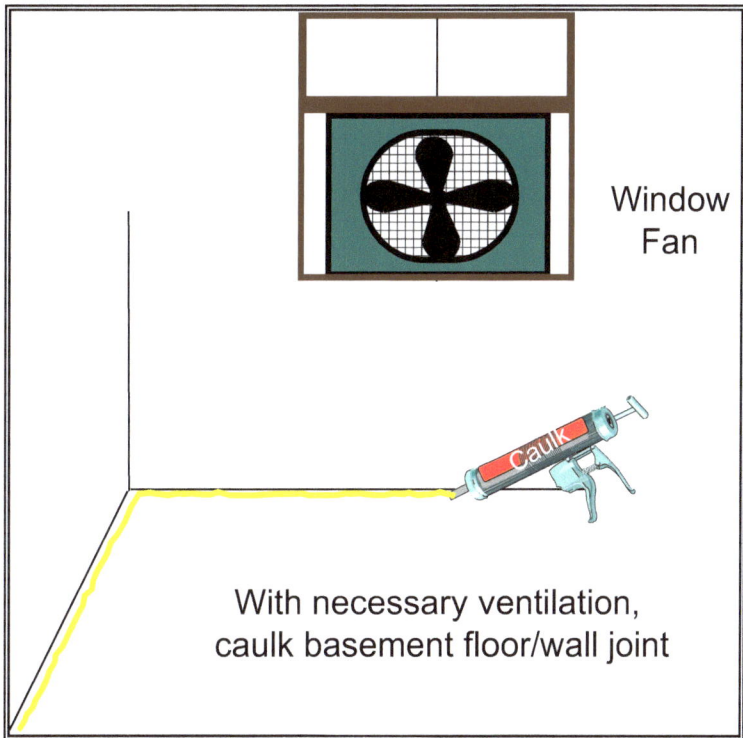

Use a window fan, or blowers that can be rented, or temporarily hook up the radon depressurization fan and use the fan to either supply or exhaust air into the work area. Caulk will release fumes as it cures so continue ventilating while the caulk dries. If you dilute the vapors and remove them from the house as they are released from the caulk or glue, you may not need to wear a respirator.

Remember, don't ventilate an area where asbestos or Hantavirus is present. This will stir up these materials and create a significant health hazard. Again, if you find asbestos, **STOP AND CALL** a professional trained in asbestos abatement.

Ventilation will also reduce the radon concentrations in the work area as well. This is particularly important when you work in confined areas such as crawl spaces, sumps or when you first cut the suction pit through the concrete floor. The only time you will need to shut these ventilation fans off will be when you perform air leak smoke tests, since the air flow from the fan will disrupt the smoke flow.

Chemical Hazards:

The materials described in this manual are not particularly hazardous unless:

1. You are very sensitive or allergic to some chemical vapors.
2. You don't follow directions and misuse the material.

To avoid problems, you should read the instructions for the use of the material very carefully (caulks, glues, foams, etc.). You should also obtain what is called the "Material Safety Data Sheet" (MSDS). All manufacturers must supply these sheets. If you are not provided one or cannot find one online, demand it. If you are still not provided one, shop elsewhere. An example of an MSDS follows this page. It describes the chemical content as well as the health risks known about the specific material. Precautions, flammability, and other good information is provided on the sheet. There is also first aid information if an

© Copyright 2023 • Center for Environmental Research and Technology, Inc.

accident does occur from your use or due to accidental ingestion. Read the MSDS thoroughly before you use the material and always ventilate the work area.

Note: The example that follows this section may look a little different from what you receive from your supplier. MSDS sheets can vary in format. Regardless of the format, each MSDS will have information relating to first aid, flammability, and toxicity. This information is required to be made available to you by federal law. Don't just shop for price. Look at the hazards that may be associated with a specific product to determine if paying a little more will reduce your health risk.

Other Hazards

Electrical hazards, power tool use, and falling from heights are the other installation hazards associated with this work.

When using power tools, make sure you are using a grounded, three prong extension cord connected to a GFI (ground fault interrupter) circuit. Buy and use a GFI receptacle box that can be put in the circuit with your extension cord. Don't use a three prong to two prong plug adapter. Use extension cords that are rated for at least 15 amps. Don't stand in water when using power equipment.

When using power tools keep the safety guards in place like those found on circular saws. When using hammer drills, hold the drill in front of you so when it twists it does not turn and kick you in the legs or elsewhere. Never use the "constant on" switch of a power tool that may have one. You will either use a ½-inch electric drill or a right-angle drill with hole saws for cutting holes through floors and walls. Position the drill against a wall or something solid so when, not if, the saw binds, the drill handle will not slam into you or twist your wrist. When going into attics, make sure that you can climb back out without having to jump onto a ladder.

You may be climbing step ladders and going into attic spaces. Use a strong step ladder, not a chair, and stay off the top step. Be careful that you walk on the ceiling joists or lay a board out on top of the joists to support and spread out your weight while in the attic. This is safer and more comfortable. It will also prevent the drywall ceiling nails from popping out.

When climbing up on the roof, use a good solid extension ladder. Tie it to the roof to keep it from sliding side to side. Place a stake in the ground at the base of each of the two feet of the ladder and tie it off to keep it from kicking out. Wear tennis shoes or some other rubber soled shoe to provide good traction on the roof. Wait for a good weather day to get up on the roof. Don't climb the roof in the snow or in the rain or if it is still damp with morning dew.

Example of a Material Safety Data Sheet (1 of 13 pages)

Safety Data Sheet

Sikaflex®-1A

Revision Date 01/20/2020  Print Date 01/20/2020

SECTION 1. IDENTIFICATION

Product name	: Sikaflex® -1A
Company name	: Sika Corporation
	201 Polito Avenue
	Lyndhurst, NJ 07071
	USA
	www.sikausa.com
Telephone	: (201) 933-8800
Telefax	: (201) 804-1076
E-mail address	: ehs@sika-corp.com
Emergency telephone	: CHEMTREC. 800-424-9300
	INTERNATIONAL. 703-527-3887
Recommended use of the chemical and restrictions on use	: For further information, refer to product data sheet.

SECTION 2. HAZARDS IDENTIFICATION

GHS classification in accordance with 29 CFR 1910.1200

Respiratory sensitization	: Category 1
Skin sensitization	: Category 1
Carcinogenicity (Inhalation)	: Category 1A
Specific target organ toxicity - repeated exposure (Inhalation)	: Category 2

GHS label elements

Hazard pictograms :

Signal Word : Danger

Hazard Statements : H317 May cause an allergic skin reaction.
H334 May cause allergy or asthma symptoms or breathing difficulties if inhaled.
H350 May cause cancer by inhalation.
H373 May cause damage to organs through prolonged or repeated exposure if inhaled.

1 / 13

Protecting Your Home from Radon

Backdrafting: Possible Effect on Ability of Combustion Flues to Operate Properly.

Chimneys and flues are designed to vent the exhaust gases from combustion appliances safely out of the home. In most homes, these gases exhaust out because the combustion gases of hot water heaters and furnaces are warm and naturally rise up the flue. This is similar to the stack effect that was discussed in Chapter 3. However, in this case, it has the beneficial effect of causing unwanted gases to leave the home. If there is a competing force in the building, like an exhaust fan running or an air leak into a defective radon system, the gases can be prevented from rising up the flue. If the flues cannot "draft" properly, these gases can accumulate in the home and can lead to carbon monoxide poisoning. Carbon monoxide can cause severe nerve damage and death. Like radon, carbon monoxide is colorless, odorless, and invisible. You cannot detect this deadly gas with your human senses.

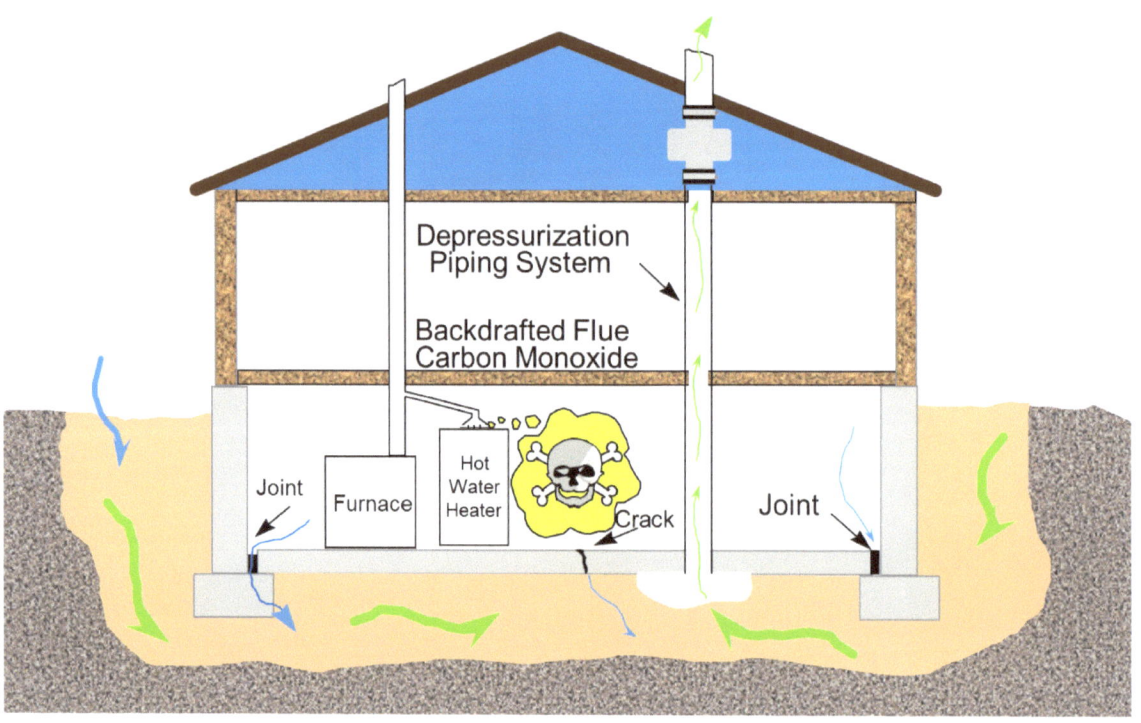

It is possible a radon system could add to the forces that compete with the proper venting of the flue. This is especially true if you have not sealed large openings in a slab such as not sealing your sump well, or there is an un-trapped floor drain emptying into the sump, or you did not seal the plastic in the crawl space well. You should test combustion appliances for backdrafting immediately after installing a mitigation system in your homes.

Testing for backdrafting and the presence of carbon monoxide is not a trivial matter. A professional home inspector, a qualified heating and cooling technician or certified energy advisor should do it. *A simple kitchen match test is not adequate.*

If a backdrafting problem is detected it very well may be due to a faulty flue rather than the radon system itself. Therefore, it is felt by the author that the backdraft test should be performed whether you fix your house for radon or not. You should also consider having this repeated every couple of years to ensure that your flues have not changed or become clogged. Also, if you decide to hire a contractor to install your radon system, make sure that this test is done before they leave. Your safety depends upon it.

Non-Thermal Smoke Used for Backdraft Test

Backdrafting potential: System alterations or breakdowns

Another consideration is that, even if the radon system is installed properly and the combustion flue works properly, this condition could change. The ability of a flue to draft properly would certainly change if a child broke the depressurization piping, a repair person working in the crawl space cut the plastic and did not repair it, or a sump lid was removed without shutting off the fan. When major breaches in the system occur, the potential for backdrafting significantly increases. This is why we also recommend you install a continuously operating carbon monoxide monitor that would alert you and your family of potentially dangerous quantities of carbon monoxide. Carbon monoxide can occur from faulty furnaces and reasons other than a broken radon system. If you're concerned enough about your family's health to consider the expense of a radon system, a carbon monoxide monitor is very cheap insurance. Be sure to purchase one that meets the ANSI/UL2034 Standards.

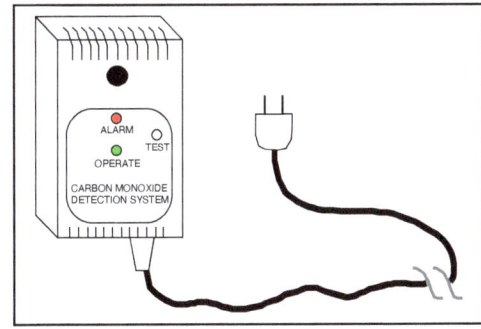

Labels recommended in this book should be placed in an easily visible location for maintenance people and future homeowners to see. Make sure the label instructs the reader to shut off the depressurization system fan before disassembling the system to prevent backdrafting during repairs. This is also why the system indicators described in Chapter 7 should be reliable and placed in a location that you will see frequently. Don't cut corners on the quality of the indicator or labels.

We recommend that you:

1. Install your system as best you can.
2. Temporarily turn it on long enough to perform the smoke tests to finish the sealing.
3. Turn it off. Arrange for an inspector to come to the home to test the flue.
4. After the flue has passed the backdraft test, turn the system on. Now start your post-mitigation backdraft test. If the flue backdrafts, **turn the system off** until a competent heating contractor can fix it.
5. Install a carbon monoxide alarm in your home according to the manufacturer's instructions.

DON'T IGNORE THESE IMPORTANT STEPS.

The authors are not saying this to satisfy their attorney's concerns, but because many "marginal flues" exist. The extra suction created by the radon system could be just enough to augment an existing problem. We have seen three homes with backdraft problems out of a few thousand. This may seem like too small of a percentage to be concerned about, *unless it is your home that has a problem!*

Last Bit of Advice

Our goal in this chapter wasn't to scare you. If you take your time and use your head, you will probably do a better job than many contractors. We have seen some strange and dangerous designs and installations over the years installed by contractors who have **not** been specifically trained in radon mitigation. If you decide to use a contractor, because you are concerned about some of these issues, use the guidance in this book to make sure that they observe the same precautions as you would, if you were to do it yourself.

Chapter 11

New Home Systems

Why install a radon control system during construction?

Basic approaches to installing radon control systems during new home construction

Planning the Sub-Slab Soil Gas Collection System

Combining Multi-Level Slabs or Slabs with Crawl Spaces

Homes with Crawl Spaces

Piping Systems for New Home Systems

Working with your Contractor in Planning the Radon System

CHAPTER 11 – NEW HOME SYSTEMS

If you have read the previous chapters in this book, you realize that installing a radon system in a home is not a trivial matter. Although radon can certainly be reduced in any home regardless of whether or not it was constructed 100 years ago or just last week, it makes sense to incorporate a radon system during construction for economic reasons as well as the ability to hide many components for a more aesthetically pleasing appearance for your new home.

This chapter is written as an overview for homeowners. More detailed programs for builders and architects are available at www.certi.us and also within *Measuring and Mitigating Radon in Colorado* downloadable at: https://cdphe.colorado.gov/radon-and-real-estate

Why not wait until the house is built when you can test the house to see if you really need a system?

You can certainly wait until the house is finished to test to see if you have a radon concern. The bulk of this book focuses on how existing homes can be fixed, even if nothing was done during its construction to facilitate the installation of a radon mitigation system. So, if you have just bought a new home, or its construction is well along, don't despair. The home can still be fixed.

On the other hand, if you wait until the house is finished only to find out that you do have a problem you will kick yourself for not having done something ahead of time. The reasons are:

- New home systems are less obtrusive because the piping can be hidden inside plumbing walls. Installing the vent pipe while the house is built will also let the roofer flash around the pipe where it penetrates the roof without voiding the roof's warranty.

- Radon reductions are typically better since the foundation joints can be accessed and sealed before the walls are built or finishing details like carpet are installed. This provides a better vacuum under your home and therefore better radon reduction efficiency.

- New home systems typically cost less to operate, since the foundation can be better sealed; thereby reducing the amount of interior conditioned air that will be drawn down through the slab and lost to the outside.

- By properly preparing the fill beneath the slab before it is poured, only one suction riser will be needed. That is, multiple suction points will not be needed, thereby reducing cost, and minimizing the number of pipes passing up through the house.

- By being sly, cunning, and clever, you can install the system in such a way that will possibly eliminate the need for a depressurization fan thereby reducing installation and operating costs. We will tell you how that is done but realize that this can only be done if you build the system into the house, not after it is constructed.

- The cost of the system can be included in your new home mortgage thus allowing you to amortize its cost over the life of the loan.

These are specific reasons for installing a system during construction. Perhaps, the overriding factor is having the peace of mind that when you finally move into your dream home that it is indeed a safe haven from the elements. We routinely install roofs on our homes to keep out nature's rain and snow. In the same manner, installing a radon system helps keep out those aspects of nature that come from the soil beneath the home. In fact, experience has shown the installation of a radon control system can significantly reduce the moisture content in the soil beneath the home that often leads to molds and mildews in basements and crawl spaces. This soil moisture reduction can also reduce mechanical pressures that expansive soils exert on foundations in areas with this concern. It certainly makes sense to incorporate these systems during construction on the basis of radon reduction alone, but you may also be able to further justify it on the basis of these other benefits.

Is there some kind of test that can be performed on my lot to determine the need for a radon control system?

A lot of research has gone into trying to determine a method of predicting indoor radon readings from soil gas measurements on vacant lots. Unfortunately, the results of this work have not yielded a good predictive model, and probably never will. The reason for this is there are too many variables. The measurement of all of these variables would cost far more than it would cost to install the radon control system. The uncertainty of predicting radon concentrations in a finished home is due to the following:

- **Soil Sampling Errors:** Radon comes from radium in the soil which is not uniformly distributed. So, soil testing may miss a pocket. Radon, as a gas, can move considerable distances through soil depending upon fissures and cracks, etc. This makes soil sampling a hit or miss proposition. To compensate for these errors, multiple sampling holes would have to be dug and both radium and radon analyses would need to be performed. This costs $$$$.

- **Soil Permeability Errors:** Radon is drawn through the soil towards the house. How much is drawn towards the home and from what distance is determined by the permeability of the soil, which is variable. Also, testing the permeability of the soil before it has been disturbed by the construction process would be testing it under its most impermeable conditions. Furthermore, running utilities in the ground toward the house will provide potential pathways for radon that could not be predicted by soil permeability tests. Gravel is often imported to a site, to assist in water drainage. This gravel can provide an easier pathway than the testing of the native soils would have predicted.

- **Variable House Vacuum:** Homes create vacuums that will draw radon and other soil gases in. The strength of this vacuum will depend upon how weather tight the exterior shell of the home will be, the climate, the amount of fresh air make-up allowed in the house, and how you live in your home.

With all of these variables, how do I know I really need to install a radon system?

All of the variables in predicting the radon concentration of a finished building from soil samples on a vacant lot are enough to cause an engineer's eyes to cross. What is typically done is to determine the radon potential for a home built in a given geographical area. This is typically determined from maps created from radon measurements in existing homes in combination with knowledge of the underlying geology. These are referred to as Radon Potential Maps that can be used either by builders or by code agencies in determining if radon systems are prudent or required. These maps rank the entire country and some of its territories into three categories of radon potential.

The zone categories are based upon the probability of the results of a short-term radon test (closed building conditions) located in the lowest potentially occupiable portion of the home falling within certain ranges of radon concentrations. The categories and their associated ranges are as follows:

Zone 1	Above action level of 4.0 pCi/L
Zone 2	Between 2.0 pCi/L and 4.0 pCi/L
Zone 3	Generally, less than 2.0 pCi/L

A copy of the U.S. EPA's Zone Map is shown below for your use. More detailed state maps can be obtained from your state health department. Caution should be exercised when using these maps in determining whether or not you plan to ask to have a radon control system installed in your new home. Remember several things:

- The maps were drawn along county boundaries for building code use. Radon is a function of radium content in the soil, which was not deposited as a function of county line boundaries. So, if you are building in a zone 2 area, don't think that you will not have a problem. The

Chapter 11: New Home Systems

authors have seen too many exceptions over the years to say that homes in zone 2 areas won't have radon concerns.

- There are health risks associated with radon exposures less than 4.0 pCi/L. You may still want to strongly consider having a system installed to further reduce the radon as well as obtain the additional benefits provided by radon systems.

Perhaps, one recommendation would be, install the system if you are in a zone 1 area, and perhaps if you are in a zone 2 area. But if you are in a zone 2 area you may want to at least install certain portions of the system. That will make it easier to fix if you move into the home and find that you do indeed have a radon problem.

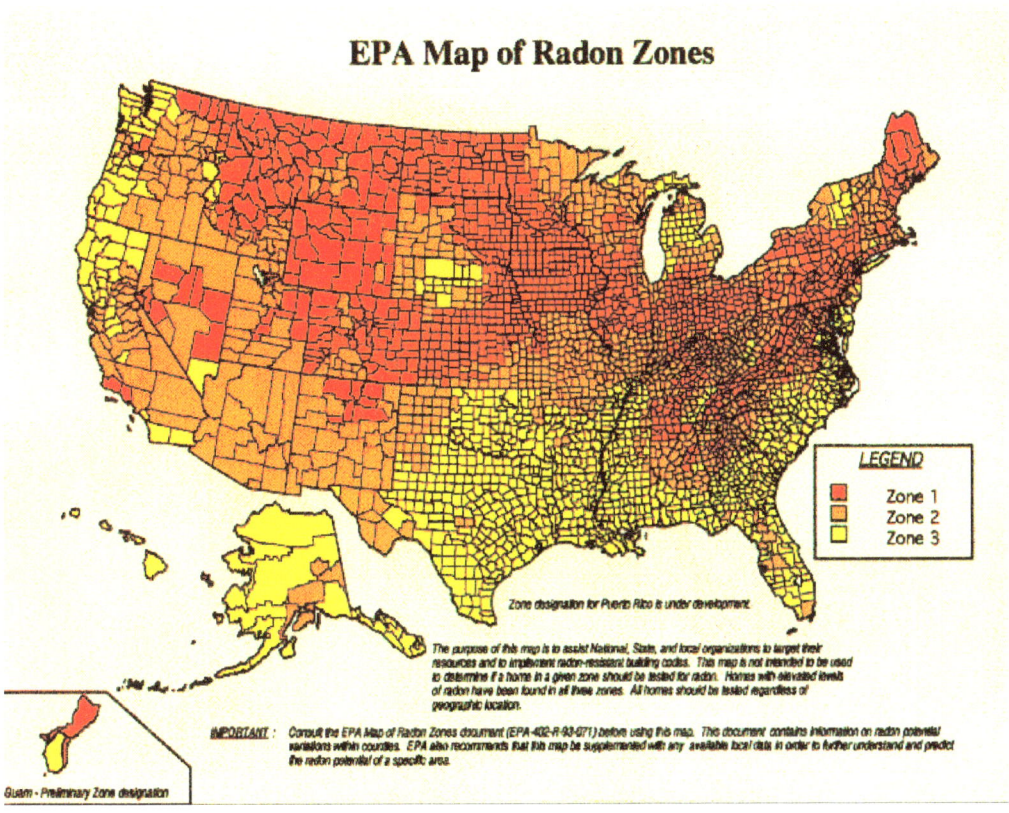

Be careful in using maps like this. Just because an area may be displayed as a low or moderate radon potential zone, it doesn't mean a home built in low potential areas will be below 4 pCi/L, it just means there is a lower probability.

Also, more and more building departments and some states have adopted building codes requiring the installation of radon systems in new home construction. These codes also have increasingly been applied to multi-family buildings such as apartments and has become a requirement for HUD finances multi-family structures. So, there may be regulations already in place that your builder will have to follow. But recognize that codes often stipulate the minimum requirements, and you may choose to have the system enhanced beyond the minimum required by code.

Basic Approaches to Installing Radon Control Systems During New Home Construction

The following illustrations describe two basic approaches one can take for new homes.

Protecting Your Home from Radon

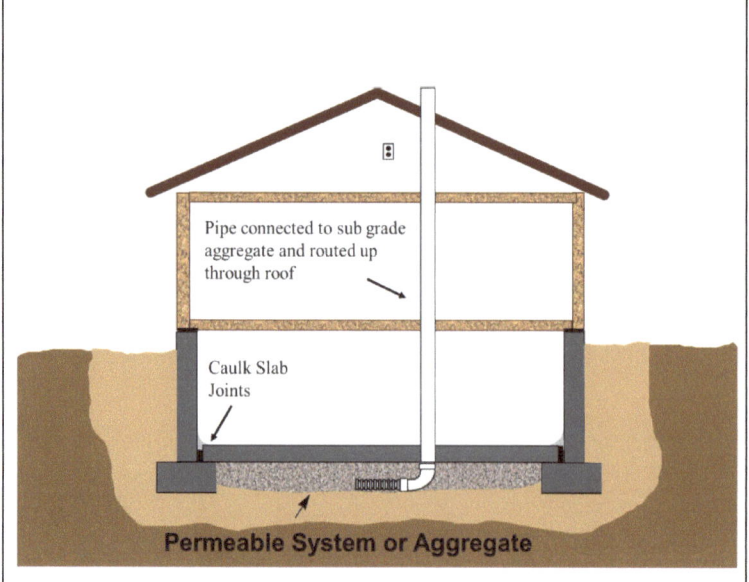

Passive

This method provides a passive venting of soil gasses from the sub-grade up through the roof. A means for collecting soil gases beneath the foundation is installed such as 4-inch-deep layer of clean aggregate or a loop of perforated pipe in a trench or soil gas mat laid between the sub-grade and the slab.

By extending the pipe up through the roof a thermal stack effect is created within the pipe which can reduce indoor radon levels by 50%.

If post construction testing indicates elevated levels, a radon fan can be easily added provided space has been planned and an electrical outlet provided to facilitate its later installation.

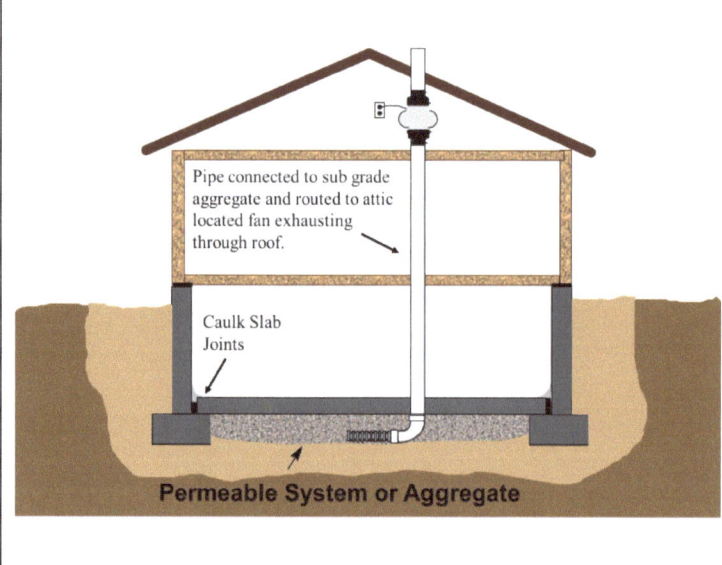

Active

This system has all of the elements of a passive system but has a fan installed to forcibly draw the radon from the soil which most assuredly reduces indoor radon to well below the action level, although post-construction testing is still warranted.

More and more builders are installing active systems from the outset as they are more effective, and it streamlines the process compared to testing and then adding a fan to a passive system and then re-testing.

An active system can also be a passive system that was activated.

Basic approach to installing radon control systems during new home construction

The figure below illustrates the basic concept of radon control systems installed during the construction of a home. The key to these systems is to ensure that soil gases and radon can move easily from underneath the building toward a single riser pipe that is routed up through the home and exits through the roof. In the case of a concrete floor that would be used in a basement or slab-on-grade home, this could be a 4-inch (100 mm) layer of ¾-inch clean gravel placed prior to pouring the floor. Other options are a gas collection system consisting of a loop of buried perforated pipe inside the footing or matting laid on the sub-grade dirt under the slab. In any case, these mechanisms will allow the soil gases to be easily collected.

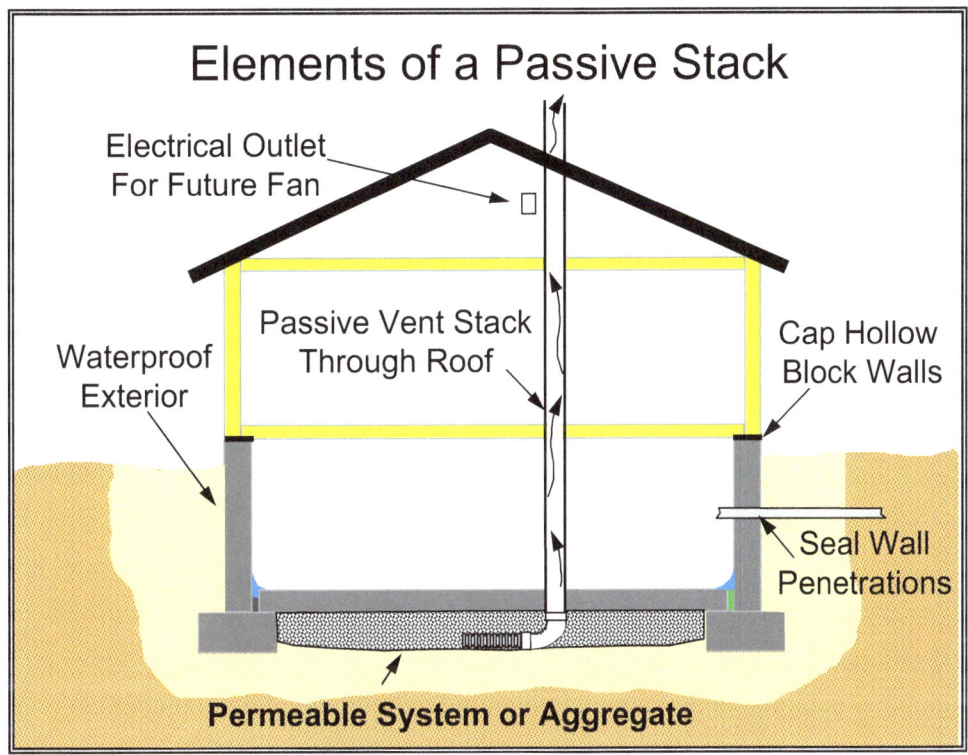

The pipe riser should be routed through the interior of the building to allow the riser to be warmed, thus creating a natural stack effect. When this riser is combined with the easy gas collecting capabilities of the system installed beneath the slab, it can draw significant amounts of radon from beneath the home. The performance of this natural convection system is enhanced by sealing openings in the slab and walls, so the air drawn up through the system comes from beneath the building rather than from within the building. These *passive* systems are further enhanced by routing the pipe through the warmest spaces in the home (like the chase where the furnace and hot water flues are located.) *Don't connect or combine the radon vent pipe with any other vents or flues.* This passive approach is not an option with existing homes unless they were constructed with a layer of clean aggregate completely beneath it with no grade beams or subgrade obstructions to air flow.

The system should be planned to allow for the future installation of a system depressurization fan if the passive system does not provide sufficient radon reduction. Provide at least 30 inches of vertical pipe in the attic for installation of a future fan.

If your home will be built completely or partially over a crawl space, the system will be similar except that plastic sheeting will be installed in the crawl space. See Chapter 4.

Protecting Your Home from Radon

Planning the Sub-Slab Soil Gas Collection System

This section deals with selecting one of three options for collecting radon and other soil gases from beneath concrete slabs in new homes with slab areas less than 3,000 square feet.

If your home will be completely or partially built over a crawl space refer to Chapter 4.

Planning Step 1: Find out what the builder is planning to do beneath the slab.

Typically, a builder has a soils test done on a lot to determine its bearing capacity and its ability to drain water away from the foundation. This information is used by an engineer to design the foundation. This may result in the use of gravel beneath the slab and around the foundation for water drainage purposes. It may also result in the recommendation for the installation of water collection systems such as French drains and sumps that can also be utilized for radon reduction purposes (as discussed in Chapter 5.) On the other hand, it may result in the soils engineer concluding that the native soils are permeable enough to allow for water drainage and no special sub-slab treatment will be necessary. This is what you need to find out to enable you to select the most cost-effective method for radon control in your new home.

If your builder is planning to place clean aggregate beneath the slab, proceed to the next section describing slabs with aggregate. If your builder is planning to use native soils beneath the slab, consider the cost of importing gravel and compare it to the techniques that utilize loops of perforated pipes or drain mats to enhance soil gas collection which are described later in this chapter.

Important Note: The systems described in this chapter are designed to operate independently of any other building system. Consequently, you will not be tying these systems into any drainage systems that may be installed on your new home as would be the case if you waited until the home was completed. Let the drainage systems do single duty for water drainage. On the other hand, you will need to cover sump pit openings and perhaps install check valves on daylight ends of French drains to reduce the amount of excess air that may enter your radon system. See Chapters 4 and 8 regarding how to properly seal these and other foundation openings.

Another Important Note: Many people have tried to build homes with plastic barriers and extensive sealing to try to keep radon out without installing a permeable system beneath the home or providing a relief vent from beneath the slab to the outside. Without providing an alternate pathway for the radon to get to the outside, sealing by itself is not a stand-alone technique in new or existing homes. It is just too difficult to obtain a 100% seal that would be needed to accomplish this, not to mention the high cost of labor and material and the lack of durability of such an approach. Remember there are two types of concrete: concrete that has cracked, and concrete that is going to crack.

Chapter 11: New Home Systems

Sub-Slab Design - Using Gravel Beneath the Slab

If your builder is already planning to install gravel beneath your slab, or if washed gravel is inexpensive and easily obtainable in your area, you will probably use this alternative.

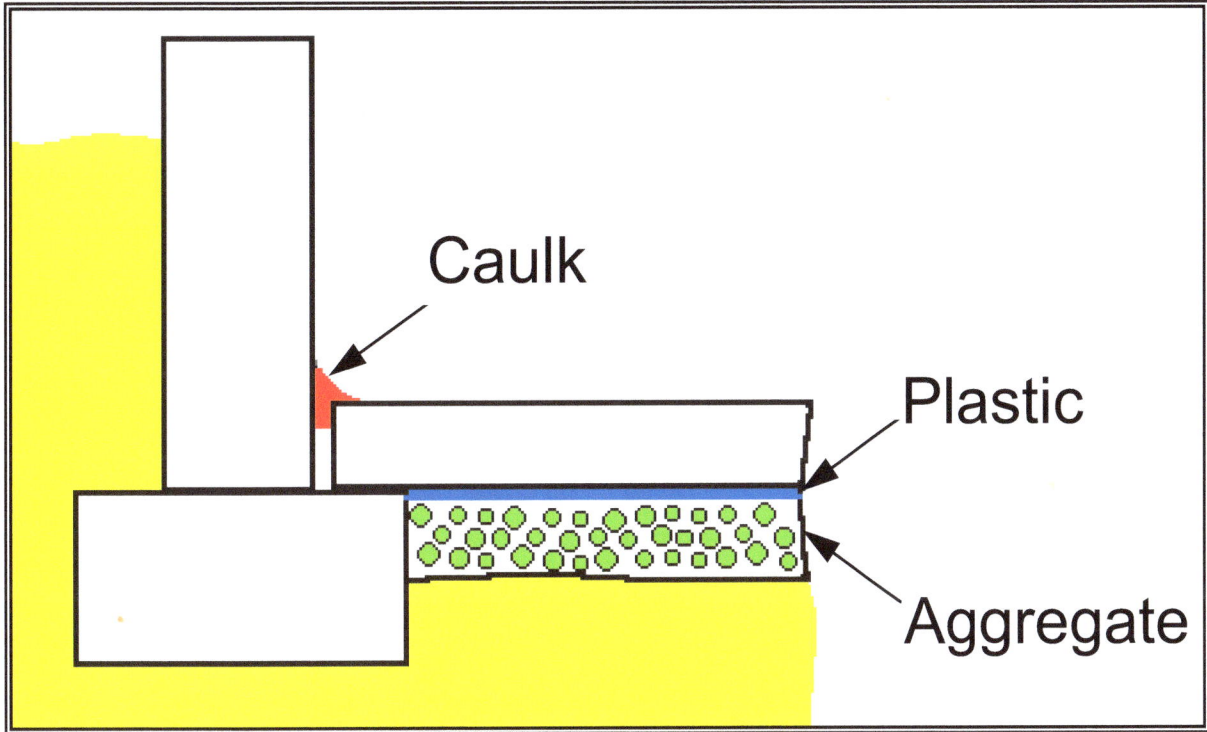

When it is installed, the following points need to be kept in mind:

- The rock should be a consistent ¾-inch in size.
- The gravel should be clean and have no loose dirt to fill the void space between the rocks.
- It should be laid to a minimum depth of 4 inches (100 mm).
- A barrier should be installed to prevent the wet concrete from flowing into the void space in the gravel. Note that this is required in building codes anyway as a moisture barrier.

    This can be accomplished by laying a 6-mil polyethylene sheet above the rock before the concrete is poured. This is referred to as a moisture/vapor barrier in the construction trades and is common practice where sub-slab aggregate is specified by the engineer. Although other codes and requirements may dictate extreme attention to sealing the membrane, for the purposes of radon reduction extreme sealing of the membrane is not required since your critical seal will be accomplished later by caulking the floor-to-wall joints and slab penetrations. See illustration above.

- The concrete itself should be reinforced with wire mesh or plastic fibers to minimize future slab cracking.
- The number of sequential pours should be minimized to reduce the number of cold joints between adjacent slabs. Don't worry about this too much because you will be able to seal these later.

© Copyright 2023 • Center for Environmental Research and Technology, Inc.

Sub-Slab Design - Ensuring full coverage of sub-slab area when gravel is used.

In order for the radon system to work properly, air beneath the slab must be able to move across the underside of the slab. There is typically either a beam or a bearing wall that runs the length of the basement to support the floor joists of the first floor.

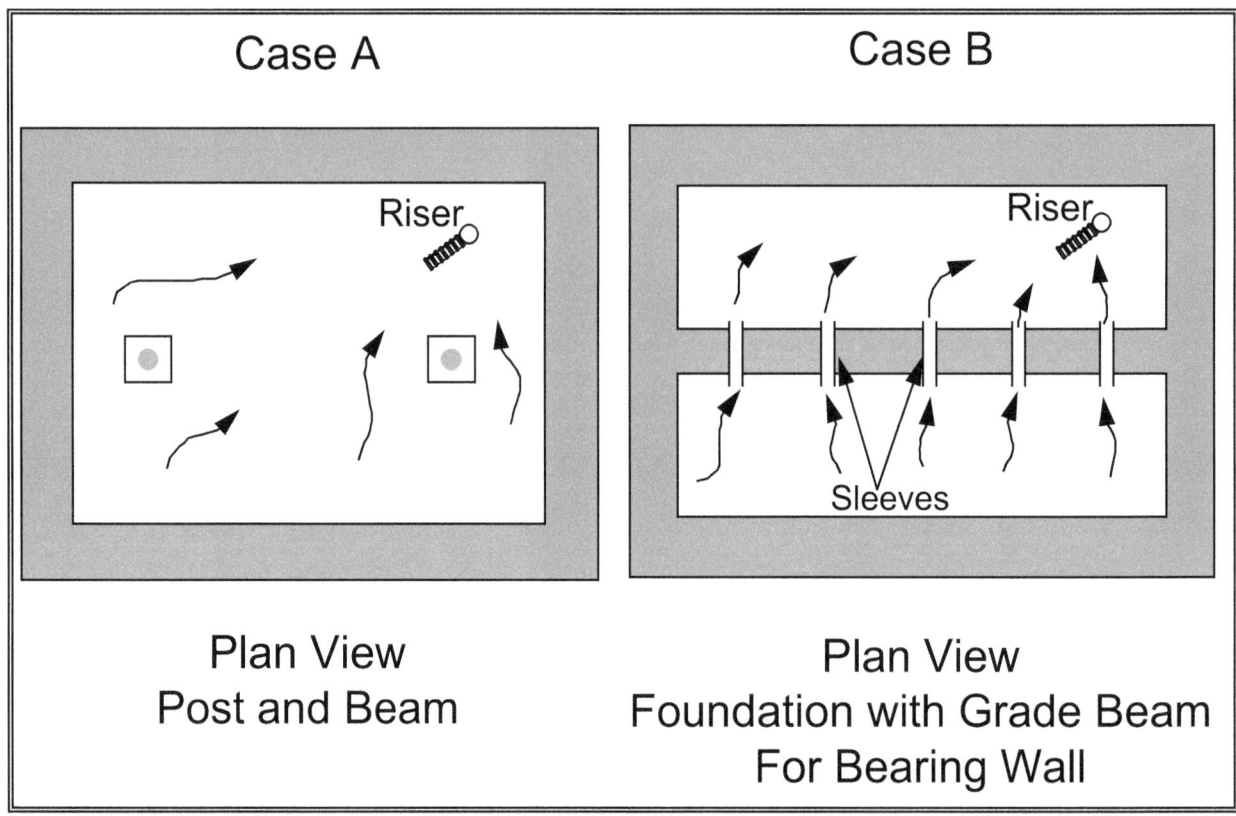

Case A: Post and beam construction: In the case of post and beam construction, a few concrete pads are poured in a line that traverses the slab area. Steel posts are set on top of these supporting pads which hold an overhead beam that the floor joists rest upon. The concrete pads that support the posts are discontinuous and therefore will not disrupt the proper flow of air beneath the finished slab. Nothing special needs to be done in this situation.

Case B: Grade beam for a bearing wall. In this case, a sub-slab concrete footing is installed running the length of the basement. This footing supports a wood framed wall that "bears" the weight of the floor joists above it. This footing does present a barrier to the flow of gases beneath the slab. To avoid this problem, the builder could either revert to post and beam construction or install sleeves through the bearing wall footing to allow for the easy flow of air beneath the slab.

> These sleeves or jumpers are easily installed by placing a 4-inch section of pipe that spans the trench or the forms before the interior footing is poured. Both open ends of the pipe must be in the 4 inches of gravel on either side of the footing to allow for good air flow. The pipe itself should be rigid 4-inch PVC, ABS, or steel to ensure that it does not sag and create a low point where water can accumulate and restrict or stop the air flow. These should be spaced on 6-feet centers with no fewer than 2 penetrations per footing.

Sub-Slab Design - Connecting the gravel to the depressurization system

It does no good to go to the trouble of placing gravel beneath the slab and ensuring good air flow if you stuff your pipe directly into the gravel. You need to allow for easy entry of the air into the pipe. In the case of the gravel alternative, this is most commonly accomplished by using 4-inch (100mm) corrugated and perforated pipe (drain field pipe) at least 20 feet (6 meters) in length.

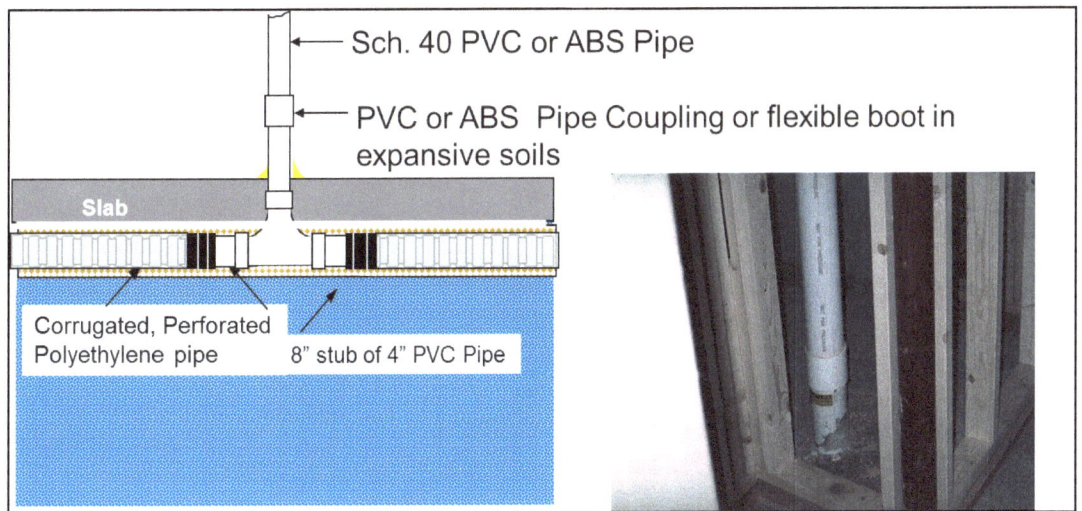

It should be installed in the following manner:

- Establish where you want the riser to come up through the slab and make a trench in the gravel to lay the corrugated pipe into. It makes little difference in which direction you make the corrugated pipe run from the riser.

- Note that one may need to plan an offset with solid pipe to assure the riser comes up where you want it rather than in the middle of a living room.

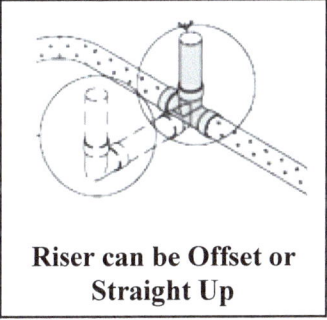

Riser can be Offset or Straight Up

- Glue a 12-inch-long solid piece of 4-inch diameter solid, schedule 40 PVC or ABS pipe to a 4-inch PVC or ABS elbow.

- Connect two 10-foot lengths of 4-inch corrugated and perforated pipe to 8-inch-long PVC or ABS stubs with a 4-inch by 4-inch rubber coupling that has hose clamps on either end. Tighten the hose clamps to firmly attach the corrugated pipe to the PVC or ABS stub.

- Glue the two stubs connected to the 10-foot lengths of perforated pipe to a Solid PVC or ABS Tee.

- Glue a 12-inch long, 4-inch diameter schedule 40 PVC or ABS pipe to outlet of the Tee. This is the riser that will stick up above the concrete and later be connected to your vent system.

- Make sure the corrugated pipe does not want to lift out of the gravel. Drive 10-inch spikes through the pipe if you need to. Don't worry about holes from the nails since the entire pipe is perforated.

- Don't seal the end of the corrugated pipe; just make sure that concrete won't get into it during the pour.

- Secure the riser to a wall (or however you can) to make sure that the concrete does not knock it over when it is poured, and it remains vertical.

- Temporarily seal off the top of your riser stub to keep construction debris from entering it.

- Label the riser pipe as part of a radon system so the plumber does not confuse it with a sewer line and connect a toilet to it.

Sub-Slab Design - Using Perforated Pipe Loop Instead of Gravel

Perhaps the native soils on your lot are sufficiently permeable for good water drainage and your builder's engineer is not specifying the importation of gravel. If gravel is cheap, you could ask for gravel to be imported and use the gravel option discussed on the previous pages or you could install a loop of perforated pipe around the interior of the building. Studies have shown this method to work very well in areas of semi-permeable soils (like decomposed granites) and also where pea gravel is put beneath the slab.

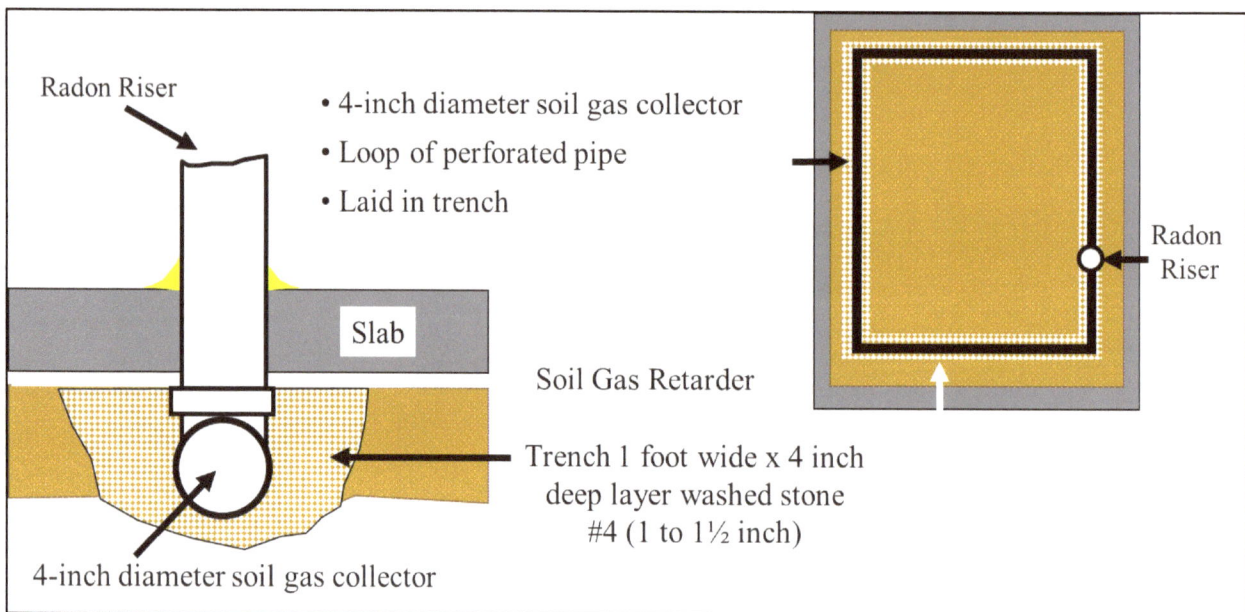

The figure above shows a cross-section of a basement that has a loop of pipe placed beneath the slab. This loop is connected to the riser at any location on the loop that is convenient for the pipe riser to be connected to the depressurization piping and routed up through the house.

These systems work well because the vacuum is distributed around the perimeter of the house and eliminates the need for soil gases to traverse the entire basement area. This fact compensates for the lower permeability of these native soils as compared to imported, large aggregates. When it is installed, the following points should be kept in mind:

- The pipe should be a minimum 3-inch corrugated and perforated pipe that is wrapped with a filter fabric cloth to keep dirt and wet concrete from filling the perforations in the pipe. (Advanced Drain System # 373-300 or any other similar pipe manufactured in accordance with ASTM # F405).

- You will have to dig a trench to lay the pipe into.

- The concrete itself should be reinforced with wire mesh or plastic fibers to minimize future slab cracking.

- The number of sequential pours should be minimized to reduce the number of cold joints between adjacent slabs. Don't worry about this too much because you will be able to seal these later.

Perforated Pipe

Pipe Loop

Chapter 11: New Home Systems

Sub-Slab Design - Perforated Pipe Option: Laying out the pipe loop

The pipe should be laid out in a loop as shown in the illustration below. Note that you don't have to treat garage areas (unless required by local codes). You want to use a loop instead of a single pipe with branches (even if the single pipe has branches off from it) to allow for air flow from two directions. These two directional air flows improves the system and lets you use less expensive 3-inch rather than 4-inch corrugated pipe.

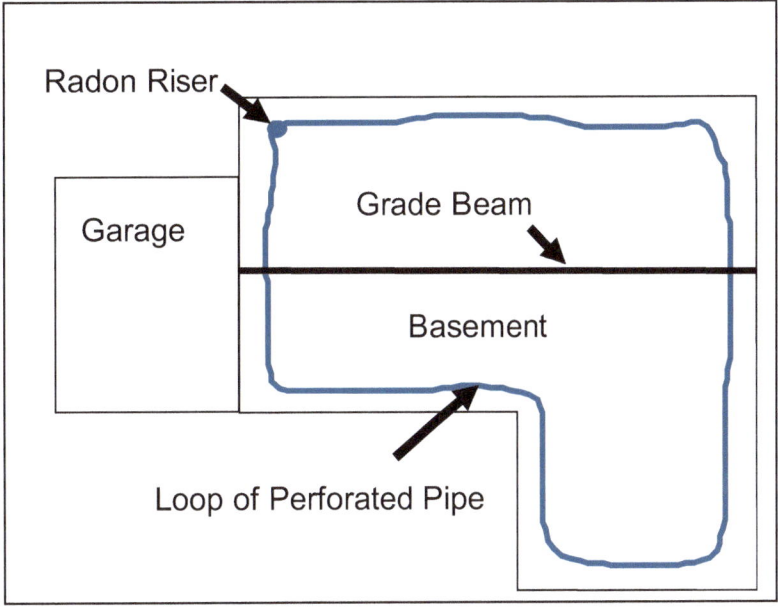

If there will be an intermediate footing beneath your slab (for example, a grade beam, as shown in the diagram) you will need to lay two short sections of the corrugated and wrapped pipe across the trench or forms before the footing is poured. Be sure to temporarily tape the ends closed to keep concrete and debris out. You will later connect to these when you install the rest of your loop.

The loop should be buried in a trench dug around the interior perimeter of the footing of the house. The trench should be dug deep enough to allow the top of the pipe to be covered by at least 1 inch of gravel. Because the pipe is flexible, you do not need to use any special elbows or fittings. Install as follows:

- Establish where your system riser is going to be.

- Lay out the perforated pipe from this point on top of the soil. Run it all around the slab area keeping it about a foot away from the foundation wall. When turning corners just flex the pipe.

- Trace a mark on the dirt alongside of the pipe and move the pipe out of the way and grab your shovel to dig the trench.

- Dig a trench that is deep enough and wide enough to lay the pipe into such that the top of the pipe is at least 1 inch below the finished surface of the dirt before the concrete slab is poured.

  Note that you cannot dig this in until all of the plumbing lines have been installed and the dirt is roughly at the concrete grade. Otherwise, the plumbers may rip up the radon pipe, or your pipe could end up with too much compacted fill above it. This means that the digging could be difficult and a pickax may be a good tool to have with you if the sub grade has been well compacted. Don't use a trencher or you will rip up the plumbing.

- Splice ends of pipes together with the snap on couplers that can be purchased with the pipe or split the ends and force one over the end of the other and sheet metal screw them together and wrap with duct tape to keep wet concrete from seeping in.

- Connect the solid PVC riser to the perforated pipe using a TEE as was described earlier (page 179) and cap the riser to prevent debris from entering during the pour and subsequent construction.

- Fill trench with clean aggregate.

Protecting Your Home from Radon

Sub-Slab Design - Soil Gas Collection Mat Option as Opposed to Gravel or Perforated Pipe

In the same manner that perforated loops of corrugated pipe can be laid around the interior perimeter of a slab, a flat mat can be laid down to collect sub-slab soil gasses. The advantage of this material is that by being flat, a trench need not be dug. This has its application where digging a trench can be time consuming and expensive. Also, if this is being installed in the winter the soil may be frozen, thus avoiding digging in frozen ground.

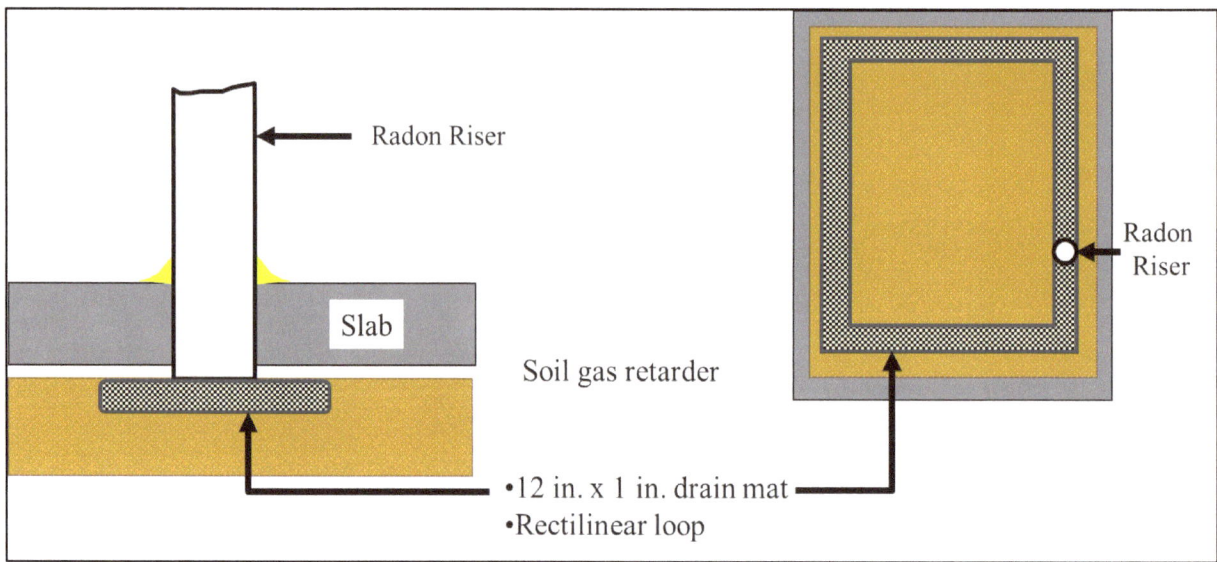

Special mats have been developed for radon reduction purposes that allow you to quickly roll out the mat in as little as an hour before the concrete truck arrives. Some come pre-wrapped in a fabric cloth that will keep the wet concrete from entering the core of the mat itself.

Other types of mats have fabric cloth on one side which will require you to spread a strip of fabric cloth over it to prevent the concrete from entering the plastic. If you use these one-sided mats, be sure to cover them with water permeable fabrics and not plastic. A strip of plastic beneath the slab will cause differential de-watering of the concrete which can cause a crack to occur in the concrete along the edge of the plastic sheet beneath it.

The pre-wrapped, 1-inch by 12-inch mats have become the preferred method of collecting soil gas when the ground is difficult to dig in. The mats eliminate the time and labor of digging pipe into the sub-grade. The minimum size of the mat that has worked well 1-inch tall by 12-inches wide to ensure good air flow. Mats less than 1 inch tall can provide too much resistance to air flow in areas with moderately permeable soils to allow for proper system operation.

12-inch wide by 1-inch-tall mat wrapped with geotech cloth

Sub-Slab Design - Soil Gas Collection Mat Option : Laying Out the Mat

The mat should be laid out in a rectilinear loop to ensure that air can be drawn towards the collection point from two different directions. It should be laid on the dirt after it has been prepped, compacted and ready for the concrete to be poured.

If there will be an intermediate footing beneath your slab, you will need to lay two short sections of the mat across the trench before the footing is poured. Be sure to temporarily tape the ends closed to keep concrete and debris out. You will later connect to these when you install the rest of your loop.

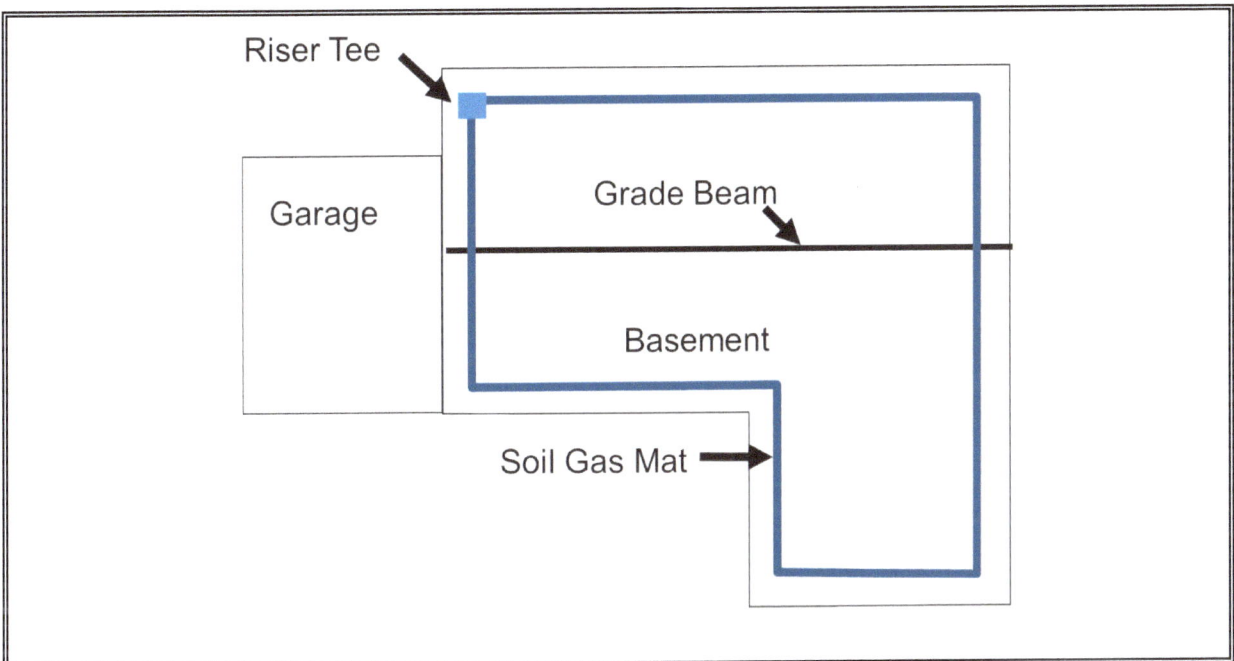

Here is how it's done:

- Establish where your system riser is going to be and begin rolling out the mat from this point.
- Lay the mat on top of the soil around the interior perimeter no further than 1 foot out from the wall.
- As you lay out the mat, smooth it down with your hands and drive an 8-inch landscape staple through the mat every 7 feet to keep it close to the ground and so it won't float up into the concrete.
- The drawings on the next page illustrate how corners and joints are made.

- When you come to a corner, cut the mat. Then cut a 12-inch long slit on the edges of the mat and fold back the fabric. Cut a similar slit in the piece that will attach to this corner at a right angle. Overlap the two cores and cut both of them with a sharp knife simultaneously at a 45-degree angle. Butt the cut edges together. Fold the fabric from both ends over the joint and use duct tape to thoroughly seal the edges of the fabric to keep concrete from entering. Drive two or three 8-inch landscape staples to hold the joint down and to make sure that the two edges of the stay together.

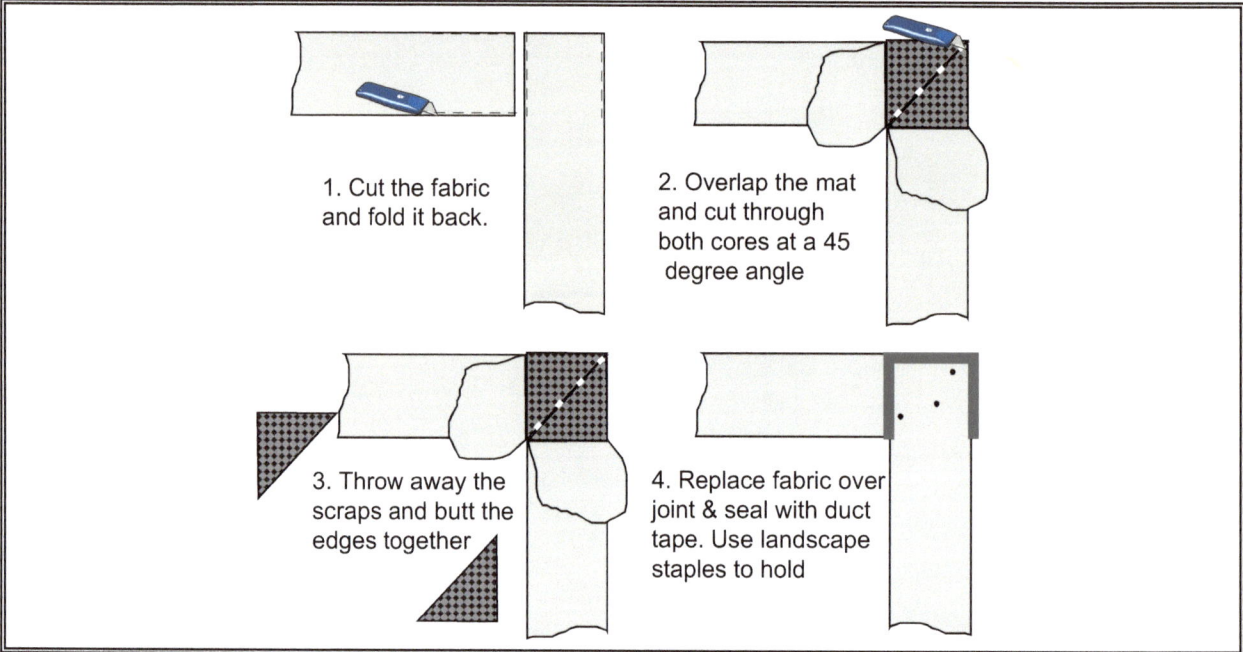

- When making splices, slit the fabric of the two ends to be joined. Lay the core from one end on top of the core from the other end with a 3-inch overlap. Lay the fabric back over the top of the splice and thoroughly seal with duct tape to keep the wet concrete from seeping in. Drive at least two 8-inch-long staples through the mat at this point, being sure to drive them through at the point the two ends overlap.

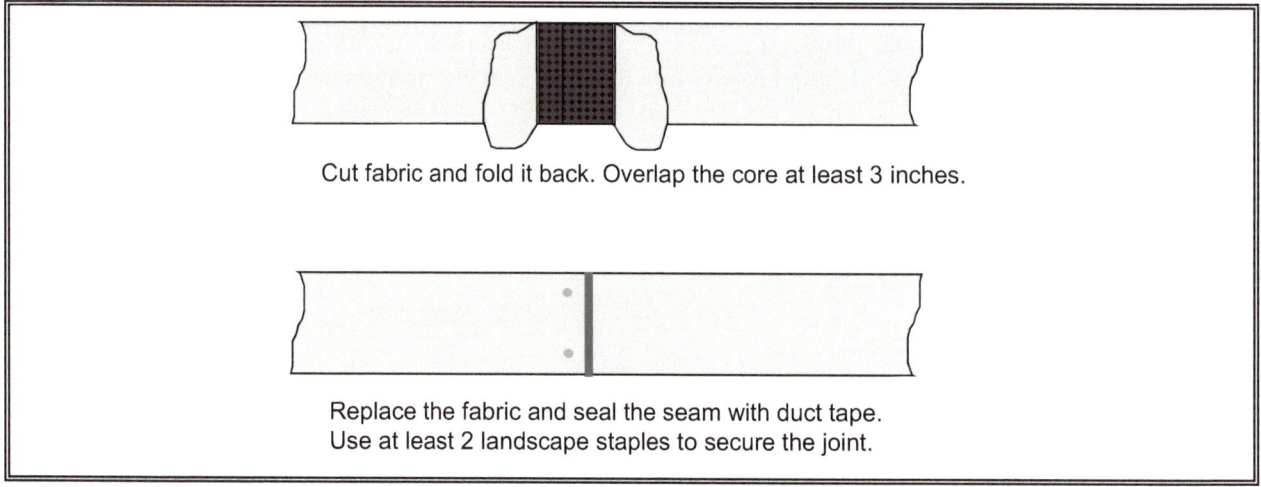

- Continue this process until you have returned to the point at which you started (which is where the riser will be located.)

Sub-Slab Design - Soil Gas Collection Mat: Making the Riser Connection

Making a connection from a flat mat to a round pipe could be difficult. Some people have used flat toilet flanges that are set on top of the mat and then covered with plastic. This practice can seriously restrict airflow at this critical junction where all of the air is coming together and is not recommended. A connector developed specifically for radon control systems in new homes allows for a good transition without a serious restriction to air flow. This is illustrated in the figure.

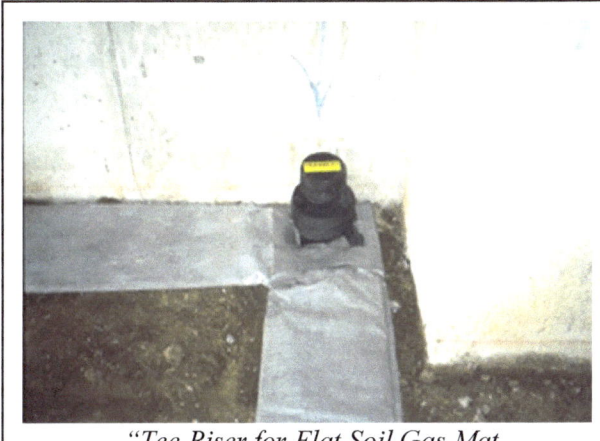

"Tee Riser for Flat Soil Gas Mat

The Tee riser has two flat openings, which accommodate the 12-inch wide SGC mat and a molded round riser to which either a 4-inch PVC or ABS pipe can be attached. It is installed as follows:

- Locate the Tee riser where you want your depressurization piping to be routed up through the house.
- Loosen the fabric on the ends by cutting a single 4-inch slit in the fabric along the side of each end of your loop of mat.
- Pull the loosened fabric back from the end exposing the core and insert the core into the ends of the Tee.
- Lay the fabric of the mat that was peeled back over the outside of the ends of the tee and seal with duct tape to keep the wet concrete from seeping in.
- Drive a 10-inch spike down through the pre-molded nail hole in the Tee to hold it in place.

When the concrete is poured it will flow right over the mat. The mats sold for radon purposes have the strength to bear the weight of the concrete as well as laborers with wheelbarrows of heavy concrete.

After the concrete is poured the top of the round portion of the plastic riser is cut off. A 4-inch, schedule 40 PVC or ABS pipe can then be inserted and secured with 1½-inch sheet metal screws and polyurethane caulk for a solid air tight seal.

Slab Design: Caulking Slab Openings

After the concrete slab has been poured, but before any walls are framed on the slab, the openings in the slab should be sealed with polyurethane caulk. This is a very important part of the system's installation because it will not only significantly improve the performance of the system but will reduce the loss of interior air should the system be activated with a depressurization fan. The caulk itself should be applied after the concrete has cured sufficiently to allow for a durable seal. Chapter 8 discusses the types of caulks and the methods of application, however, as a review, the key places to seal during new home construction are as follows:

- The floor-to-wall joint. When concrete cures it will shrink leaving a gap between the floor slab and the foundation. This is a significant area of leakage and should be sealed before any walls are stood upon the slab. If any isolation material is used, such as ½-inch asphalt impregnated fiberboard, it is very important to seal this joint.

- Plumbing penetrations. Generally, foam is wrapped around pipes where they penetrate a slab to isolate them from the concrete when the slab is poured. Cut the foam flush with or below the top of the slab and caulk around the pipes.

- Plumbing block-outs. Often, a one-foot square opening is blocked out where a drain line penetrates the slab for a shower, toilet, or bathtub. This allows the plumber some room to move the drain to fit the fixture that is being installed. These large open areas can be sealed by cutting pieces of plastic (4-mil high density polyethylene sheeting, or 30-mil PVC sheeting) to fit into the block-out and caulking them to the edges of the block-out and the drain line itself.

- Control joints and gaps between adjacent slabs. Generally, slabs are poured all at once and then before the concrete has set straight grooves are tooled in the slab that are about a ½-inch deep. Sometimes the concrete is allowed to cure and then a concrete saw is used to make ½-inch deep cuts through the top surface of the slab. These grooves or cuts are referred to as control joints. They cause the slab to be weaker along these joints so when the slab cracks, the cracks will occur within these grooves rather than on the surface of the floor. At least that is the theory. These joints should be filled with polyurethane caulk. This will allow the slab to crack along these lines as it is supposed to, with the caulk providing a barrier to air leakage. The flowable or self-leveling form of polyurethane caulk works best for filling these control joints because it will flow into the channels and level itself with the top of the concrete for a neat appearance.

Chapter 11: New Home Systems

Combining Multi-Level Slabs or Slabs with Crawl Spaces.

There are often multiple levels in a home. These may consist of more than one slab or a slab and an adjacent crawl space. These may all be tied together and connected to a common riser. (See Chapter 9 for some additional details on combining systems). The elegance of installing radon systems during new home construction is that this may all be accomplished without running unsightly pipes through finished spaces and concealing them. This is because, with proper planning, the crossovers can be all done beneath the foundation, and slab.

System crossovers are typically made with 4-inch corrugated and perforated pipe that is wrapped in a filter fabric cloth. In this instance, the perforations are used to ensure that condensed water does not build up in these crossover pipes and render a portion of a system inoperable. When using these pipes, remember they have to be below slabs or, in the case of connecting to a crawl space system, it must be under the plastic barrier installed in the crawl space.

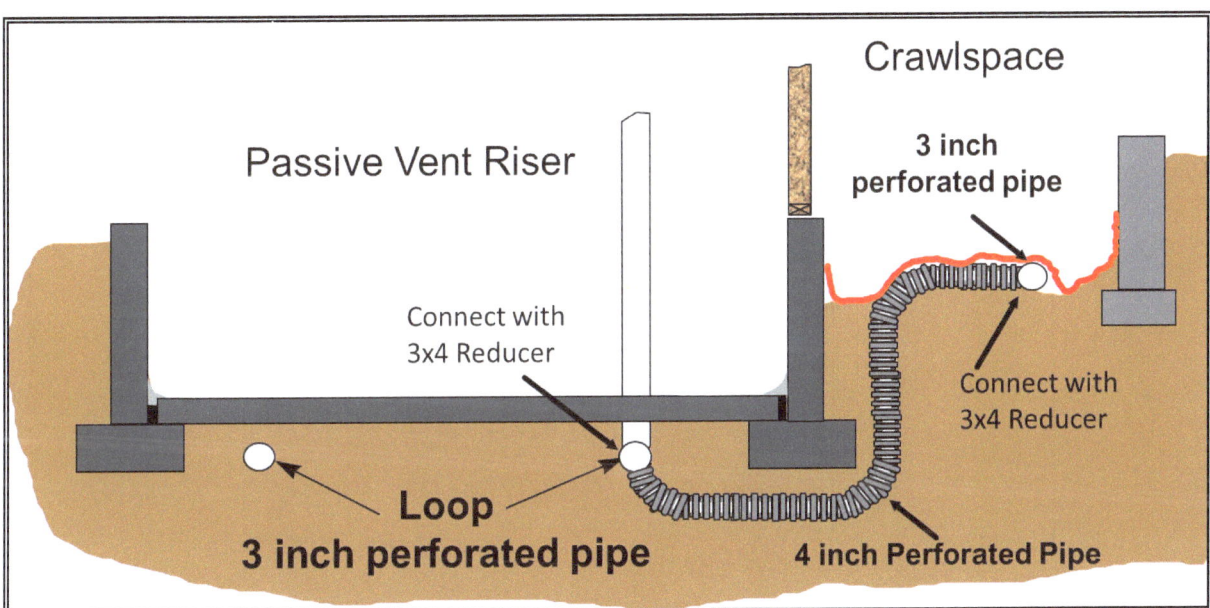

Connecting to 4-inch gravel layers:

Insert at least two 4-inch perforated and corrugated pipes at least 10 feet into the aggregate layer and route the other ends to the area being tied into it.

Connecting to sub-slab perforated loop:

Install a snap-on Tee that can be purchased from the same people from whom you buy your perforated pipe. Note that you will also need to buy a 3 to 4-inch reducer to allow your crossover to be 4 inches in diameter.

Connecting to sub-slab SGC drain mat:

Cut a 12-inch slit in the fabric in your loop and insert an appropriate length of mat into it. Tape the edges of the fabric to keep the concrete from seeping in and secure with landscape staples. Run the lateral branch to the next slab area and repeat the process. If you are connecting this to a crawl space system, you can either lay the mat in the crawl space instead of the perforated pipe or purchase a special flat to round adapter that will connect your flat mat to round pipe.

Homes with Crawl Spaces

Homes with crawl spaces are treated in the exact same manner as have been discussed in detail in Chapter 4. The only additional comment to be made here is that the plastic should be installed after all the wiring, plumbing, & mechanical systems have been installed to keep construction debris, etc. from damaging the plastic during construction.

> **Note:** Passive venting from beneath a plastic sheet does work. However, without an active fan drawing a vacuum from beneath the plastic, the radon reduction will not be as good. Another aspect of venting from beneath a plastic sheet in a crawl space without a fan is that the plastic will move up and down with wind and changes in vacuum in the house. This may not sound objectionable at this point but wait until midnight when the wind begins to blow, and the plastic is rustling up against the floor joists beneath your or your child's room. Trust us, this will happen.

People have tried putting a layer of sand on top of the plastic to hold it down, but you lose that space as clean storage. Given the additional benefits of drying up the crawl space when an actively operating fan is used as well as avoiding rustling plastic in the middle of the night or sand in the crawl, we recommend installing a fan on systems that include crawl spaces.

You may also find that in some of the codes being adopted as options for radon control systems, they do not specify that the edges of the plastic sheeting be sealed to the walls. If you do not ask the contractor to seal the edges you will lose some interior air which will increase operating costs. But more importantly, the edges could easily be pulled back in the future and cause a potential for your combustion appliances to backdraft.

By sealing the edges of the plastic to the walls, you will incur some additional up-front costs, but it will be well worth it in terms of system efficiency and safety. It will also negate the need for special sealing of openings through the sub-flooring, sealing of furnace ductwork located in the crawl space and gasketed closures on access doors which should more than offset the cost of sealing the edges of the polyethylene sheeting. So, our recommendation to our readers is to seal the plastic as described in Chapter 4.

Chapter 11: New Home Systems

Piping Systems for New Home Systems

After the soil gas collection system or systems have been installed, your builder or one of the sub-contractors can connect a 4-inch (100 mm) PVC or ABS pipe to the risers installed and run it up through the house. All of the key elements of running this pipe are covered in Chapter 7, but let's review a few key points:

- Use 4-inch schedule 40 PVC or ABS Drain Waste and Vent Pipe (DWV)

    In some areas, 3-inch pipe would work given the amount of sealing you can do during construction that will reduce air flow requirements, but the larger 4-inch pipe will provide a greater surface area to enhance the natural stack effect and improve the chances of not needing a fan. Furthermore, if a fan is needed, the larger pipe will allow for a much quieter system.

- If any of the vent piping has to be run horizontally, slope your pipe back to the suction points to avoid water accumulation.

- If routing the vent up through the roof for the maximum passive stack effect, route it up through the roof and terminate it at least 10 feet away from openings into the home.

- Install screens on the discharge, but no rain caps.

- If installing a Passive System, make allowances for a system performance indicator in the event that the system may need to be powered by a fan.

- Make allowances to drill a portion of exposed pipe inside the conditioned space of the home for connecting a manometer, or plan to use the low-voltage fan with built in indicator if a fan is added later.

- Label the piping where it is exposed, and yes, behind walls at every level. See example below:

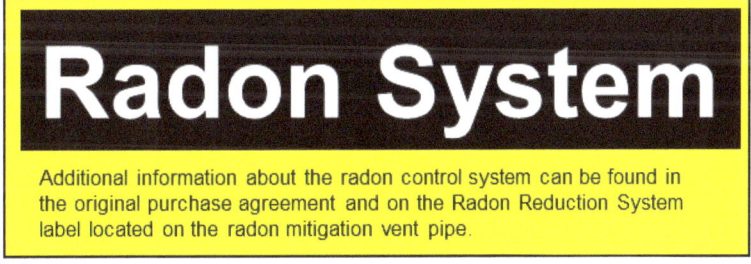

- Route pipe through warm spaces

The efficiency of a Passive system will be enhanced if the pipe is run through a warm space. That is why the pipe is generally brought up through the slab in the furnace room. This will allow this exposed portion of the system to be in a concealed area. It will also allow you to install a future system performance indicator very easily. Running the pipe up through warm spaces will significantly improve the chances of your system operating passively and saving money. The trick is to plan ahead for the framers to provide enough space in the chase to allow for the safe routing of the pipe. Note that fire codes require specific separations from flues.

If you use the flue chase, and we recommend this, when the pipe enters the attic space turn horizontally away from the flue and then turn the pipe vertically again to exit the roof at a point 10 feet away from the flue discharge. ***Also, allow at least 30 inches of vertical room in the attic for proper installation of the fan***. The fans discussed in Chapter 7 are appropriate for this use if post construction radon testing would indicate the need for further reduction by adding the fan.

Working with your Contractor in Planning the Radon System

Radon systems are understood by many homebuilders but not universally. Share this book with them; it can save both you and your builder some headaches. Homebuilders want to build a quality home and to meet your desires as long as you are reasonable. Here are a few hints:

- You will have to pay extra for this system. Radon control systems are not necessarily required by codes and, even if they were, the builder would add the cost of this into the base bid.

- The builder is likely to be concerned about liability and warranties on anything that is put into a house. First of all, if you have the builder install a passive system there is no guarantee it will sufficiently reduce the radon to below 4 pCi/L unless it is activated. So be specific as to who will pay for the fan installation if post-construction testing reveals levels that are unacceptable to you. Most builders will want you to put the fan in or hire your own contractor to do so. This helps keep the builder out of the liability loop, which is desirable for several reasons. First, many builders are not knowledgeable about radon systems. Second, their general liability insurance policies may not cover them for this type of work.

- Perhaps you might suggest the builder hire a certified radon contractor to work as a sub-contractor. Generally, when this occurs the radon contractor will guarantee to you, as the home buyer, the effectiveness of the entire system. This can help reduce the liability and warranty concerns that a builder might have while still providing you a quality system. Although this can add additional costs to the system, it can reduce the anxiety level that your builder might have.

- Builders who are not familiar with radon control systems may have some difficulty integrating the specific steps of installing the radon system into the overall construction schedule of the home. The flow chart on the following page may assist both you and the builder to understand when certain critical events need to occur to assure proper installation scheduling.

The bottom line is that if you want a system, and you especially should if you live in a high-radon potential area, you can get it done. It may take some negotiations with your builder, but it is in both of your best interests to accomplish the task. You get a healthier environment in your home, and the builder avoids liability by putting it in.

Chapter 11: New Home Systems

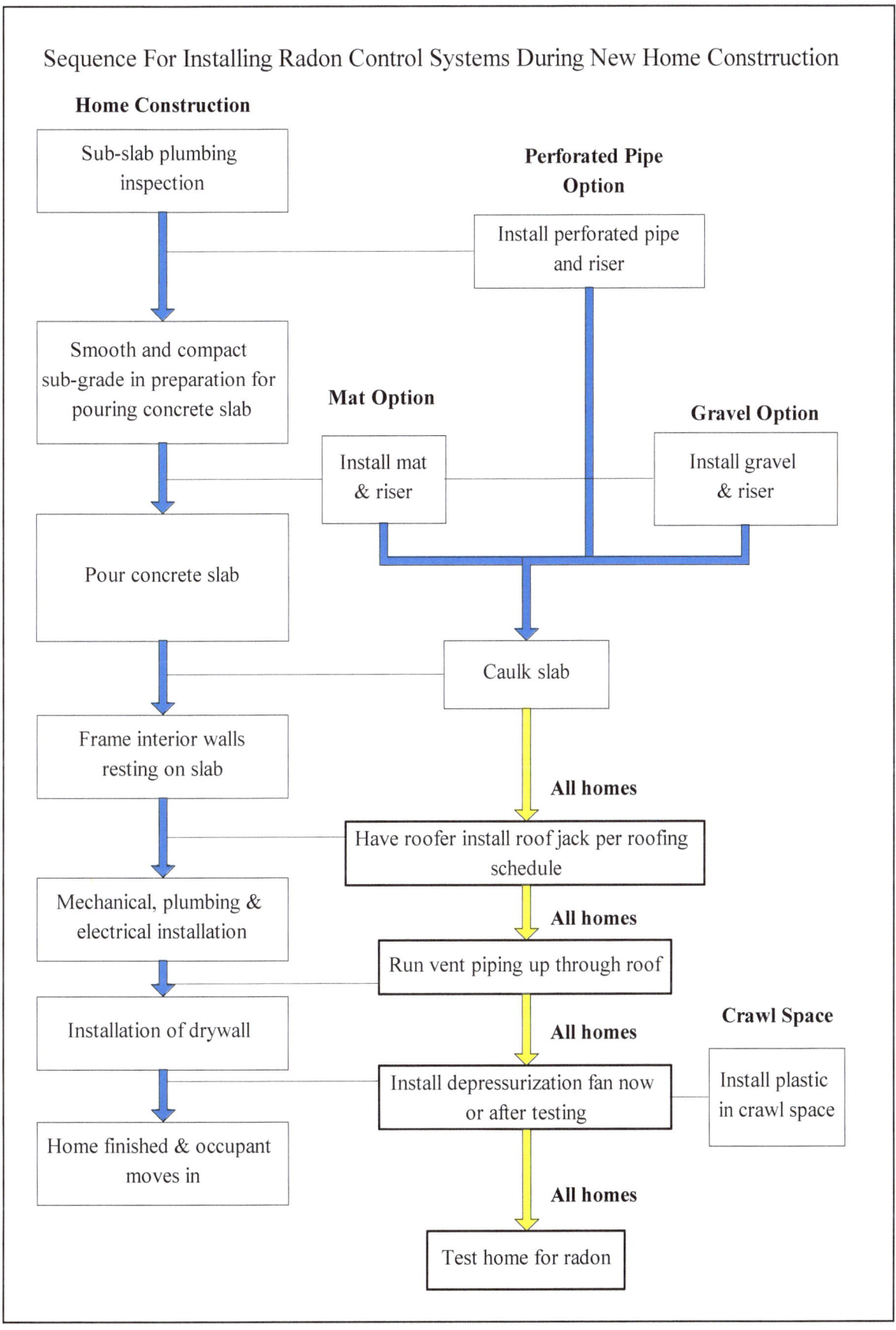

Chapter 12

Getting Help from Contractors

Do I need the help of a contractor?

How to select a radon contractor

CHAPTER 12 – GETTING HELP FROM CONTRACTORS

Do I need the help of a contractor?

After reading this manual, you may determine you do not have the skills or inclination to accomplish all or part of the work necessary to install a quality radon reduction system. There is no reason to feel that you have wasted your time reading this manual. Actually, as an informed consumer. you are now in a better position to evaluate proposals that you may receive from contractors. In fact, this book has been used for that purpose many times since the first edition was printed in 1993.

If you feel confident in doing all of your work yourself, great! Go for it. On the other hand, you may feel comfortable in doing only part of the work yourself and hiring a contractor to finish it off. If you hire a contractor, you have two basic options. First, you can hire a tradesperson who is skilled in certain applicable areas. Examples of this could be as follows:

- You do the dirty work of installing the plastic in a crawl space or tying into the perimeter drain and then hire a plumber to route the piping up through or alongside the house.

- You install all of the system, including setting the fan in place, but hire an electrician to connect the power.

- You hire a contractor to core the hole through your concrete floor for a sub-slab depressurization system. Then you install the rest of the system yourself.

These are just a few examples of how you may use normal trades people to help you with the system. However, if you do this, take the time to share the information in this book with them to increase their understanding of the critical aspects of the system. This is because the tradesperson may not fully understand nor be trained in some of the critical characteristics of radon systems, such as the need not to create water traps in the piping or to insulate the piping in cold spaces, etc. We have seen highly capable people get creative without the benefit of experience and make mistakes that could have been easily avoided if they had read through certain parts of this manual. On the other hand, with proper guidance, very good systems can be installed.

Another option is to hire contractors who specialize in the installation of radon mitigation systems. If you do this, and we encourage this, make sure that they are properly trained and have the credentials to do this work in your area. Although you could use a radon contractor to perform part of the work for you, radon mitigators are normally used when a person wants someone to do the whole job. This approach has many advantages because these individuals will generally not only design and install the system for a fixed fee, but they will also guarantee the reductions to less than 4 pCi/L or even lower. On the other hand, if you hire individuals to do part of the system, they will not provide warranties other than the manufacturers' warranties that come with the individual components. Hiring a radon contractor can provide a certain level of confidence in the performance of the system.

Certified Radon Contractors

There are several states that require radon professionals in either radon measurement or mitigation to be certified and/or licensed. Check your state radon information site by doing a web search using key words like "Radon" "(Your State)", "certified contractors" and after sorting through the ads you will find a URL for your state radon program. Go there and look for a list of qualified contractors.

If your state does not have a regulatory radon program, you can also defer to lists of certified radon contractors at either of the two following national certifying bodies:

- The National Radon Proficiency Program (NRPP) (administered by the American Association of Radon Scientists and Technologists) www.nrpp.info

- The National Radon Safety Board (NRSB) www.nrsb.org

Chapter 12: Getting Help from Contractors

Locating a person on these lists is a good start, but as a wise consumer you should also qualify other aspects of the contractor's capabilities and reputation.

Things to Consider when Selecting a Radon Contractor

What is a certified contractor?

An individual who is nationally certified or state licensed has attended an accredited training program and passed an independent, written examination. Furthermore, they agree to follow specific Mitigation Standards that describe what procedures must be, or should be, followed to maintain their certification.

Do State Offices or National Certifying Bodies Inspect regularly inspect contractors work or compliance with Standards?

No, they do not. This would take an enormous effort and staffing requirement. They have the means for reviewing a questionable radon mitigation installation should a complaint be received from the public.

How do I know a person is truly certified?

Verify that they are on the current Internet list of certified contractors. Once a person has been certified, they must fulfill certain continuing education requirements to maintain their status. Not everybody on the work crew has to be certified as long as at least one person who is certified oversees the work.

Should I hire someone with considerable experience?

Not necessarily. Experience is good, but conversely it doesn't mean that inexperience is bad. Many people now entering the radon mitigation field have had considerable experience in remodeling, plumbing, or other related fields. Although they may not have a lot of radon related experience that does not mean that they are not conscientious contractors who, with training, are able to offer you a quality installation.

If everyone follows the Radon Mitigation Standards, then shouldn't price be my only consideration?

If you are concerned about a functional, durable, and aesthetically pleasing installation, price will not be the only consideration. One contractor may cut corners by using thinner wall pipe, or not caulk as much of your slab as another more conscientious contractor might do. One contractor may not care that a pipe is routed through a hallway where it is exposed, where another may take the time to run it up through a closet and carefully cut each of the shelves to conceal it.

What things should I look for to see if a contractor is cutting corners?

First of all, compare the elements of a contractor's design to the elements described in this book. We are not so self-righteous to think that the methods described in this book are gospel, but on the other hand, they come from a lot of experience and research. We welcome innovation, but we take considerable issue with contractors that don't follow building codes. Here are some things to look out for:

- The depressurization piping system is routed through a fire wall (garage wall) without the use of a fire barrier or maintaining the air tightness of that wall by caulking around the pipe.

- If the contractor is not a licensed electrician nor has one on the crew and he does not use the low-voltage fan system or plug the fan into a nearby outlet, he may wire the fan himself. In all of the areas of the country that we are familiar with, the installation of the 120-volt fan system requires an electrical permit. The installation also requires a licensed electrician, and likely a post installation inspection by a local building inspector. Non-code electrical wiring is one of the most frequent means of cutting corners on cost. Homeowners often foster this when the contractor asks them if they want to save some money by being quiet about this or other building code issues. Faulty or incorrect wiring can be very dangerous to you and your family. Be extremely wary of these types of contractors who don't follow codes. If they knowingly and openly violate codes, what else will they do that they won't tell you about?

- They won't bother to properly prime the joints of the pipe before gluing them or insulate the pipe when it passes through extremely cold attics.
- They will put in cheap system indicators that only sense a problem when the system is turned off. It will not indicate a problem when it is obstructed, damaged, or in need of service.
- They put in much larger fans than are necessary. It lowers the radon but can result in a higher operating cost.
- Their warranties solely match manufacturer's equipment warranties with no warranties on the actual performance (radon reduction efficiencies) of the system.
- They don't carry worker's compensation or liability insurance. If they do not carry worker's liability insurance and one of their employees is injured on the job, you can be held responsible for medical bills and personal damages. If they don't have liability insurance you may have a tough time getting someone to pay for any damages they may accidentally cause, like fire, for instance. It should be noted that just because a contractor may have liability insurance, they will not be covered for radon-related work unless they have purchased a special rider to their general liability policy. If they do not have a radon rider, the insurance they have may very well be worthless in the case of a claim.

What kind of warranty should I expect?

Most radon contractors offer performance warranties. They will generally arrange for a short-term test to ensure that they have reduced the radon to less than 4 pCi/L. They will often perform this test themselves for their own information but must advise you of the benefit of an independent test that you could either perform yourself or hire a radon measurement professional to do. The results of the short-term test generally determine contract compliance for the purpose of final billing.

Furthermore, most radon contractors will also include, in their bid, a warranty that the radon levels will continue to be below 4 pCi/L for a specified period of time. The determination of when the system goes out of warranty is often made with the use of long-term test device placed in the home for one year. Most performance warranties cover the first year of operation. Some contractors may offer longer warranty periods.

When you evaluate warranties, realize that the only component that can wear out is the fan. Most radon fans themselves come with a three-to-five-year warranty from the manufacturer. Once the radon has been reduced to less than 4 pCi/L, there is little that can go wrong unless you remodel your home or change the type of heating system you have. So, long-term warranties may be of marginal benefit compared to their cost.

Also, realize that a warranty is only as good as the company that is offering it. If the company is on shaky financial ground, the warranty may be meaningless. Ask for references on any contractor you consider hiring. This will help provide you with insight on their professionalism and ethics to determine if they will indeed stand behind what may appear to be a "too good to be true" warranty.

Will a contractor charge to give me a bid?

Generally, radon contractors will look at your house and provide a bid at no charge, unless they have to travel a great distance. However, if your house is very large and has multiple foundations or has been added onto several times over the years, they may spend additional time in your home performing diagnostics to design your system. They may charge for this extra effort. Make sure this cost is understood up front. You may also want to ask if they will apply some or all of the design fee towards the cost of the system if you decide to hire them to do the work.

Any other advice?

- Always try to get more than one bid.
- If one bid is significantly lower than others you receive, you should ask yourself why before you automatically sign a contract with the low bidder.
- Ask for references from other people that they have worked for.
- Check with local, consumer protection-based agencies.
- Have them carefully explain the system routing and appearance to be sure you know what it will look like. Remember, the cost of the system is driven more by the amount of finish work you want, rather than the amount of radon that has to be removed. Make sure there are no ugly surprises.
- Be leery of contractors who speak poorly of their competition or claim that they are the only ones who know anything. Maybe they are the best in town, but normally contractors that try to build themselves up by tearing someone down have something to hide, like their reputation and lack of ethics.
- Be wary of contractors who ask for their competitors' bids so they can copy them or provide a quote, which is a few dollars less. The few bucks you save may not be worth the headaches of dealing with an unethical contractor.
- Be sure that they obtain necessary permits from the local building department.

Protecting Your Home from Radon

Bid Evaluation Form:

To help resolve issues with contractors ahead of time and also to compare bids we have put together a table that you can fill out to assist you in choosing between several bids. You can also use this as a checklist for final job completion:

Item:	Contractor _____	Contractor _____	Contractor _____
Proof of worker's compensation insurance			
Proof of general liability insurance with radon provision.			
Years in business in your city			
Years in radon business			
Number of mitigations			
Years of related experience (what type)			
Guarantee to reduce radon below 4 pCi/L?			
How will the house be retested and by whom?			
Long-term warranty and, if so, for how long?			
How will warranty compliance be determined?			
Does warranty cover parts and labor?			
Warranty transferable to future homeowners should the house be sold during the warranty period?			
Is the warranty extendable?			
How long will installation take?			
When can it be installed?			
Will the work be done in phases and, if so, who will test to determine the need for additional phases?			
Will a backdraft test be done on the combustion appliance, and if not, why not?			
CONTINUED ON NEXT PAGE			

Item:	Contractor _____	Contractor _____	Contractor _____
Will a carbon monoxide monitor be installed?			
Will a building or electrical permit be taken out? If not, why not?			
Are you comfortable with the pipe routing?			
Is the contractor using schedule 40 pipe or weaker schedule 20 thin wall pipe?			
Will the piping be labeled on each floor?			
If the piping is to pass through the roof will the contractor warrant the integrity of the roof?			
Will the location of the discharge pipe be located where discharged radon will not come back in through windows, etc. See Chapter 7.			
If the pipe passes through a garage wall, will a fire barrier be used?			
How much caulking is the contractor planning to do?			
Will a system performance indicator be installed? What type?			
Has the contractor agreed in writing to follow the applicable standards? Which ones?			
Has the contractor shown you their current certification card?			
Cost:			

Are Radon Contractors Crooks?

We did not write this chapter to lead you to think that radon contractors are crooks. On the contrary, there are a large number of very qualified and conscientious contractors in the industry. We wrote this so you can more easily identify the good ones from the not so good ones. So, whether you fix the house yourself or hire all or part of it out, the important thing is that you get the work done for the benefit of you and your family.

Resources

Additional Reference Material

Helpful Videos

Links to Radon Standards

Links to State Resources

Contact Us

Appendix

RESOURCES

Need more help?

If you would like to discuss your radon concerns or any part of this book, please feel free to contact the authors at (719) 632-1215.

Interested in entering the radon industry?

If you are interested in pursuing various aspects of the radon profession, such as becoming certified, contact the Center for Environmental Research & Technology, Inc. at 800-513-8332 or visit their website at www.certi.us for course information.

www.ingramcontent.com/pod-product-compliance
Lightning Source LLC
LaVergne TN
LVHW071048170325
806102LV00003B/21